Out of Loneliness: Murder and Memoir

Mary Woster Haug

The Humble Essayist
Press

The Humble Essayist Press
Blairsville, Georgia

Stories move the walls that need to be moved.
Nicole Maines

Becoming Nicole: The Transformation of an American Family
by Amy Ellis Nutt

CONTENTS

PROLOGUE

Memorial Day, 1962, Bev Waugh, a twenty-four-year-old laundry worker, stepped on the gas, rounded her Chevy around a corner, and rammed into Myron Menzie's car, smashing its wheels against the curb and crumpling its back fender into the other car's front wheel well. Menzie, a young Lakota man, gripped its steering wheel, still pushing his boot against the brake. Clinging to him was Gina Lee, his pretty, teenage fiancé and Bev's lover.

Just minutes before the collision, Myron had sped down the Highway 16 hill into Chamberlain, South Dakota, a small town nestled in the banks of the Missouri River. In the last few months, he had grown used to Bev waiting until he and Gina left the drive-in movie theater or the Rainbow Café then trailing them back to Pukwana, Gina's little hometown east of Chamberlain; used to her habit of circling the block and blinking the lights when she drove by the two of them parked in front of Gina's house. He hoped to ditch Bev somewhere to avoid another scene with her. He was tired of her games. But he didn't fear her. Although Bev was three years older than Myron, her age gave Bev no advantage over his easy masculinity—thick, black hair, dark Lakota skin, broad shoulders, and powerful hands on the steering wheel. Underneath her short hair, western shirt, and the rifle in her car, Bev was just a girl, at least in Myron's eyes.

Bev was exhausted. She had spent the day circling Gina's house. The cardboard skunk swaying from the rear-view mirror did not hide the odor of tobacco and motor oil on her fingers wrapped around the steering wheel. She clenched the stick shift with her right hand, pressed the knob into her palm as she thought of the lies Gina told. "I have to wash my hair," she had said that morning when Bev asked to see her. But she was never home when Bev called.

Bev thought about hunting jackrabbits, tromping through the tall grass on the river bluffs with a rifle over her shoulder. She had even loaded her borrowed gun and leaned it barrel down against the passenger door just in case. But she was too nervous to hunt. Bev leaned over the steering wheel, glassy-eyed yet focused, distracted but determined. Her chest tightened when she pulled closer to Myron's car and bumped his fender with hers, just to scare him a bit. Or make him pull over so she could talk to Gina.

Myron pressed the gas pedal to the floor board, stepped on the clutch, and shifted into second gear. He made a quick turn off the highway, into a driveway, and parked behind a cluster of bushes. He listened for the rattle of the muffler on Bev's car but heard nothing. He looked in the rearview mirror. No sign of her.

Dusk was falling as Myron pulled back on the highway and drove to Main Street still littered with candy wrappers and crepe paper streamers, remains of the Memorial Day parade. He drove north past the flower shop and the Rainbow Café where high school kids gathered after school for cherry cokes and cake donuts. He continued down Main Street past Peggy's Dress Shop, City Hall, Casey's Drug Store, and the Brown Derby Café. Old ranchers lingering after a round of beer at the Silver Dollar Saloon smoked cigarettes and chatted on street corners. Dogs ran wild, barking and snapping at the heels of other dogs. Boys with basketballs under their arms jogged toward the gym, the long days of pick-up games ahead of them.

Myron merged onto the truck route, angled south past the Fleet store, the Mussman Hotel, and Swift's Body Shop before looping back to Highway Sixteen. He made a quick turn left on Sanborn Street, a placid neighborhood of four-square houses with screened porches and bicycles scattered in the grass. The Post Office of red brick and white pilasters sat kitty-corner from the Melcher Law Office. A block away the steeple of the United Church of Christ was a pyramid rising through the treetops. Leaves rich with the promise of spring were butterflies fluttering in the breeze. Potholes, remnants of a particularly brutal winter, peppered the streets. Myron swerved around them.

On Sanborn Street, men leaned against cars parked on the front lawns, beers in their hands. The smell of charcoal smoldering on grills rose from backyards. In the houses, mothers shaped hamburger patties, filled bowls with potato salad, and squeezed lemons into water pitchers. They gossiped about high school girls "in trouble" and whispered about men who drove down country roads with women who weren't their wives. Some speculated about friends who spent their days in bed with "migraines," coded word for drunk.

Seeing no sign of Bev, Myron relaxed and fiddled with the radio dial until he found WNAX, the country music station in Yankton, a town downriver. Myron turned up the volume and slipped his fingers under Gina's skirt massaging the flesh above her knee as he hummed, "Crazy for thinking my love could hold you." Did Gina squirm at his touch, her breathing growing soft and rapid? Or did she stiffen and hold her breath waiting for him to stop? Was he so focused on the feel of her smooth skin he didn't see Bev's vehicle round the corner to ram his car against the curb? The sound of engines groaning, tires grinding against pavement, then silence. And three lives mangled by desire and despair.

Part One: Beginnings

SEINING MEMORY

> . . . love is a joint experience,
> but that does not mean it is a similar
> experience.
> The most outlandish people
> can be a stimulus for love.
>
> Carson McCullers
> *The Ballad of the Sad Cafe*

> True
> wisdom
> comes to
> each of us
> when we
> realize how
> little we
> understand
> about life,
> oursel
> ves, and
> the world
> around us.
>
> Socrates
> *The Apology*, by Aristotle

In the fall of 2012, fifty years after Bev Waugh murdered Myron Menzie, I stood outside the Brule County Courthouse in Chamberlain, South Dakota. I

3

had come here to ask the Clerk of Courts for the transcript of Bev's trial. I had come with a thirst for understanding that tragedy. I rested my hand on the still-warm hood of the Malibu, unwilling to go into a building after a three-hour drive. Why not surrender to a September day in central South Dakota when the air possesses clarity of color possible only in arid lands? Why not linger in this place where the autumn sun spills over the bluffs and brushes the river in its lucid light? I have always felt the pull of this landscape, but that day the pull may have been intensified by my reluctance to begin a search that might reveal uncomfortable memories.

I hadn't witnessed Bev's transition from a girl with a pony tail to a mannish person wearing western shirt, cowboy boots, and jeans. Her metamorphosis was complete by the time I was in high school and became aware of her dragging Main on Saturday nights. Bev was little more than a carnival freak I observed from the distance, relieved that I was not like her yet on the deepest level recognizing myself in her boyishness. But Bev gave no reason to suspect that she would make that Memorial Day memorable for more than honoring veterans.

That morning, I had marched through a tunnel of flags on Main Street. Ahead of me, cowboys in boots and Stetsons sat tall in stud-spangled saddles on the backs of restless horses. Boy Scouts, red neckerchiefs knotted around their necks, marched ahead of tractors and fire engines decorated with red, white, and blue streamers. Children followed the parade grabbing candy tossed by the volunteer firemen. The straps of a snare drum crisscrossing my breasts and back dug into my flesh. It was sunny and unseasonably hot and sweat dampened my upper lip and ran down my back. My uniform was damp and scratchy. The smell of wet wool mingled with the odor of horse manure left in piles on the concrete.

Later that night, I loitered with a gang of friends in the parking lot at the Dairy Queen, a popular spot along Highway 16. Every summer, cars would be bumper to bumper as tourists drove through town on their way to the Black Hills. But in May it was a still a sleepy road in a quiet place.

Had I been paying attention that night, I might have seen Bev tailing Myron into town. But I didn't notice anything. It was the beginning of summer in a teenage hangout where the taste of adolescent longings lingered in the air, moist and sweet as sugar and cream. Girls in pony tails and bobby socks flirted with boys in crew cuts and letter jackets. Boys in cars wooed with heavy-lidded eyes that swept over the girls' bodies, slight nods of their heads signaling approval. They beckoned to girls. "Hey babe, come over here." They were men in training practicing

James Dean squints that hinted of danger though their soft cheeks still reflected vulnerability. Gathering at the Dairy Queen was the prelude to nights on lover's point, a flat piece of land overlooking the river where the lights of the bridge glittered on the black water and the windshields steamed over in the heat of summer and lust.

~~~

A picture of Bev Waugh on the front page of a yellowed newspaper prompted my journey to this modest courthouse of blonde bricks and black trim. The photo captured the image of a woman with delicate features, the contours of her face soft, her skin unblemished, shoulders and waist narrow. "My tiny one," Gina called her referring to her size-six boots and diminutive frame. My words for Bev were brawny, masculine, and fierce, a maverick in cowboy boots and western shirt. Seeing Bev's photo prompted feelings of fear mixed with confusion. How could I reconcile my memories with the tiny woman in the photo, a woman my cousin Leo described as having the potential to be "drop-dead beautiful, a real knock out"? Perhaps what matters most is not my faulty recollections but the reasons for my distortion of her. Why? That's a question I needed to ask, the itch I needed to scratch.

I discovered the paper on a steamy July day in 1999 while cleaning out my mother's home in

Chamberlain following her move to an assisted living facility. The air conditioner had been turned off, and the heat and the dust in the carpet and drapes triggered a migraine. I soaked a piece of paper towel, pressed it to my forehead, and collapsed on the worn carpet in the living room surrounded by garbage bags filled with magazines, tattered linens and dish rags, out-of-date calendars, and cookbooks. My brothers had already loaded trucks with furniture including my mother's upright piano and Wurlitzer organ, the two material possessions that most defined her. As I watched them drive away, I felt utterly alone. I had never spent a day in this house without hearing my mother play ragtime on her piano. Now all that could be heard was the wailing of the wind, nature's muted saxophone blowing against the window screens. At the end of the day what remained was silence and a withered balloon dangling from the ceiling, the word *Grandmother* collapsed in wrinkles of latex.

My mother had tucked the newspaper with Bev's photo in a stack of magazines piled in the corner of our front porch. Why? Mother took little pride in a tidy house, so she may have misplaced it in the room's clutter. More likely she hid it during the trial because the story revealed sexual details too salacious for her children to read. I sometimes imagine my Irish Catholic mother creeping into the room after her children had gone to bed and reading of a sexual expression that I had assumed shocked her. Years later, I learned that a lesbian couple was among Mother's friends, so it's possible she was curious about the desire that these two women felt for one another. But not judgmental. "It's their business, not mine," she said. That comment further complicated a woman who often surprised and confused me. I sorted through a lifetime of her possessions with an archaeologist's eye for significant and revelatory artifacts. Despite my search, my mother remained an enigma or a koan, a paradoxical riddle that Zen Buddhists use to unravel meaning from contradictions.

I first realized my mother was a puzzle I'd never solve when I was in college. I was drinking coffee at the Rainbow Cafe with Mother and her friends when one of the women caught me off guard by asking, "What's a 69?"

My mother's friend likely assumed that a college girl would have the answer. She was mistaken. My sexual ignorance had already been exposed the night a gang of women in my dormitory took a purity test consisting of a series of questions about anatomy and sex. One response brought howls of laughter when I asked, "What does it mean to goose somebody?" My quiz score went downhill from there.

I had assumed my mother was equally naïve until that day at coffee. Her friends waited for me to say something. I glanced at Mother. She looked away, her lips corkscrewed, a signal that usually meant she would disapprove of whatever I did. "Well, it's, um, it's. Well, you know. Oh, maybe you should ask someone else."

Still not looking at me, Mother said, "Oh, just answer the question."

Her abrupt command prompted me to give an answer that must have been short and vague and likely inaccurate. As I drove home my mother said not a word about the coffee conversation.

That memory came to me as I sat cross legged in her now empty house, a newspaper over my knees. Carefully unfolding it to keep the fragile crease from tearing, I scanned the article and read a portion of Gina's testimony in which the prosecuting attorney asked, "What did you and Beverly do when you parked at the river?"

"We talked."

Above me, dust motes shimmered as they swirled in the sunlight streaming through the windows. Questions spiraled through my brain in the same way. Most of my memories involved the shock of an "inverted" love affair that led to violence. How could I have known or thought so little about the love story behind it? I had never imagined a conversation between the women. Was it possible that they, lesbians, might flirt and date the way "normal" people did?

Another question: How was it that Gina an attractive honor student, cheerleader, and teachers' pet, could be in a relationship with Bev, an awkward loner who flunked a grade; who after her eighth-grade year turned sixteen and dropped out of school. Thoughts of the mismatch between Bev and Gina brought to mind the novel *The Ballad of the Sad Café* by Carson McCullers. She writes of a love triangle involving Miss Amelia, a tall, masculine, and eccentric woman; her cousin Lymon, a short, hump-backed, schemer, and her former husband and ex-con, Marvin Macy. The community regards the triangle the lovers have formed as grotesque in the way some townspeople considered the relationship between Bev and Gina to be freakish. McCullers, however, doesn't try to make sense of or to judge their attraction. She simply accepts the incongruities and often pain of being in love. "There are the lover and the beloved, but those two come from different countries."

My understanding of Bev and Gina came through rumors that circulated the coffee shops and school corridors. Likely each time someone told a story about them, the truth became more garbled like the "gossip" game we played at slumber parties. One night, one of my friends shocked me by saying, "Well, you know, Bev is a hermaphrodite." I rushed to the *World Book Encyclopedia* and was stunned to learn that real people could be born with both male and female genitalia, not just creatures from mythology. What would my life have been like had I been born that way? I could disguise my physical duality from others with the right clothing, but I could never disguise the aberration inside me. God's mistake some might have said. In the same way Bev could not, or would not, hide the man behind the woman. So, we considered her a creepy cross between a female and a male like Tony Perkins in *Psycho*.

In truth, Bev's masculine clothing and hair style had disturbed me because I was a tomboy, more comfortable in cut-off jeans and sloppy pony tail than skirt and lacquered hair. Unlike some transgender males, I never longed to be a boy. I just wanted to do what boys could do and not be constrained by social expectations. Still the gossip about Bev triggered a brief bout of teenage angst over my own sexuality and reshaped Bev into my extreme opposite—muscular and middle-aged. This thought reassured me that I wasn't "one of them," whatever that meant. Fifty years later, a photo challenged my long-held perceptions of Bev Waugh? Who was she? Grasping an answer to that question was capturing gossamer threads of dust—one image slipping through my fingers as another floated by. I tucked the newspaper in my purse and turned the key in the lock to Mother's house for the last time, closing the door on one version of this story and opening the door to another.

~~~

I hadn't considered writing Bev's story until I found the newspaper with Bev's photo and read this passage in the testimony.

"Gina, what else did you and Bev do when you parked?"

"We cried."

The air whooshed out of the room leaving me short of breath at words that exposed my indifference to the pain that these women suffered. Once again, I asked how could I have known so little about this story and these women? That question brought me to this courthouse.

The courthouse windows shone in the morning light; the lawn on the edge of turning brown was neatly clipped. Cedars and honey locust trees drooping in the late summer heat flanked the entrance. The building looks much as it did that day in December 1962 when I took my first driver's license exam here, a ritual that for many teens accelerated a sluggish adolescence into a high-speed chase after cars and freedom, booze and sex. Bev once told Gina that she had come to this courthouse to apply for a marriage license for the two of them. Her story wasn't true. In 1962 these words were still included in the South Dakota Constitution: *Only a marriage between a man and woman shall be valid as recognized in South Dakota.* Bev probably didn't know about the constitution. Likely, she didn't understand the laws. She did know that people like Myron and Gina's mother, Sadie, were trying to convince Gina to break up with Bev; she knew that Gina avoided her at work and no longer answered the phone when she called. Another possibility? Bev was becoming so deranged she believed her own lie. But what if the story were true? What if the clerk of courts held back giggles as she said, "Bev, you and Gina can't get married? It's illegal. Don't you know that?" If this scenario happened, it's easy to imagine Bev dashing out of the building, her face flushed, the smell of burning rubber trailing as she sped away.

The last time I walked into this courthouse was on a sunny morning in June of 1968 when my husband, Ken, and I applied for a marriage license. I forced a smile when the clerk teased us. "So where are you two lovebirds going on your honeymoon?" I wrapped my arm around Ken's waist, not out of joy, but to anchor myself. We were waiting for a diagnosis that explained my father's unrelenting stomach pain and drastic weight loss. For the first time in my life, grief and fear overshadowed moments of joy. Other times would follow.

Years later, I stood in the same office seeking information on a murder trial. A woman in her forties, a hint of gray in her hair, a pencil behind her ear, came from a back office. "Hi. Can I help you?"

"Yes. I was wondering if I could obtain copies of the transcripts from a murder trial in the fall of 1962. The murderer's name is Beverly Waugh."

She looked at me, eyebrows scrunched. "Who? What was that name again?"

Her response stunned me. How could she not know Bev's name? I realized the clerk was too young to have a memory of Bev's startling transformation. Nor had she experienced the shock of an unusual romance and murder. "Well, could you please see if there are files on her and or the murder?"

"You said the year was 1962? Most of our records are destroyed after that many years. I'll check but doubt we have anything."

I slumped into a chair and pressed my head against the wall, devastated at the possibility that no official documents existed concerning the murder, the trial, and most importantly, background information on Bev. I had become obsessed with the need to understand Bev and my response to her, to document the way in which our lives intersected, and to interpret how our childhood in this place had shaped us. But why? Many people from Chamberlain remembered this story. They weren't driven to research it and certainly not to write about it. Perhaps because I was pushing seventy years of age at the time, I found myself reflecting on the good fortune of my life. I was in a long, loving marriage. I was approaching the end of a thirty-year career teaching English at South Dakota State University. Our daughter, Maura, had transitioned successfully into her profession, marriage, and children. We were financially secure. Why did I have this fortune while Bev and others suffered? A religious friend said that God chose me for this life. I disagree. It was damn luck, or as some say, I won the ovarian lottery. I was born to parents who provided me a stable childhood along with the resources and the awareness of how a college degree might prepare me for a rewarding life. Bev's parents endured a life of impossible challenges that were then passed on the Bev. Most of all, I felt somehow responsible for giving Bev, and by extension Gina, a voice in telling their stories; responsible for disentangling the myths from the truths of their stories.

The clerk scurried back into the room, a flash drive in her hand. She must have noticed my earlier disappointment because she smiled. "I think you're in luck. You can sit at this computer and see if this is what you need."

I popped the flash drive into the computer and clicked past a couple of screens. A legal document popped up one screen. *7217 The State of South Dakota, Brule County, plaintiff versus Beverly Waugh, defendant. . .. that the offense of murder. . . has been committed and there is sufficient cause to believe that Beverly Waugh is guilty thereof. She will be held to answer the same at the next term of the circuit court. . .and she will be transferred to the women's ward at the county jail in Davidson County.*

A file appeared on another screen listing subpoenas issued to people whose names I recognized, as well as affidavits filed and instructions given to the jury. The file also included the judge's order appointing Samuel Masten as public defender as well as the assignment of trial errors Masten would later file with the court. The last page number— 80—was labeled transcript.

A hand-written letter in tidy cursive popped up on the next screen. It began, *Dearest, Hi. Well this finds us apart again. It's Wednesday night and I've pinned the top of my hair.* My God, I had found a letter Gina wrote to Bev. I scrolled quickly through more screens and discovered several letters the women had written to one another, letters I didn't even know existed.

In one letter, Gina wrote fourteen pages whimsically describing such ordinary tasks as changing the sheets on a bed, fighting with her two sisters, making "tater salad" and fried bologna. She doodled hearts and flowers, rain drops and weeds on many pages, including one with a musical staff and the poignant and prophetic inscription *I even drew music you'll never hear.*

The letter ended *Do you love me now? I'm good. Love and Kisses, Gina*

The realization hit me. This was Gina's story as well and I had an obligation to tell it as best I could.

Bev's letters, scrawled in a cramped, childish hand, began *Hi Sweet One, Well I read your big letter hon.* This letter, too, was fourteen pages long, but if Gina's breezy thoughts and words appeared to have come easily to her, Bev's letter suggested effort not only to match the number of pages, (Matching the number of pages they wrote was apparently a friendly competition between the women.) but to express her feelings with the flair Gina possessed. *Yep, my gal had a pretty orange dress on. I like it, but mostly what's in it. Yep I hope that woman of mind let me see her tonight.*

It ended with *I love you always, a whole lot. God Bless you darlin and be good. Your tiny lover, Bev*

That the letters gave me access to their private lives felt like both a gift and a burden. They provided a pathway into the women's thoughts, the story told in their own voices. But did I have the right to use them? Was I trolling in protected waters looking to snare the big fish so I could peel back its skin and scales and remove its vulnerable innards and then mount the trophy on my wall? I would often struggle with my motives as I worked on this book.

The clerk copied the letters and promised to transfer the transcripts to a flash drive and mail it to me. I left the courthouse and slid into my car. I sat for a moment thinking about what this material meant. So much information could be found in the transcripts like the family background, police investigations, legalities of the trial, and testimony from family members, doctors, and even Gina and Bev.

"Let sleeping dogs lie," my mother often said, a comment that both amused and annoyed me with its deliberate attempt to hide anything that exposed uncomfortable truths. "Truth will out," I answered with the unmerited certainty of youth.

As an older woman, I am less certain of the value of truth or how to define it. Any story of human tragedy is multi-faceted and intensely personal, and our response is filtered through our own experiences. Despite my reservations, I was driven to uncover a larger truth beyond murder that I sensed needed to be told. I started the car and drove north toward Main Street.

~~~

People in my youth defined our community as the Heartland, where crime was low and "neighbors cared for neighbors, unlike cold, big cities." Women were "housewives" and if they had other dreams, they said nothing and immersed themselves in family and church. Men went to work at banks, the feed store or lumberyard, law firms and clinics, or farms and the sales barn. Businesses closed early on Wednesday, Church Night, and teachers let homework slide so students could attend Catechism classes or Luther League. On weekends most of the town watched the Chamberlain Cubs compete in football and basketball or attended high school plays and grade school music concerts. But after Bev followed Myron down the Highway 16 hill, we were reminded that we lived in a place not far from the frontier, a place where a man still solved his own problems, sometimes with violence.

Bev grew up on the north side of Highway 16. Although today lovely homes are tucked in the bluffs north of the highway, in my childhood Highway 16 ran through the middle of town and divided Chamberlain economically and socially. On the south side where I lived was evidence of middle-class prosperity and possibilities with houses freshly painted, manicured lawns, and cars free of dents and rust in the driveways. Bev grew up on the far north end where poverty and dead ends, peeling paint, scrubby grass, and car engines on blocks in front yards prevailed. Years ago, when my family and I crossed the highway, my stomach tightened the way it did when we drove across the reservation border near our land. Although a man from the reservation was good friends with my father, he and all my native neighbors lived on the edges of my life. I feared them the way I feared what lay behind the rustling of tall grass in the ditches. Not knowing is fearing. The Waugh family must have sensed that crossing the highway to the orderly homes and clipped grasses on the south side was like driving on the wrong side of the road, the confusion and fear of being lost in a place where people have the time, energy, and money to mow lawns and paint houses.

I turned east and drove up Merrill Street past the bowling alley recalling a night I drove the family station wagon up this hill to a slumber party at Sally's house. She was a perky blonde with flawless skin. We sprawled under the pink canopy over her bed and spritzed dime-store cologne in curvy bottles on our wrists and neck. Posters of Troy Donahue and Frankie Avalon covered her bedroom walls and music blasted from KOMA, a rock 'n roll radio station out of Oklahoma City. Paul Anka sang, "Put your head on my shoulder, whisper in my ear, Baby." His smooth tenor provoked yearnings I had not yet explored with my boyfriend knowing I would have to confess my sin to Father John. We chatted about Donnie, the athlete with crinkly eyes and dark crew cut, and drooled over Tom, blonde and handsome as Troy Donahue and just as unattainable. We whispered about The Duke, the high-school "hood" whose direct stare and questionable reputation made me squirm with fear and curiosity. Although in retrospect I suspect his reputation was unwarranted but necessary to provide a sense of danger missing in boys with crew cuts and shy smiles.

After a while, Sally said, "This is boring. How 'bout a game of Truth or Dare?"

Although we knew this game could turn ugly and hurtful, none of us risked saying no for fear the queen of our class would drop us as her handmaidens. When my turn came, Sally said, "Either you tell us which girl in this room is your best friend or drive past Bev Waugh's house and honk the horn."

Bev frightened me with her swagger and sneer and the unfounded rumors that she shot dogs and cats that roamed the neighborhood. But I wasn't brave enough to admit that Sally wasn't my best friend. "I accept that dare," I said.

It was after midnight when we drove to the bluffs above the Waugh home. The girls hopped out of the car to watch from the safety of the hilltop. "We want to make certain you don't chicken out," Sally said, a bit of sadism in her giggle. I turned off the headlights so no one in the house would be awakened by a flash of light across the windows and shut off the motor. No streetlights lined the dirt road that led to Bev's house, and the car coasted into a tunnel of darkness guided only by the dim light of the moon weaving through the clouds.

Venturing close to an abyss with no sense of what lay at the bottom, I felt my hands shaking on the steering wheel. The car lurched and swayed. Why was I doing this? But what options did I have? Sally was waiting at the top of the hill. She would ridicule me for being a coward and then demand the truth for failing the dare. I turned the key in the ignition, pressed down on the accelerator, spun a wheelie, honked the horn, and sped back up the hill. I kept my eyes on the rearview mirror looking for lights in the windows or worse, headlights racing toward me.

~~~

Fifty years later, my stomach tumbled once again as I pushed on the brakes to keep the car under control and eased the Malibu down the gut-dropping hill. Just to the right of me, a cement plant belched clouds of dust and the rumble of trucks penetrated the silence. In the front yard, a rusty Oldsmobile huddled in the weeds along with cars perched on their rims. Maybe Bev learned to fix engines here, her hands greasy and nails ragged, her jeans dusty from working under the car. It could be that a brother squatted on his heels explaining car parts to her. The same brother perhaps who taught Bev how to slip a bullet into the slit on the stock, hold the gun to her shoulder, and sight a target. She may have discovered for herself the pleasure and pain of the gun's butt shuddering against her as the bullet was released and the thrill of dropping a jackrabbit with a single shot.

Dense trees and overgrown bushes blanketed the bluffs and wrapped the house in shadows. Squares of cardboard in broken window panes shaped the crooked smiles of jack-o-lanterns. The house tilted toward the ground shedding feathers of paint over dandelions, and thistle bunched in clumps against the foundation like cattle clustered along fence lines. The air was muggy and smelled of something rotting perhaps garbage stacked in piles against the garage or maybe damp leaves from a recent rain. The smell of decay collided with the fresh piney scent of wood being cut in the lumberyard nearby. This was a place infused with a sense of beginnings and endings.

Nobody looked up from under the hood of a car to see who was pulling into the yard. No hands pulled back the ruffled curtains. No eyes peered through the glass except those of a cat curled up in the window. Its indifference to my presence both comforted and unnerved me. I parked the car, pulled the newspaper from my purse, and studied Bev's photo thinking of what we had shared. We had both tromped the bluffs through scrubby cedars and thick grass, shopped at Kramer's General Store, and sipped cokes at the Rainbow Café. Perhaps we had sat in the same desk in the back row with the other end-of-the-alphabet kids—Yeatons, Verschoors, Waughs, and Wosters. We had attended the same church, dragged Main on Saturday nights, and necked at the drive-in movie theater at the top of the hill. Despite our common experience, something about this clearing in the woods made my skin prickle. At the same time, I had an odd sense of coming home after a long absence.

A memory came to me. I am a small girl rubbing my fingers over the smooth surface of a rock wondering what mysteries lay inside its shell of stone. I poked a stick under the rock to pry it loose from the sod, not knowing what might scuttle from underneath—dung beetles and spiders or snakes and maggots. But I couldn't stop digging because sometimes I dislodged a rock, turned it over, and found a hollowed-out space lined with mica like stars in a sky of gold and blue stone. How many years of patience and determination were needed to form this lovely universe within a rock? In the same way,

I would need to patiently prod under the layers of the tales told of Bev. Perhaps then I might discover the stars in Bev's sky hidden by my fear of her.

The sun began to descend over the bluffs and the woods closed in on me. Behind me, a shadow seemed to move between the glass and cardboard of the windows. I panicked, put the car in reverse, pushed hard on the pedal, and crashed into a stand of trees. The tires sank into the mud. Branches screeched over the roof and fell across the windshield. I felt twitchy, agitated. I pumped the gas pedal and pulled away spraying mud clods. In the thick shrubs, a doe watched me pass by, her fawn lingering near her. The doe lifted her ears and tail, alert, but unafraid. Her brown eyes followed me up the hill and into dusk's fading light as I drove toward the river.

The native people called the Missouri River Smoky Water. Historians have dubbed it The Big Muddy. Writers speak in metaphors describing it as a vein that runs through the heart of the state. I think of it as a long, twisting seam that both connects and divides South Dakota. It is the place where corn fields surrender to grasslands, where Miles Davis gives way to Johnny Cash, and sedans are replaced by pickups. It is the place where the West begins. Here, cowboys still herd cattle on horseback and livestock graze in the miles of grass. Hawks whirl and rise in the updraft and zoom down to snare mice or rabbits. In my childhood, the wide sky was a blue comforter that warmed me. The quiet openness of the grasslands instilled in me a love of solitude. Its natural rhythms, deeply spiritual and earth-centered, offered a sense of belonging to the very soil and sky around me, a sense of home I have felt nowhere else. At the same time, the isolated, open landscape exposed me and taught me to shelter my soft parts by keeping my secrets close. How did the landscape shape Bev? Perhaps the expanse of the country instilled in her a sense of freedom. Or boldness. Or maybe she experienced the schizophrenia of living in an open space while closeted in a body misaligned with her soul.

I turned on to a gravel road, parked in a worn patch of grass, and walked toward the beach near the railroad bridge where my friends and I had gathered the night of the murder, our voices squeaky with fear. I slipped off my sneakers and walked up to my knees into the water, struggling to keep my balance as the waves pushed against me. Memories flooded over me. The river was where we girls met to share gossip, to skinny dip, taste our first beer, smoke our first cigarette, and for some to first experience sex. Naturally we met at the river that balmy night in May 1962. Now, years later, I could almost hear my friends chattering. One girl said, "Bev opened

Myron's car door and asked, 'Are you a man or a mouse?'" That was not true. Nor was it true as one girl claimed that Bev shot at Gina as she ran away from the car. We didn't challenge these stories, however. We had never known of murder and so everything seemed possible.

As the river's current muscled toward the Gulf, the undertow dragged tiny grains of sand between my toes. I felt pulled as well by a need to seine the pools of memory where Bev had always lingered but from which she had rarely emerged. Why had she come to me now? Some believe that ideas are everywhere and that these ideas drift from person to person looking for someone willing to birth the idea into a story. Perhaps in some mystical way, Bev's story chose me, not the other way around.

The low angle of the sun's light transformed the sky from coral to a pale then inky blue until only an outline of the river bluffs remained. Something moved in the dusk. I narrowed my eyes and for a second saw a tiny figure lurking behind a pier. I froze with an irrational fear it was Bev. Why would she be here? And what did I have to fear from her? But it was only the first light of the rising moon casting shadows on the bridge. Still, Bev made her presence known in the rivulet that cut a path through the shale behind me, swirled around my ankles, and then flowed into the river. In the same way, I had once circled the edges of Bev's life, merged briefly with her in days of teenage angst, then branched off in a different direction before looping back to this place where our stories began.

ORIGINS

Strangely
enough, here was
this girl with a good
reputation in town,
she has been a good
girl, she was never
in trouble, she
wasn't like the
other girls. But she
had this cancer
inside, that's the
trouble. That's the
thing we have to
understand. Are we
going to strike back
at this child or are
we going to try to
understand it?
Samuel Masten, closing argument

Over the years, I often typed Beverly J. Waugh, SD, in my computer's search bar hoping to discover new information about her or to find an address or phone number so I might arrange an interview. But always with no luck. Then one frigid December night

29

when the wind blew through the branches of the pine trees and battered snow pellets against my office windows, I tried again. These words popped up on my computer screen: Beverly J. Waugh, 76, died November 3, 2014. Guilt, grief, and regret pummeled me the way the blizzard pounded my house. My fingers on the keyboard were cold and shaky. How had I allowed the opportunity to meet Bev slip away from me? Laziness? An unwillingness to ask her to dredge up her painful past? An abiding fear of her?

I traced the letters in Bev's name on the computer screen, its surface supple beneath my fingertips. Her attorney Samuel Masten had said of Bev, "She came out of loneliness; that's where she lived." Had she died in loneliness? What secrets did she take to her grave? How could I flesh out the person she was? What was her story?

Bev Waugh was born to Frank and Helara Waugh on January 2, 1938 in the home of her grandmother who served as midwife as she did for all the Waugh children. In his opening statement, Masten spoke of the "panic. . . in the heart of a woman until that first look when she knows 'this is a good healthy baby.'" He described the happiness and relief Helara experienced at Bev's birth. "There was born a baby girl. There was joy in the mother's heart because she was a nice, normal baby. God had made her."

Bev, however, told Gina that she was born in the Waugh family car along the side of the road as her parents drove to St. Joseph's Catholic Hospital in Mitchell sixty miles away. Hospital care was expensive. The Waughs were Catholic and they may have dreamed of a birth where nuns in veils and starched gowns scurried through the halls carrying bed linens, white, crisp, and smelling of bleach and sunshine; may have longed for the comfort of a priest bringing communion, leaving the dry taste of a wafer on Helara's tongue and laying his hands upon Bev's head in blessing. Most likely her parents let that dream die as they had many other dreams. Did Bev fabricate the story of her birth to impress Gina with its television-worthy drama? To suggest the family could afford the bill for a hospital delivery? Or did it reflect her sense of being an oddity, even her birth being outside the norm? Perhaps Bev invented the story of her birth the way she created a male persona. She needed to change all the stories of her identity.

Bev attended elementary and junior high school in Chamberlain. She said she "didn't much like school." Her grades reflected that. She dropped out after eighth grade and took a job at Kulm Laundry. People who knew Bev through work or her bowling league generally liked and accepted her. However, few considered her to be their friend. Her boss testified that she was a hard worker and good employee. But with little education, she had few prospects beyond work in a laundry earning ninety cents an hour, the same salary I earned in high school working as a fry cook at the A & W. I spent my money on record albums and movie magazines. Bev paid her mother five dollars a week, room and board, to supplement the family income.

Those of us who didn't know Bev feared her differences. She grew up in a run-down house in dark woods, an outsider in society and even in her own gender. Eventually the arc of history would bend toward equality for gays and transgender men and women. But for Bev, the arc bent toward failure and isolation. My origins are rooted in the grasslands in a humble, yet cheerful house with flowered wallpaper and a kitchen where canaries sang in cages and the sun shone through Dotted Swiss curtains. I was white, middle-class, and heterosexual. My life bent towards success and a sense of belonging to the community.

Bev's family history was complicated and contradictory, as most histories are. On the one hand, Masten described her childhood as "quite normal for any child growing up." On the other hand, the Waugh family struggled not only with poverty but with addiction and mental illness. Her brothers Darrell and Jerry worked sporadically on farms or for the railroad, and sometimes they laid bricks or shingled roofs with their father. Her little sister, Norma, was dark and small like Bev but feminine and pretty. "How can sisters be so different?" townspeople often asked. "Different as an old mare and a filly." Despite these differences, Norma testified that she and Bev were "as close as sisters could be." Norma and her husband moved around for several years, but she brought her two small children to Chamberlain often to visit her family. "Bev liked the children real well," Norma testified. "She thought the sun rose and set on Frankie, the little boy, and always brought him surprises and sacks of candy."

Helara suffered from a nervous condition and often, as my Irish family would say, "took to her bed." In the 1950's, few medical terms described the depression and anxiety many women like Helara, and my mother as well, sometimes experienced from menopause. Or maybe from the overwhelming work of managing a home and a large family while having little power or control over their own lives. Helara must have been exhausted by the burdens of finding money to pay the rent and utilities and to put food on the table. Except for gatherings with extended family, Helara kept to herself, spending much of her time at home resting on her bed, digging in her flower garden, or tending to her chickens and geese whose eggs Bev sold to co-workers for twenty-three cents a dozen.

The oldest son, James, was often in legal trouble for fighting and was twice committed to the state hospital in Yankton for deliriums. "He was awfully nervous, even as a small child," Helara testified. It's not clear from court transcripts what caused Jimmy's deliriums. His doctors may have diagnosed schizophrenia. Townspeople blamed his trouble on booze.

Jimmy liked to fish under the Highway 16 Bridge where trucks rumbled above him and the bobber floated on waves that glinted in the sun like fish scales. He became a legend among little boys including my youngest brother, Kevin, the day he dug an eyeball out of a carp's socket, popped it in his mouth, and chewed. "Don't taste that great," he said, his eyebrows lifted. Did he spit it out and chuckle as the boys ran into the thickets of cedar that folded into the creases of the bluffs? Did he do this so they would leave him alone? Or was he just having fun with them? They came to fish with him the next day for they were not afraid of Jimmy. Those boys saw a man few of us knew. In a letter to Gina, Bev gave a glimpse of that man when she described how Jimmy coaxed his mother from her bed to dance the Twist. I can almost hear "Oh let's twist again, like we did last summer" blasting from the radio and children laughing and clapping at the rare sight of their mother smiling and shimmying while *Jimmy jump around like a frog.*

Bev's father Frank was fifty years old when Bev killed Myron, close to my father's age. As young men, they surely shared dreams of owning a comfortable home filled with children who loved and respected them. While my father was able to prosper in the post-war years by buying land and building his herd of Herefords, Frank was an alcoholic who had suffered two heart attacks. He worked sporadically as a brick layer and roofer. In the letters Bev wrote to Gina, she often expressed disgust with her father for failing to support the family. *Guess the old man didn't work again today.*

Although he spent most of his days at home, Frank seems to have existed in the shadows of Bev's life. He didn't testify at the trial, and neither Bev nor her mother refers to him in their testimonies leaving no record of what he thought or said about the murder or his daughter's gender shift. Bev rarely mentions good times with her father except in one letter when she jokes about Frank singing his favorite song *That's My Pa. Jittered up and ready and about half wild.*

Frank spent part of his time casting a line into the muddy backwaters of the river that spread over the wide basin below their house. *The man was fishing today guess he got a bunch of them, mostly bullheads.* Most self-respecting fishermen would toss bullheads back into the water. My father, however, fished for them in early spring when the waters of the dam were deep and cold. He brought them home for my mother to roll in cracker crumbs and fry in butter. He may have been prosperous, but he was not profligate. We ate whatever he brought down with his shotgun or snagged with a hook, even a prehistoric-looking fish with long, spiky whiskers and mottled belly.

Frank watched television for hours hollering at Bev to lower the volume on her radio. *The old man want me to turn my radio down. Guess he couldn't hear the tv too good hon. Guess I better so he stop yelling at me.* Sometimes she defied him and turned up the volume ignoring his yelling until he gave up.

I often imagine Frank sitting in a dark room in the flittering light of a tv, a cigarette between his yellowed fingers, the smoke spiraling upwards and then spreading across the ceiling. In the bedroom, Helara lies on the covers in her housecoat, her hair in pin curls, hands folded over her belly. She stares at the ceiling. In the kitchen, Jimmy babbles, sometimes to a sibling passing through the room, often to himself. Rock-a-Billy music blares from Bev's bedroom. Frank is too tired to yell at her about her music, her haircut, and her cowboy boots, too weary and confused to understand who she's become. The sweat from the beer bottle drips over his fingers, and he leans his head against the back of the chair, takes a swig, and closes his eyes. He waits for something he can't name but senses will be disaster.

~~~

In speaking of Gina's family, Masten told the jury, "Like the Waugh family, Gina's parents were so happy. . . they had a normal baby. They couldn't see inside. . . to the girl who developed into what we saw on the witness stand."

Gina grew up in a tidy house in the tiny town of Pukwana, named for an Ojibwa word meaning "curling smoke of the peace pipe." It's unclear why the founding fathers named the community after a word from "The Song of Hiawatha." Likely it was chosen by a railroad employee with an Eastern education who knew and loved the poem.

In Gina's childhood, Pukwana boasted of a public school, two churches, a couple bars, a post office, a feed store which candled and sold eggs, and a cluster of wooden grain bins with slanted roofs. Today, only the grain bins and the bars, including Puk U which sponsors the annual lawn mower races, remain.

Other buildings on Main are boarded up, the paint peeling, the windows shuttered, and the foundations settling into the ground like old women in their easy chairs. Despite Pukwana being only a few miles east of Chamberlain, it was a place we drove past not a place we visited.

Her father, Joe, was a blacksmith who often had to travel for work. Gina wrote to Bev that the family was especially thrilled when he took a job in Gregory County. *He's going to be paid four hundred dollars for the week.* Her mother, Sadie cut meat at Joes Super Value in Chamberlain. This was a time when women stayed home. If they worked, most women except those who lived on farms and ranches did not have jobs that required physical labor. Although I don't remember people gossiping about her, many likely disapproved of her breaking social conventions by working in a traditionally-male occupation. I recall walking past the meat counter and seeing Sadie cutting big hunks of beef into sirloin and T-bone steaks. I must have wondered why she wasn't home like other mothers. Likely I felt sorry for her children coming home from school to an empty house. At the same time, her white coat, bloodied hands, and surgical skills with a knife impressed me.

Described by the newspapers as "a slender, attractive red-head," Gina was an honor student and popular with her teachers, often running errands for them during the school day. She was elected cheerleader and participated in school plays. A dreamy girl, she doodled flowers and weeds on her homework, sketches she would later draw on the letters she wrote to Bev with the inscription, *The rains will make the posies grow—and the weeds.*

In his opening statement, Prosecutor Hollmann told the jury that Gina's family was a typical family for the time. Gina had two younger sisters, Susie and Linda. The girls probably played jacks on the front stoop or rode their bikes down the middle of the streets with baseball cards rattling in the spokes. They squabbled over who had to do the dishes or mop the floor. Although the family was Episcopalian, they attended Sunday service at the Lutheran Church, the only other church in town besides Catholic. Gina was close to her aunts, uncles, and cousins and gathered with them every Memorial Day to decorate family graves and to share a picnic afterwards.

In his closing statement, Masten questioned the prosecutor's description of Gina as an innocent who bore no responsibility for the murder. He called her a greedy girl who manipulated Bev for the gifts and attention she gave her. In blaming her for the tragedy, he used the most damning biblical passage referring to the mark of blasphemy. *We probably can't touch Gina but she's got the mark on her hand, she can walk through life with it. Her penalties are going to be heavy.*

~~~

On December 8, 1945, the year Bev started first grade, my mother gave birth to me in the hospital where Bev claimed to have been born. Very few babies were delivered by doctors in those days including my oldest brother and sister who were born in the Bode House, a maternity-care home on the river banks. For each birth, Mother spent two-weeks in confinement under the care of "a mean little lady" who wouldn't allow Mother to open the windows in the stifling days of summer.

"Breathing in the air coming off the muddy river water in July will make you sick," the woman warned.

Sweaty and sleepless, tossing and turning to find a comfortable spot despite her swollen belly and aching back, Mother crept to the window at night, opened it a bit, and stuck her nose to the screen gulping fresh air. No doubt she stewed about the length of the labor ahead of her. Or fretted over the baby she had left in the care of neighbors while she lay in her bed twenty miles away. Perhaps if they'd had the money, the Waugh women would still have chosen a home birth for the intimacy and comfort that family can offer. Did Mother, the youngest, sheltered child of a large Irish family regret being cut off from them during her labor and left in the care of a woman who intimidated her. Did she long to hear a familiar voice? To see the reassurance in her mother's eyes that she would survive the pain?

Mother's labors were always intense and lengthy, my birth erased from her memory by ether's "twilight of sleep" a nun drizzled over the mask covering her face. She never expressed regret at not having witnessed my birth, at not hearing my first cries. Natural births puzzled her. "I was so happy to be out of pain, I didn't care. I knew I'd see you soon enough."

My parents brought me home to a house where the green fragrance of alfalfa and of bread baking in a sunny kitchen infused my days and where the family gathered for meals around the time-battered oak table that now graces my dining room. Some would consider us a typical mid-century, rural family, but a photo taken in front of my uncle's house in Kansas City captured the accidental details that reveal ways that we were alike and yet very different from others. We gather in front of an old car, all looking to the left. None of us remembers what drew our attention. My father, Henry J. Woster, looms large in the photo. Born in Nebraska to a Bohemian family, he moved to the grasslands of South Dakota when he was a small boy. Despite the distance from his cultural homeland, he clung to his Eastern

European roots in his love of stories, music, and a taste for exotic foods that we shared despite or maybe because of my mother's disdain. Pickled pig's feet, pickled herring, rye crackers, tomato juice laced with sauerkraut juice, sardines soaked in oil, and oyster stew on Christmas Eve. "Issh. How can you eat that smelly stuff?" she griped. Her complaining made our alliance taste even sweeter.

In the photo, he stands with one foot on the bumper and rests his elbow on his knee. The set of his broad shoulders and the way he gazes to the distance with steady eyes hints at confidence in his ability to overcome whatever challenges might lie ahead. When hail flattened wheat crops and blizzards buried our cattle in deep drifts, I wept in fear we might lose our farm. He hugged me. "As long as I have my health, Toots, I can face anything." He must have been thirty-six years old when the picture was taken. He couldn't have imagined facing cancer.

My brother Jim wearing cuffed jeans and loafers leans against the trunk, his ankles crossed, hands in his pockets. The photo hints at the cool teenage rebel he would become with duck's ass hairdo and white t-shirt, the sleeves rolled up. But he squints in a worried way that became familiar after my father died and he assumed responsibilities for the farm and his mother and siblings. He juggled those tasks while also providing for his wife and three children and building a career as a cattle buyer and television personality. Only now do I understand how young he was and how heavy the burden we placed on him.

My sister, Jeanne, leggy and lean in trousers and plaid blouse, stands to the right of the photo a few feet away from the family. She crosses her arms, a quizzical look in her eyes. There is something about her that suggests a young Katherine Hepburn—classy and confident. Jeanne was a serious student and gifted pianist. As the first girl among our extended family and friends to attend the university, she was something of a celebrity. Growing up, I often felt as if I were standing below her stage, my face washed out in the spotlight.

Terry, round-faced and handsome, huddles against Mother and wraps his arms around her legs. The shy, middle-child, he escaped the chaos of a noisy family by reading books he stashed in the glove compartments of trucks and beneath the eaves of the granary roof. He learned to listen while the rest of us clamored to talk. He learned the power of language through books he read, both skills useful in his long career in journalism covering state government and writing columns in daily newspapers.

Missing from the picture is Kevin, born three years later. He claims that the photo shows us looking for him to complete the family. Perhaps he's right. Five was a good number of children for

Catholic families then, a manageable brood for the mother and proof to the parish priest that no birth control was being used. Poetry was embedded in Kevin's marrow. Or perhaps the stunning images he writes come from a place of sorrow. Only sixteen when our father died, he was shattered and dropped out of school. Despite his struggles, he managed to sustain our mother through her early days of widowhood, mostly by making her laugh. He eventually went to college and majored in journalism making his mark as a newspaper and television reporter and columnist.

Marie (McManus) Woster and I stand in the middle of the photo. Mother was the youngest child of an Irish clan, adored and overly protected by her parents and much-older siblings. When she was three years old, she slammed her pinky finger in the barn door. The whole family gathered around her fretting over the indentation in her tender flesh. Her oldest brother even hustled home from his work at the Lyman general store to check on her. She didn't find it odd that her brother ran three miles across the prairie just because she smashed her finger. "Why wouldn't he?"

In the picture she wears a housedress, thick support hose, and clunky shoes. If my father's face is relaxed, his mouth slack, my mother's is tight-jawed and her eyes wary. She may have been dreading the drive back to South Dakota. My father had a heavy foot, and Mother gasped and gripped the door handle as he passed one car after another, the wheels whizzing over the yellow line. She was most certainly fretting about her children's health. Had we been exposed to whooping cough in the shopping mall? Did the milk taste a bit sour? Was the red blotch on Terry's neck a sign of measles?

I am wearing coveralls and a hat with a furry brim and ear flaps. Paranoid about a recurrence of the rheumatic fever I had suffered that year, Mother overdressed me in all weather. She wraps her long fingers around my upraised arms and pulls me to her belly as if pushing me back into her womb. I plant one foot in front of me and raise the heel of the back foot, a sprinter at the starting line. She claimed I would dash down the road so fast she couldn't catch me. On a trip to the Black Hills, she strapped a halter around me before we walked the path to base of Mount Rushmore. Her back straightened when a woman hissed, "She's a child, not a dog."

"I know that. But I'm keeping her safe. Mind your own business."

Years later in telling this story, her voice quivering, she said, "You were fearless and I was afraid you'd run off a cliff or something."

On that trip to Kansas City, my mother noticed a red streak running down my calf. I have a vague

45

memory of my parents arguing under their breaths over the seriousness of the streak. She fretted about blood poisoning. "Henry, look. The red line is getting longer. She needs a doctor." My father believed it was a simple boil or perhaps my skin was infected by the sliver from an old fence embedded in my skin. Still, we went to the emergency room before we drove home. A doctor prescribed hot packs with Epson salts. He chuckled when Mother asked if I should have a penicillin shot. I have no memory of receiving a vaccination. Whether I did or not, my mother likely still worried about me. My parents said nothing as we walked out of the hospital. On the harried drive through city traffic and stretches of empty highways, the car was hushed.

That moment may have planted in me seeds of fear and uncertainty over impending disasters, whether illness or accidents. This uneasy feeling germinated over the years and grew into a fight-or-flight tendency I've struggled with all my life. The Kansas City picture reveals not a reckless child likely to dash down country roads or toward steep cliffs, but rather an anxious one who shuts her eyes and clenches her hands; a little girl who sensed that something unspoken and terrifying lay beneath silence; a girl who became a woman who protected her fears with laughter and sarcasm.

Despite these tensions, my childhood was rich

with the freedom of living in a place with wide skies and the love of a large, extended family. I have fond memories of cousins playing Canasta around the dining room table, of pulling taffy in the kitchen, or churning ice cream in the front porch on winter nights. But mostly I have memories of music— Mother bouncing on the piano bench playing "The Flight of the Bumblebee" with such ferocity the photos on the top of the upright tumbled to the floor. My siblings and I giggling as my lanky father danced around the living room, a windmill of arms and legs singing *I'm a ding dong daddy from Dumas.*

COWBOYS AND FATHERS

> I've seen some really good cowboys farm,
> and I've seen some really good farmers run cows,
> but I've never seen one do the other well.
> Bob Kinford
> *Cowboy Romance: Of Horsesweat and Hornflies*

> Susie just told Dad to pick up the papers, so he did. Yes
> dear.
> Gina's letter to Bev

One summer when I was a little girl, I donned a fringed vest and a cowboy hat and walked to the bridge that spanned the Missouri River. I sat on the abutment waiting for the rodeo cowboys who would stay with my family. Nestled in the banks of the river, Chamberlain was in many ways a typical little town in the middle of America in the middle of the twentieth century. But hints of its frontier past could still be found in the miles of bluffs where the Arikara once built lodges and the Lakota hunted deer in the ravines; where buffalo migrated through the grasslands; where fur trapper Hugh Glass ended his crawl at Fort Kiowa, battle-scarred but triumphant after wrestling a grizzly. It was here that Lewis and Clark camped on their journey up the river to map the territory Thomas Jefferson had purchased. The map drew men to the Great Plains to plow virgin sod, build railroads, decimate the buffalo herds, and drive

Indians off land they had inhabited for centuries. Embedded in this landscape is the story of grittiness, conquest, and violence, a place where domination defined a history and a man. It was also a place where we could trust our neighbors to show up when prairie fires swept over our pastures; to harvest crops when illness struck; to carry our caskets to the graves they had dug. Violence and compassion grew in equal measure in the arid soil of the Northern Plains.

Finally, a caravan of pickups appeared on the western horizon. They rumbled over the bridge trailing gasoline fumes and the smell of animal hide. They pulled trailers with bucking broncos and Brahma bulls, feverish-eyed and restless animals who stared at me through the slats of the trailers. They had been bred to resist ropes and riders, and they pulled against the restraints that held them. The trailers swerved with the commotion. Country music—Hank Williams or Patsy Cline perhaps—drifted out the windows and mingled with the sound of girders rattling beneath the weight of the trucks. My heart pounded when I spotted the lariats and saddles stacked in the trucks' bed along with sleeping bags and cowboy hats in the back windows. Men squished in front seats squinted in the smoke that circled through the cabs. Did they notice the little girl in fringed vest and a felt cowboy hat tied with a string under my chin? Could they know how rodeos had sparked my dreams of leaning over my saddle urging a quarter horse to race through a figure-eight of barrels? Or the rush I would feel in controlling a thousand-pound animal with a mind of its own?

The rodeo cowboys descended from those who had once worked the open range, sleeping under star-speckled skies, pistols tucked under the saddles on which they lay their heads. They were drifters, cut loose to ramble like the tumbleweeds in a song my father sang. When progress brought pickups and trailers, cattle drives became obsolete. Men who once herded cattle from Texas to Nebraska were now vagabonds traveling the rodeo circuit from Houston to Kansas City, Cheyenne to Calgary, and to small towns in South Dakota. They slept not under the stars but on the floors of strangers. Still, if wandering was the ballad for open-range cowboys, domination was the rodeo cowboy's anthem. Masculinity was the theme that underlay both scores.

The next morning, I crept among the men who slept sprawled over our living room floor, still in dusty jeans and shirts, holes in the toes of their stockings. They smelled of sweat and horse liniment and something sour on their breaths. Some slept on their backs, cowboy hats covering their faces. Others snored softly. Their dusty, weathered boots were lined up on the porch. I ran my finger over the scalloped uppers of one boot, brought the boot to my nose, and inhaled a smell of horse hair and hide. These men inspired my romantic vision of the cowboy who was part knight in shining armor and part mountain man. They chewed tobacco, rolled their own cigarettes, and killed snakes and other varmints. They sat easy in saddles moving to the horse's rhythm in a way that made my stomach fill with the heat of longing; moving in a way I would one day understand is the motion of lovers attuned to one another's bodies.

By the second night of the rodeo, the cowboys moaned in their drugged and restless sleep. White tape covered their hands and elastic bandages were wrapped around their ribs. On a bull rider, plaster white as bones, encased his arm from his wrist to his shoulder. Earlier that day I watched from the grandstand as the bull rider settled on the back of a Brahma bull caged in a chute. He tied one end of the rope around the bull's belly and wrapped the other end around his hand. Then he lifted his free hand above his head and nodded to the rodeo crew to open the gate. He dug his spurs into the bull's sides as the animal spun and bucked out of the chute, the bell on the rope clanging. Swirls of dust rose beneath the animal's hooves. The cowboy swayed back and forth, an air dancer at a tire store. Before the eight seconds were up, the cowboy flew off the bull, hit the dirt, and curled into a ball. The bull spun around, kicked his legs, then landed his back hooves on the cowboy's side, breaking bones in his arm and shoulder and bruising his ribs and liver. Silence fell over the arena as the cowboys carried the rider to an ambulance. "Let's keep that cowboy in our prayers," the announcer said. People around me lowered their heads, but I couldn't take my eyes off his trampled hat lying in the dust.

He came home from the hospital later that night but said little about his injuries except to tell my mother, "Don't worry Maam, I'm fine." She settled him into my father's recliner, gave him aspirin and iced tea, and checked his bandages every few hours. The next morning, I wrote my brand with a crayon on his cast, an *m* over a *w* lying on its side. It was an imitation of the *w* over a lazy *b*—The Woster Brothers' Brand my father seared into our cattle's flanks. He tipped his cowboy hat. In the same voice he used after my mother served him steaks and apple pie, he said, "Well, thank you, Maam." Even today when I think of the word courtly, I picture a battle-battered cowboy digging his spurs into an animal's hide one moment and treating a little girl like a lady the next.

~~~

At the rodeo grounds, Bev ambled among the tourists who wore ten-gallon hats, boots inlaid in patterns of gaudy colors, and jeans creased down the front. Many had purchased these outfits at Wall Drug, a kitchy but popular tourist spot with advertising billboards stretching from South Dakota to Viet Nam. "We've always wanted to see a *ro-Day-o*," they said. I scoffed at the way they pronounced the word rodeo and the way they said *Coyo-te* instead of Ca-yot, or *creek* instead of *crick*. Like country music and jazz, boots and wing tips, language was a dividing line between westerners and city slickers, between men and pansies.

These were the James Dean years when teenage boys like my brother Jim wore black loafers instead of boots, white t-shirts with cigarettes rolled-up in the sleeves instead of shirts with pearl snaps, and black leather jackets, the collars turned up instead of sheepskin. They styled their hair in a slicked-back Duck Ass, which we called a DA. According to my cousin Leo, Bev "combed her hair exactly like Jim's" except for the twisted curl hanging over her forehead. She wore a western shirt and tucked a wad of Copenhagen in her bottom lip; the outline of a jackknife pressed against the back pocket of her jeans. She had somehow morphed into a combination of both—the outlaw—Gina's nickname for her—and the hood. Bev must have puzzled and amused the rodeo men. Was she a cowboy or a greaser? A man or a woman? There was no such duality in the cowboys. They were singularly masculine, at least in my image of them.

My brother Jim described Bev as having a bull-rider's waist, thin but muscular with a low center of gravity that gives a rider better balance so he can stay on the bull's back while the animal bucks, twists, and rattles the rider's bones. Bull riding is a battle between a two-thousand-pound animal and a determined cowboy, a sport that evolved from the Mexican tradition of *japereo*. A bull rider who stays on the bull's back for eight seconds is said to have "grit" like John Wayne.

The opposite of being gritty was "henpecked," or "pussy-whipped" as high school boys called it. Bev complained to Gina that her mother, Sadie, had too much control over Gina's father, Joe. "Your Dad is a good guy," she wrote Gina. "Too bad he doesn't stand on his feet. And show her that he wears the pants around the house. I think he would if we got married and she tired to break us up."

Did Bev recognize that Helara and Sadie, however, showed true grit during the painful days of the murder, the depositions, and the trial.

Likely as she wrestled with redefining herself as a man, Bev looked for an example to follow. That Bev said nothing about her own father's strength suggests that she rejected him as a model. What potential for grit did Bev see in Joe? He had little influence in terms of controlling Gina. She ignored the curfew he imposed and often stayed out with Bev until early morning. He said nothing when she blamed her sister for coming in late, although he suspected she was lying. He said nothing about the relationship between the women. Frank appeared to be detached as well.

Did fear of being seen as weak like her father spur Bev to be violent with Gina that spring of 1962 when the relationship between the two began to unravel. They had argued earlier that day, and Gina slipped a note into Bev's back pocket. *Hon, don't you love me anymore? Really, you called me an awful name today. You are sweet but you seem so crabby.* Later that night, Bev drove to Gina's house. When she spotted Gina walking down the sidewalk, Bev chased her, wrestled her to the ground, and knotted Gina's hair between her fingers the way a calf roper wraps a tie rope around the calf's legs to keep it from escaping. Just then Myron pulled up in his car and rescued Gina. As Bev drove home that night, she may have thought about the bowline knot the cowboys used to keep their horses tied to fences. No matter how hard the animals struggled to escape, the knot held. What knot could she use to tether Gina to her?

~~~

My father, Henry Woster, was a cattle breeder and a farmer, not a cowboy. He smelled of grease and manure. He wore gray chino pants, a shirt buttoned at the cuffs, chamois gloves, and a straw fedora. The sun burned his face except for the patch of pale skin across his forehead protected by his hat. He rode the metal seats of tractors bouncing over the dirt clods of fields in rhythm to the songs he sang. One day his singing drifted to the adjacent field where my cousin Leo was tilling the soil. He hopped off the tractor and strode toward my father who blushed and quit singing. It's an endearing story now, but as a little girl, I was mortified. Unlike Roy Rogers, a showman at best, real cowboys didn't sing as they worked. But in truth, I was rhinestone cowgirl who didn't even own a pair of spurs, much less a horse. Even worse, I was a nervous rider who gripped the saddle horn with both hands and bounced like a baby in a Johnny Jump Up as the horse trotted through the pasture.

If my father was not a cowboy, he was a straight-up man who could "do things." A neighbor boy watching my father turn the tractor with only one hand on the steering wheel knob once asked, "Why doesn't he have power steering?" His father answered, "Because Henry Woster doesn't need power steering." He could castrate a bull calf with a minimum of bleeding, pull a calf feet-first from a jittery, pain-ridden heifer birthing her first calf, and rip open a feed sack with bare hands. He expected his sons to be men who could "do things" as well. He crackled with impatience when my brothers acted like teenage boys, which they were. "One boy's a man; two boy's half a man, and three boys are no man at all," he muttered the day my brother Terry and cousin Leo were mowing the hay fields and played chicken on the tractors. Neither boy would turn his tractor away. They collided, bending the tie rods and denting the radiator. For several days, they lowered their heads whenever they walked by my father afraid of the anger and disappointment on his face. At the same time, he was the father who comforted his little girl by telling a lie.

He told that lie one branding day when I perched on the top railing of the fence wishing it were my father not my uncle Frank who rode a horse into the corral. My uncle tucked his jeans into his boots and tied a neckerchief inside his collar. He held the reins loosely in one hand and pressed his knees against the horse's flanks. They ambled toward several yearlings bunched up and bawling against the fence. Horse and rider were deciding which calf "to cut out of the herd." In cattle cutting, horse and calf face each other, hooves deep in the dust, reacting to one another's slightest movements in an intuitive dance until finally the calf lowers its head in defeat. Like a boy leading a girl onto the dance floor, my uncle guided the horse and calf to the chute where my father waited. The letters on a branding iron glowed red in a pile of coals in the dirt.

My father had explained to me that he branded the cattle so he could identify and claim a cow that might break through a fence and wander to a neighbor's pasture. Or worse rise from a ditch at night and collide with a vehicle. I secretly hoped that he worried about cattle rustlers and imagined him brandishing a pistol and chasing the thief through the dark, although he didn't own a pistol. What he didn't prepare me for was the brutality of the branding.

He pushed a calf through a chute toward an upright metal table with large hooks on the top. He clamped the hooks around the calf and flipped the table. The animal lay on its side bellowing and banging his head against the hooks that trapped him. A hiss of hot iron against hair, a sizzling of hide, and the smell of something scorched as he burned our brand into the calf's flank. The branding took seconds, but the bellowing of the calf seared my heart the way the branding iron seared the calf's hide.

A child who grows up on a farm or ranch knows the reality of animals and pain. I had seen my father put a rifle to the skull of a heifer bloated and struggling to stand, heard the crack when he pulled the trigger. I had heard stories of cousins shooting a doe thrashing in the ditch, its crooked leg bent beneath her body, eyes wild with pain. These were quick, deliberate, necessary acts of mercy. But these yearlings weren't suffering. They were simply innocent, compliant creatures submitting to a man who had power over them. How could my father be so cruel? When he saw that I was crying, he pushed through a cluster of calves pawing the dirt and snorting. He climbed up on the railing, took off his glove, and wiped my tears. "It doesn't hurt him, Toots," my father assured me. "He's just a bit scared."

I believed the lie for years.

I was probably ten-years old the day my father walked into the house, hung his hat on a hook, and collapsed into his easy chair with a book in his hand. He said nothing about his swollen lips, missing teeth, and face covered in purple bruises. In the same way, he said nothing about those days that he sliced his hands fixing barbed-wire fences or felt his limbs grow numb as he hauled corn to the feed trough over grass glazed with ice and snow. Men, even men who sang as they worked, suffered pain in silence. Later I asked my mother what had happened. She shook her head and whispered something about a steer and a metal bar leaving me to imagine this scenario: Barrel-chested steers bunch together in the corral, the way they do in the pastures when storm clouds gather. They flick their tails at flies crawling over their hide, lower their heads, slobbering and eying my father warily. The summer sun is intense and my father's shirt soaked. The fabric clings to his back, defining the muscles in his shoulders. Dust swirls around his face. He spits but the taste of earth lingers on his tongue. He uses a cattle prod to move a steer toward the chute, leans his shoulder against the animal's flank, and shoves it into the chute. Then he threads a bar through holes in the sides to keep the animal from backing out. He may be tired and frustrated with grappling a balky animal, and so he is careless about securing the bar. The steer kicks with its force of twelve-hundred pounds and knocks the metal rod into my father's face. Spitting blood, choking on bits of shattered tooth, he staggers but doesn't fall. Angry at the steer and at himself for being careless, he picks up a wooden board and whacks the steer on the back until both are exhausted. He drops the board, leans over his knees, chest heaving. Then he lifts the gate, watches the animal limp toward the pasture, and then staggers to the house leaving a trail of blood behind him.

SILENCE AND SHAME

A girl in the years of her puberty becomes quiet within
and begins to think about the wonders happening to her
body.
Anne Frank
The Diary of a Young Girl

Well, you knew you were a girl, didn't you Beverly?
In a way, yes.
Bev's testimony at the trial

This shedding of my womb-lining is my offering,
my prayer, my blood. My purification ceremony.
Carmellia De Los Angeles Guiol
"In My Culture, Having A Period Is Powerful"

On a steamy July day in 1958, rare, humid
weather on the western prairies filled the air with a
sense of abundance, and the sweet, milky-scented
corn rose from our fields like Jack's beanstalk, rich
with life and promise. I should have been nestled
among the trees in the shelter belts where the lush
scent of ripening plums hung in the air and the sun
was a mother's hand warming my back. Instead, I
curled up on my comforter, pressing my fingers into
my abdomen as if to loosen the knot twisting in my
belly.

A few months shy of my thirteenth birthday and later to start my period than many of my friends, I listened with interest as they described the cramps and soothing heat of hot water bottles pressed against their tummies. I spotted Midol tablets in their purses and watched as they dropped quarters in dispensers on the bathroom walls. The gears grinded as Kotex boxes tumbled into the slots. I was somewhat prepared when it came to remedies, but I knew nothing about the biological process of menstruation.

I left the bedroom and walked to the kitchen where Mother sang as she unfolded dough over the counter top, sprinkled it with sugar and cinnamon, rolled it into a log, and sliced the dough with a string. I peeked around the corner and whispered, "Mom, I think I started my period."

"Go back to your room. I'll be there in a minute."

She didn't look at me when she handed me a box of Kotex and a thin elastic belt with hooks dangling from two strands. "Here, use these." Her voice was brisk, the tone she used when she was annoyed or disappointed with me. She walked out of the room, the smell of flour and yeast trailing her. I sat up, pulled my legs to my chest, and rested my chin on my knees. The wind coming through the windows washed over me warm as bath water and sweat trickled down my back and pooled in the elastic band of my underwear. I sensed my body was moist and fertile as summer hayfields. At the same time, I shivered as if winter had arrived early.

I picked up a notebook and wrote down the words my friends used for menstruation: reassuring words—the monthlies, my friend, the visitor— and nasty words—on the rag, the curse, and the plague which made me think of locusts eating our wheat fields to stubble. Was menstruation a good thing or a bad thing? How did Mother feel when she first spotted the blood in her underwear? What had my grandmother told her? Most of my friends complained that they learned little or nothing about menstruation from their mothers. Probably Bev, too, had seen her mother purse her lips and look away when Bev asked questions about her body. If so, she was likely unwilling to ask her mother, "What does this mean? How do I use this pad?"

I tugged at the tape on the cardboard box Mother had given me. Tucked between the pads was a pamphlet with a list of do's and don'ts for girls who were menstruating: Do take warm baths, do use deodorant, do wear your prettiest dresses. Don't participate in strenuous activities like softball and don't go swimming for at least three days after your period starts. I was a tomboy in cut-off jeans who still climbed trees, sailed rafts over the muddy-watered stock dam, and hiked through the north pasture where the wind rustled the wheatgrass and grasshoppers brushed against my bare legs. The words in the pamphlet said to me: don't be the girl you used to be.

An illustration in the pamphlet showed how to use the pad and sanitary belt. My real teacher was the frustration of bending and twisting my body to snag the pad to the clips on the belt. The ordeal left me sweaty, exhausted, and miserable. I walked into the kitchen, a bowlegged toddler in diapers. My mother must have noticed, but still she said nothing. That night I lay in bed watching the moon slip in and out of the clouds. My teacher said that the moon was locked in a cycle of twenty-eight days that ended by disappearing into the earth's shadows. I was trapped in a monthly pattern of blood, a victim in a horror movie obliterated by a slimy blob absorbing everything in its path.

Sometime later I chanced upon my mother's panties floating in the sink, a silky jellyfish in a rose-tinged sea. But she never spoke of her periods, and her silence suggested something shameful about the carmine-colored stain in my undies. What purpose did the bleeding serve and why was it such a dark color? Maybe it wasn't even my period but something awful—an infection or cancer. I would never ask Mother those questions. We would never speak of this moment. To this day, the earthy fragrance of cinnamon triggers memories of silence and dried blood in underwear.

Bev had enrolled in school later than her classmates and then repeated a grade. She must have been twelve or thirteen years old when she was in fifth grade and had her first period. While I was a six-year-old child playing jacks and Hopscotch, Bev was likely the only girl in her class to be menstruating which must have made her feel even more of an outsider.

Was Bev disappointed, confused, or even terrified when her breasts ached and her nipples pressed against her t-shirt; or when she doubled over her school desk, her belly muscles coiling inward and something seeping between her thighs? I can't assume that Bev struggled to deal with menstruation. It's possible that Bev didn't mind. Or maybe she felt crampy, cranky, and fatigued as I did even though I didn't do physical labor like Bev. Very likely, Bev's feelings toward menstruation were complicated by her identifying as a male. She spent her days lugging heavy, wet laundry across a room, tromping the corn fields with a gun over her shoulder, and riding a horse across the river bluffs. How could she not resent the feeling of a bulky pad pressing against her jeans and her breasts swaying as she ran down the corn rows chasing a pheasant.

Helara never questioned the changes in Bev's outward appearance and so it's unlikely she talked to Bev about "all that was taking place inside her body" as Anne Frank wrote. That silence must have made Bev unable to confide in her mother or her sister Norma. She couldn't even confide in Gina because she had not yet admitted to her lover that she was a woman, not a man.

~~~

A week after I began menstruating, my family stopped at the library as we did every week after our swimming lessons. Tiny Miss Arp sat at her desk in the middle of the room, white hair pulled back in a bun, an ink-stained rubber tip on her finger. Her face was pale as Talcum powder. Wire glasses perched on the end of her nose. She always tucked a lacy hankie that smelled of lilacs in the sleeve of her blouse. Despite her size, she possessed a silent authority over this book-filled room, a power that often intimidated me. I scurried past her in fear she'd notice how water dripped off my pony tail and onto the library floor leaving a trail of white, chlorine-smelling spots on the hardwood. If she saw the stains, she didn't scold me. I was an avid reader and that atoned for my sins.

But mostly I admired her for choosing the perfect books for me to read, books I realize now that had guided me on my path to adulthood: *Anne of*

Green Gables, Black Beauty, Little Women, To Kill a Mockingbird, and *Anne Frank: The Diary of a Young Girl.* Because Bev mostly read magazines like *Sports Afield,* she probably didn't go to the library where Miss Arp might have helped her as she helped me with book recommendations, not about gender bending perhaps, but a Beverly Cleary story of a young woman solving her problems.

In my memory, African Violets bloomed on the shelf in a corner and crystals hanging in the windows cast rainbows over the books, the way words dispersed enlightenment. I ran my fingers over the spine of Anne Frank's diary, slipped the book from the shelf. In my mind's eye, I see a photo of a young girl on the cover. Dark hair framed her narrow face and the corners of her mouth suggested a pensive, knowing smile. But I think now that the picture I recall may have been the cover of a later edition. Sixty years of memories often merge into a single image, perhaps an aunt's face, a stock pond in pastures, or a mother rolling sweet dough over a counter.

Anne Frank was a Jewish girl hiding with her family in an attic in Amsterdam during the Holocaust. She wrote her diary during those two years of silence and fear. I scanned the first few pages and despite our overwhelming differences, I felt an instant connection to Anne. She was thirteen, nearly my age when her father gave her the diary with the red-and-white-checkered cover. She was private and often lonely. "I never discuss myself with anybody. That is why I have to talk to myself." Although my family was large and boisterous, I often felt alone and unable to share my feelings or ask honest questions.

But in another way, she was nothing like me. She eagerly anticipated menstruation. "When I get my period, I'll be really grown up... the important news. . . I'm probably going to get my period soon. I keep finding a whitish stain in my panties." I had no idea what the "whitish stain" might have meant and couldn't understand her enthusiasm for something so gross and burdensome. How could she celebrate this?

I took the book to Miss Arp's desk and handed it to her. She studied the cover a moment, then looked up and smiled. "This is an excellent choice." She stamped the return date in purple letters and numbers on the back page and gave it to me. I floated down the stairs the word "excellent" echoing in the stairwell.

Back home, I crept into the walk-in closet, sat under clothes hanging on a rack overhead, and rested my back against my father's bass drum, the diary in my hand. The smell of dried calfskin hung faintly in the stale air and cobwebs sparkled in the sunlight. The sounds of my childhood enveloped me—Mother playing the piano in the living room, the sizzling of a blow torch as my father welded machine parts in the shed, and the bellowing of cattle trudging down the cow path to the feedlot. Under the noise, I could almost hear Anne's voice saying to Kitty, the name she gave her diary, "I hope I will be able to confide in you as I have never been able to confide in anyone. And I hope you will be a great source of comfort and support."

That summer Anne became my confidant and my best friend. I carried the book everywhere—to the granary roof where the smell of wheat in the bins below was yeasty and clean; under the plum trees where black beetles scurried over clods of dirt beneath my bare legs; in the back of the pickup, the words jiggling with each bump over the ruts. I read the diary so often I could almost hear her fountain pen whispering over the pages as she scribbled the thoughts of adolescent girls. "Could anyone know how much went on in the mind of a young girl?"

Like me, Anne needed a place to be alone. She often climbed the ladder to a space above the attic and stuck her nose in a crack in the window to smell the woody fragrance of the chestnut tree. She peeked through a slit in the curtain to watch men and women running to catch trams and children pedaling bicycles down the sidewalk. Their jackets flapped behind them; the dinging of little bells merged with the sound of boats slicing through the still water of the canal. Beyond the rooftop was "a strip of blue so pale it was almost invisible." She must have wondered what lay beyond that skyline and feared, perhaps knew, that she would never live to see whatever was there. Unlike Anne, I could climb to the top of the granary roof and watch a parade of clouds march across the sky. I could hear geese in flight and smell the musty aroma of cattle in the feedlot below. The distant swell of the horizon suggested an unlimited, if uncertain, future.

I have since visited the secret annex on the Prinsengracht canal, a cloudy, sluggish waterway in central Amsterdam. Many of the original furnishings in the rooms have been destroyed including the bookcase that hid the secret door to the annex. The musty starkness of the rooms captured those bleak years of isolation and fear the family had endured. Traces of Anne lingered in pictures of movies stars pasted on the wall and in her words that echoed in the stillness. *Those who have courage and faith will never perish in misery.* I stopped short when I spotted the lines Mr. Frank had drawn on the wall to mark his children's growth. In that room miles and years from my childhood, it was as if I felt my father's broad hand resting lightly on the top of my head as he penciled my height into the wallpaper in my bedroom.

In this place, I finally understood my friend. Hidden in an attic for two years, Anne had already relinquished the freedoms of an adolescent, the joyful and painful rites of passage that I had experienced. Perhaps the physical process of puberty was the only sense of normality in that secret annex, a hint of her immortality in the children she might bear one day.

It is impossible to imagine that Anne died at fifteen without knowing that years later, her diary would fall into the hands of a farm girl on the other side of the world. Impossible to think that she would never know how her words "the sweet secret. . . so wonderful, and not only what can be seen on my body, but all that is taking place inside" would both puzzle and yet comfort me as I navigated puberty.

~~~

If silence was the approach my mother took to my puberty, her sister, my Aunt Evelyn, shared a few stories about her experience with menstruation. "Your grandmother was so prudish that she made me and your mother rinse our menstrual rags in a bucket outside and then hang them to dry behind the shed where our brothers wouldn't see them. One day, I ran across the yard, the wet rags dripping between my fingers. I heard my brothers laughing and looked over my shoulder to see if they were near. I tripped and landed in the dirt. I had to rewash the rags and then my clothes."

She laughed so hard, she snorted.

Her laughter made me laugh as well. But in my mind's eye, I saw her kneeling in the dirt, brushing the dust off her face and the blood from her scraped knees, then running back to the house with the rag scrunched in her hand. I imagined my grandmother's disappointment and worry that her sons might have witnessed the moment, not because of her daughter's humiliation, but because of her sons' embarrassment. Evelyn's story of shame eventually helped me to understand my mother's silence and discomfort with her body.

Mothers and aunties in other cultures celebrate a girl's passage into womanhood with ceremonies. Today, on the Yankton Sioux/Ihanktonwan Oyate Reservation in South Dakota, girls experiencing their first menses celebrate Isnati Awica Dowanpi, the coming-of-age ceremony. Dakota women quit practicing this ceremony many years ago, most likely discouraged by European settlers or forbidden by Christian missionaries as something primitive or pagan. But twenty years ago, the Dakota grandmothers revived the rituals of puberty with the "intent of calling home the spirit of the culture."

"As a grandmother and great-grandmother, I

just wanted to come and spend a few hours," said Madonna Thunderhawk of participating in the ceremony. "At one time, all of this was underground. We only got the American Indian Freedom of Religion Act in the late '70s. So, we stand our ground to have these things out in the open again."

The girls set up the moon lodge on the banks of the Missouri River where eagles swoop overhead and cottonwood leaves chatter in the wind, a place where the past and present merge. Because the young women are considered at the peak of their power, they spend four days isolated from men who might steal that power. They study the Dakota language, gather healing herbs and plants, and make pemmican with buffalo meat and berries. They are not allowed to touch food or drink while in the moon lodge, so the mothers feed their daughters in a ritual one mother described as bittersweet. "I can treat my daughter like a baby one last time before she becomes a woman."

On the fourth day, their mothers or aunties bathe them in sage water and instruct them in the ways of dating, marriage, and pregnancy. They tell the girls stories of their own experiences, providing reassuring models of how to become women. Finally, they give the girls their Indian names and dress them in brightly colored clothing with beaded ribbons the girls have sewn. They then introduce the girls to the community as the newest members of the Brave Heart Women's Society. They celebrate this ceremonial coming of age with feasting and dancing.

My Aunt Evelyn, like the Dakota aunties, engaged and instructed me with stories about her life as a young girl, wife, and mother. She modeled the strength of women as she talked of marrying during the Depression years and of following her husband from railroad town to railroad town; she described living in shacks where dirt seeped through the linoleum and winter frost blanketed the windows. "Either I was scrubbing dirt off my daughters' knees or scraping windows so the sun could shine into the house. Of course, if I'd left the windows alone, I wouldn't have seen the dirt on their knees. Oh well, guess the joke's on me." Irish humor grounded in pathos and irony often prompted her to laughter and tears. She chuckled. Then wiped her eyes.

A small and spunky Irish woman, she taught that a woman should never allow a man to control or demean her. On my wedding day she took me aside and offered one bit of advice. "Keep your cast iron skillet handy and in a place where he can see it. A whack on the head can change his attitude." I assumed she was kidding, but then again. . .

After my uncle died, Aunt Evelyn took a job as a housekeeper for the bishop of her diocese. She was fond of him and respectful of his authority in the Church. But she had her limits. One night he looked at the dinner she served him and said with a bit of disgust, "Evelyn, what is this?"

"Bishop, you have two choices. Eat it or wear it."

I adored Aunt Evelyn for being so defiant. I adored her because she talked to me as if I were her contemporary, sharing family secrets of cousins drinking and sibling's financial problems. My mother's family protected her from unpleasant truths about her family's struggles with alcoholism and depression. She passed the culture of shame and silence on to me. Aunt Evelyn revealed those family secrets because she wasn't ashamed of them. She didn't cling to the false security of silence.

I envy the Dakota girls, separated from the clan and pampered and instructed by older women. Envy the time they had alone to prepare for the changes to come in their bodies and in their lives, envy their being taught to embrace the power of being a woman. But at least I had Aunt Evelyn and Ann who helped me to understand that blood is the common bond among women, and if we're comfortable with our gender, we should honor that bond.

The Dakota girls were taught that menstruation was a natural, mysterious, powerful process and a cause to celebrate. My mother learned to feel shame at menstruation. But if she felt too uncomfortable with her own bodily functions to guide me through the process, or if she couldn't celebrate my transition into womanhood, I'm quite certain that with four children under the age of six, she rejoiced each time she bled.

RITUALS, TABOOS, AND TRANSFORMATIONS

> What a gal I have.
> Yes hon were really happy together
> and it is a wonderful felling hon.
> I found a wonderful gal that I really care about.
> And I'd like to have a life with my hon.
> The more time we spend together the stronger our love
> grows.
> Bev's letter to Gina

> They [lesbians] are more immature than the majority of
> individuals
> and would probably be more temperamental
> and more changeable as a result of this immaturity.
> Testimony of Dr. Richard Leander

The Lettermen sang "The Way You Look Tonight," and I dreamed of being in the arms of Michael Sean O'Donnell, my head tucked under his chin as we twirled around the junior high school gym. My father walked by singing "I will feel a thrill just thinking of you and the way you looked tonight." How did he know my generation's music? He winked, grinned, and said, "When I was a young man, Toots, I sang that to a special girl." Then he walked away leaving me to envision my mother playing the piano in her family's parlor while her tall suitor, my father, leaned over her shoulder, his breath warm on her flushed cheek.

If my mother was hands brushing my feverish forehead with cool fingers, my father was the heart of my childhood, the one who sang love songs and with threads of fanciful words wove stories of airplane rides to the North Pole, of bottomless lakes, and of prehistoric sea creatures roaming the prairies. He took me to *The King and I* when I was ten-years old. We sat in the front row sucking on lemon drops he had stuck in his coat pocket, our tongues sugar sticky and thick with bits of pocket lint. On the drive home down River Street, we sang "Shall We Dance?" His rich tenor blending with my thin, little-girl voice was sweet honey drizzled in weak tea. For that moment, stars glittering on the dark river were chandeliers lighting a ballroom, and the wind, violins playing arpeggios. He was a bald-headed king in silk trousers and slippers; I, a pale-shouldered woman in a ruffled gown that lifted behind me as we romped around the room. I couldn't imagine a day when I wouldn't dance with my father wherever he led me.

By my thirteenth birthday on December 8, 1958, I had already negotiated, or more truthfully survived, the many firsts of puberty: first bra—white cotton and padded, first period and hot water bottle pressed to my belly, first curly hair in private places, and first crush on a pudgy boy who shared a desk with me. But that year my birthday marked a special rite of passage into the teenage rituals of sock hops and slow dances, walks in the moonlight, and shy glances at a boy across the classroom. My father had agreed that Michael Sean O'Donnell could meet me at the movies. He was new in town, a ginger-haired boy with cornflower-blue eyes, freckles, and a crooked front tooth; a boy who made my stomach flutter with hummingbirds feeding on nectar.

My mother enjoyed the rites that celebrated childhood—baptism, first communion, and birthdays with cakes decorated with horses and cowgirls. For my thirteenth birthday, Mother baked an angel food cake, covered it in green icing, draped a string of silver candy beads through the frosting, and nestled a Cinderella doll in the center. She hid the cake in the pantry the way she used to hide my other presents—cowgirl outfits with gun and holster under her bed at Christmas and colored eggs under the yellow tulips at Easter. But she couldn't conceal the fragrance of sugar and vanilla that saturated the house. Why didn't I follow the aroma to the cake, trail my finger through the icing, and lick the sweetness with my tongue? This might have prepared me to be more gracious when she carried the cake into the dining room, her face lit by the candles.

"Mother, a Cinderella cake, really? I'm thirteen."

She slammed the cake on the table and stomped out of the room. "I just want to put a brick on your head so you never grow up."

When she came back from the kitchen wiping her eyes, I didn't apologize. I blew out the candles and opened my gifts from her—Bonnie Doone anklets and a lacquered jewelry box with a ballerina that twirled to "Swan Lake" in front of a mirror. My father gave me a diary because I told him about the red-and-white checkered diary Otto Frank had given Anne on her thirteenth birthday. Mine was midnight blue with a brass lock in the shape of a heart and a tiny brass key. He penned a poem on the front page: *What Should I write/What should I say? To my little girl on her thirteenth birthday/In seven more years, you will be twenty/between now and then, I'll say plenty.*

My father loved words and was an inventive storyteller, but I had never known him to write a poem. His wistful words unexpected and tender touched me. He died only two years after I turned twenty. What was the "plenty" he had promised to tell me? Would he give me financial advice? Lecture me on social responsibility and personal morality? Could he have imagined how I would disappoint him? How a time would come when we would seldom speak?

I threw the diary away when I went to college so my little brother couldn't read it. I knew about snoopy siblings. I had read my sister's diary she had hidden behind shoe boxes in our closet. Her description of a friend kissing a boy so hard "her lips were bruised and purple" was titillating. I wouldn't give Kevin the same illicit thrill. For some reason, I ripped the page with the poem out of my diary and kept it for years in a small pine box with a silver horse glued to the lid. I sometimes took it out and traced the words written in his feathery handwriting on parchment that grew more fragile each year.

I lost the box in a move to a new house but never forgot his words.

After the presents and birthday cake, I ran to my room to get ready for the movie. I dressed slowly, relishing each step of the first-date ritual: slipping on a blouse and a cardigan sweater, pink and fuzzy, and then stiff jeans with the cuffs rolled; tucking dimes in the notches in black loafers and polishing the toes with Kleenex. I swiped my face with foundation, an extra heavy layer over the acne that dotted my cheeks, dabbed my lips with hot-pink gloss, swept my waist-length hair into a pony tail tied with a satiny ribbon, then clasped a rhinestone bracelet on my wrist. Finally, a spritz of Avon Eau de Parfume.

For once the reflection in the mirror pleased me as I twirled like a ballerina, my pony tail swirling behind me. Even it danced that night. Nothing could go wrong.

When my father dropped me off at the State Theater, horizontal sheets of snow swept over the sidewalk. Michael Sean O'Donnell paced in front of the movie posters his jacket collar turned up. In my experience, boys held the power in matters of romance. Could he possibly be as nervous as I? I opened the car door expecting my father to insist on picking me after the movie. Instead, he said, "He can walk you home, but I want you in the house thirty minutes after the movie ends." His words were firm, but the corners of his mouth hinted of a smile. He may have been nostalgic and a bit worried, yet amused by my first romantic adventure.

I dashed across the street to wait with Michael Sean for the doors to open. The marquis lights made the freckles on his pale skin glow; flakes of snow glittering on his eyelashes were powdered sugar on strawberries. Later, sitting in the movie theater with Michael Sean, I didn't care that a musty odor wafted from the thread-bare drapes that hung over the screen, didn't care that my shoes stuck to pools of soda under the seat. What could those things matter when Michael Sean O'Donnell was so close that I could feel his chest rising and falling, could smell the soap on his skin? When we reached in the popcorn box, our hands brushed against one another's. Love was the taste of butter and salt.

Everything was perfect. Then it wasn't. Snap. A spring in the seat cushion pushed against my bottom. No amount of twisting and shifting could relieve the pressure. I imagined jumping up, screaming, and running out of the theater, a puncture wound in my buttocks. Miraculously the spring held. That catastrophe averted I revived my adolescent script of a perfect date ending with my first kiss. He would reach up to unscrew the porch light, and I would wrap my arms around his neck and thread my fingers through his hair. His lips would be cool and soft, his breathing shallow and warm against my face. But instead, he said goodnight, turned away, jogged down the sidewalk, and faded into the shadows between the streetlights. We never met at the movies again and he never told me why. At the end of the school term, Michael Sean moved away. Heartbreak following joy was my rite of passage into adolescence.

~~~

On December 24, 1958, three weeks after my disastrous date with Michael Sean, Gina had her first date with Myron Menzie who had just transferred to her high school. Myron was the star football player; Gina was a sophomore cheerleader. In a small town in South Dakota in 1958, their romance on the one hand was as traditional as homecoming coronations and winter formals. On the other hand, the young couple shattered an unspoken but unambiguous taboo against interracial romances.

The Menzie family came from the Rosebud Reservation in southwestern South Dakota near the Nebraska border. This is a place of wide ranges and rolling hills where cottonwood trees line the banks of the narrow Keya Paha River, Turtle Hill in Lakota language. A senior in high school, Myron was handsome, athletic, and smart. He'd already been awarded a scholarship to attend a teachers' college in southeast South Dakota that specialized in technical training. Likely, he hoped to study industrial arts, perhaps be a teacher and a coach.

What did Myron and Gina do that night? The Chamberlain movie theater and cafes were closed on Christmas Eve. No high school basketball games were scheduled or keg parties in the pasture planned. Perhaps they went to the truck stop on Highway16 to sip hot chocolate frosted with marshmallows. Maybe they read the license plates on trucks that pulled up to the pumps wondering what it would be like to be a teenager in Michigan or New Mexico. Gina may have learned how to flirt as most of us had from magazines like *Seventeen* that suggested "wear dangling earrings to catch his attention, tease him and let him do manly things like carry your books." Or "Look him in the eyes and then slowly move down to his lips and let them linger there."

Perhaps they strolled through town on a night when the sky was studded with stars, a night so still they could hear the sifting of snow as it fell from the trees, the flakes melting on their faces. Love that night may have been as simple as a boy and girl walking hand-in-hand on a winter evening, as gentle as the feeling of the boy's hand on the small of the girl's back as he guided her up the steps to the front door, as certain as the boy reaching up to loosen a light bulb. In the moonlight, the winter trees were skeletal and eerie, but the young couple were aware of nothing but the warmth of the other's body against their own.

I don't know when I realized that romance between races was a line that "good girls" did not cross. A few older girls from Chamberlain were rebellious or courageous enough to go steady with boys from the Crow Creek reservation. Their jet-black hair hung long and straight to their waists and beaded earrings shaped like feathers dangled from their earlobes. They wore faded jeans and tawny-colored moccasins. Mothers pursed their lips and shook their heads slightly when they saw the girls walk down the sidewalk, their long hair swaying. I envied their exotic look. One summer, I wanted to buy a pair of turquoise moccasins beaded with patterns of bright yellow lightning and sunshine. I pleaded with my mother. "Why won't you let me buy these? Lots of girls wear moccasins. What's wrong with them?" Mother said nothing. She tromped out of the store. I never asked for another pair of moccasins.

Nothing in the transcripts and letters suggests that inter-racial dating presented a problem for Gina and Myron. It's not clear how Sadie felt about Gina's romance with Myron. But if she had the same objections that many mothers had to daughters dating native boys, she probably overlooked them especially once Gina had accepted an engagement ring from Myron. That would solve the problem with Bev.

Why didn't Gina have the same concerns about dating a native boy that I had? What was different in Pukwana that made their romance seem less forbidden? Maybe the young couple were oblivious to the disapproval. Or didn't care. Being a much smaller community than Chamberlain, there may have been none of the class divisions— arbitrary and absurd economic, social, intellectual, and racial distinctions—that dictated whom people could date. Samuel Masten, Bev's defense attorney, alluded to such class differences between the Waugh and Lee families in his questioning of Gina. "It was poor circumstances and a rather poor home located on the back of the hills down by the river, right? But you have a nice place over there in Pukwana. You recognize, Gina, that Bev is not of the intellectual level that you are?"

Gina nodded, "Yes."

Masten likely intended to suggest to the jury that Gina possessed the power in her relationship with Bev and that somehow made her responsible or at least complicit in the murder. He would return to this line of questioning often throughout the trial. But he never addressed the power that being white gave Gina.

~~~

By the time Gina and Myron began to date in1958, Bev was transitioning into a male appearance except for her hair which she still wore long. Barber shops in those days belonged to men, and Bev likely feared entering that sanctuary. Imagine Bev leaning against the window of Elmer's Barber Shop, her face watery in the frosted glass. She longs to be among these men, to feel a barber patting her cheeks with shaving cream and running a razor through the foam. She longs to feel the cool sting of aftershave on tender skin, to grab her crotch and rearrange herself when she stands up. Once, like bartenders, barbers listened while men unburdened themselves about financial problems, troubled children, or a much-regretted rendezvous on the river bluffs with another man's wife. It may have been the one place where a man could relax into the pleasure of a man rubbing his shoulders, gliding a straight edge through the foam on his face, or patting aftershave on his skin; where he could be touched by another man without fear of being called a fag or a queer.

I walked into Elmer's Barbershop only one time when I was very small and wanted a nickel from my father to buy a package of gum. Old Spice and Bay Rum bottles shimmered in the mirrors, their fragrances wafting through the transom above the door. On a calendar, a leggy blonde in fringed shorts and midriff top pursed her lips around a bottle of Coke. She looked under long lashes at men who wondered what it would be like to go home to such a woman instead of wives with sagging bellies from too many babies or slices of pie.

Sitting in chairs along one wall, boys read comic books—*Superman, Captain Marvel, The Green Lantern.* Bazooka bubbles ballooned, pink and translucent fish bladders, from their lips. Men smoked cigars, flicked the ashes in ashtrays, flipped through the pages of *Sports Afield*. During the school day, perhaps they read *Playboy* kept in a drawer under the cash register. From the radio came the crack of a bat and the men cheered and shook their fists as Ernie Banks rounded the bases at Wrigley Field. It felt almost sinful to enter this sacred place, the way I felt creeping into the church and writing my name in the filmy bottom of the holy water fount.

My father sat in a barber chair a towel draped around his neck. He smiled when he saw me in the mirror, turned around, and reached in his pocket for a coin. One man looked at my coveralls, my hair tangled from roughhousing with my brothers, my muddy sneakers, and said, "Elmer, get the clippers. This little girl wants her hair cut short like a boy's. Maybe she wants to be a boy." When my father dropped the coin in my hand, I ran out of the room through their laughter. For the first time, but not the last, I felt uneasy surrounded by men who made boyish girls a target of ridicule.

~~~

That winter of 1958, Bev's bowling team won the city tournament and the team would be recognized at the annual banquet. Perhaps to please her mother, Bev wore a dress for the trophy presentation. It may have been a shirtwaist dress in deep-blue cotton with a gathered skirt and sleeves trimmed in satin, a popular style that year. Or maybe she chose a slim skirt and blouse with a Peter Pan collar, my homeroom teacher's standard uniform.

Dressing for special occasions tortured me. The girdle's rubber pinched my skin as I inched it over my legs and hips, my muffin top falling over the girdle's waistband. The metal clips attached to the nylons dug into my thighs and left indentations that lasted the night. I snitched powder and mascara from my sister's drawer along with a delicate-smelling cologne to spray behind my ears. An hour later my eyes were smudged with black and the powder caked by sweat.

Did Bev go through the daily ritual that most girls followed to be pretty enough to attract a boy? Did she wash and rinse her hair in lemon juice until the strands squeaked, then twist them in spirals and pin them with bobby pins? Was her scalp covered in snail-shell curls like Buddha? Did she sit on the edge of the tub shaving the fine hair off her legs and armpits, pluck her eyebrows in front of a small mirror, and brush her hair one-hundred strokes? Bev likely did not do any of these things. What kind of boy would date her?

Bev must have been miserable rummaging through Norma's vanity drawers for eye shadow and lip gloss when she'd rather be sorting lures in a box of fishing tackle. How strange the scent of the cologne for her, sweet and cloying, so different from the rusty smell of blood on a freshly-killed pheasant. When she looked in the mirror, her face glistening with powder, did she see only the sharp angles of her boyish, yet female body? Did she still feel like a misfit among girls comfortable with their curves and soft places?

My mother bowled in a league and must have attended the banquet, but I don't remember her saying anything about it. However, Gina's mother, Sadie, a member of Bev's team, testified that people laughed when Bev walked into the room. She turned and ran out the room, a wounded and frightened deer cornered by predators. "Don't leave," one woman called. "We're sorry but we've just never seen you look so girly." Even when a member of her bowling team grabbed her arm and begged, "Stay, please," she fled to her car and sped down Main Street to her home on the river bottom.

Sadie testified she didn't see Bev crying, so she couldn't swear it happened. "But she looked real nice. That was the last time I saw Bev wearing a dress. After that she wore a man's suit to dress-up affairs like weddings and funerals."

Today there are websites and books with tips on binding breasts and choosing clothing that conceals curves. There are stores that sell packing devices that give the feeling and the appearance of a penis.

Many websites offer strategies for avoiding womanly mannerisms like smiling with an open mouth or leaning forward while conversing. Perhaps Bev's father and three brothers unintentionally modeled for her ways to act like a man—grin through tight lips, use a firm grip when you shake hands, and lean back in the chair. Both Bev's cousin Larry and my cousin Leo recalled how Bev sat at the counter in the Rainbow Café with knees spread, calves wrapped around the stool's legs. "I thought it odd she sat that way. But then most things about Bev were odd or at least different from other girls," her cousin said. For Bev, that macho position likely exuded power, power denied to girls who wore dresses and sat primly with knees together.

The night of the bowling banquet may have been when Bev acting on instincts fully transitioned from a womanly to a masculine appearance. I sometimes think of her standing in front of a mirror, wiping the lipstick off her mouth with the back of her hand. She must have felt liberated as she slipped out of pointy-toed flats and a dress and girdle that cinched her waist so tightly she couldn't breathe. Perhaps she felt the pleasure of ripping off the nylons that chaffed the inner thighs. Did Bev know that some lesbians in cities wore their hair cut short and slicked back like the school's hood Duke and my brother Jim? Did she think of them when she grabbed her mother's sewing scissors and hacked at her hair, the strands whispering as they fell in black pools around her feet.

Bev turned her bra backwards, her breasts flattening beneath the band as she snapped it. She pulled her jeans up over her narrow hips, stuffed a rolled-up sock down the front, then stood in the front of the mirror practicing how the Duke narrowed his eyes and let a cigarette dangle from the corner of his mouth. She practiced his swagger as she walked through the living room. Bev's short hair dismayed her mother. "Oh, Beverly, what did you do?"

"It's too hot at the laundry. My long hair makes me sweat too much."

Did it occur to Bev that it wasn't the length of her hair that worried Helara, but what each change in her appearance said about her daughter? According to Larry, Helara had begun worrying about Bev in first grade, had even talked to her teacher about her daughter's preference for jeans and boots. "Don't worry," the teacher said. "It's just a phase. She'll outgrow it." Helara had believed the teacher then or least had convinced herself her words were true. That night watching Bev walk through the dark and climb into her '53 Chevy, Helara may have known her daughter was traveling down a dangerous road.

~~~

Perhaps nothing captures our sympathy or imagination the way a tragic love story can. In *The Ballad of the Sad Café,* McCullers writes of an unlikely, even grotesque, love story. Love, she writes, may be a shared experience but not a similar one. "There is the lover and the beloved, but these two come from different countries."

Her words capture the improbable romance between Gina, a pretty, high school valedictorian from a middle-class family and Bev, an eighth-grade dropout whose family struggled to pay bills. The women met in early June of 1959, when Gina began work as a bookkeeper at Kulm Laundry. If Bev's gender bending confused Gina, she chose to ignore it whether from youthful naivety or willful ignorance.

Bev operated the large tumblers there, hauling wet laundry from washing machine to dryer. Gina likely glanced up from her bookwork to watch Bev trudge around the room, boots clumping on the concrete floor, biceps straining against the weight of the wet linens. Gina may have noticed how Bev held her cigarette between thumb and index finger and tilted her head back to exhale smoke, may have watched the smoke rings circling to the ceiling while Bev flicked the ashes on the floor. In contrast to this macho behavior, Bev's short hair revealed sweet, childlike ears and the fingers that held the cigarette were almost dainty. Gina admitted at the trial she "wondered all the time if Bev was really a boy."

Bev likely noticed the pretty girl at Kulm's leaning over her desk studying numbers in a ledger book, her auburn hair a grassfire spreading over her shoulders. She may have imagined putting her hands around Gina's narrow waist, feeling her ribs just above the circle of her fingers, imagined kissing the lips Gina puckered around a pencil.

Who struck up the first conversation? Bev had already dated women and that may have given her the confidence to push through the racks of clothes in plastic bags and stop at Gina's desk. "Hey, wanna drive to Mitchell and see a movie or something sometime?" Did it surprise Gina to hear Bev's soft voice, expecting it to be deep and rough? Did her breath quicken when she smelled tobacco and Lava on Bev's smooth skin? Despite her curiosity about Bev blurring the line between male and female, Gina turned down the invitation.

They chatted often during coffee breaks after that, quick conversations about silly subjects. Gina complained about her younger sisters fighting over whose turn it was to do dishes or scrub the floors. Gina laughed when Bev told her about the family dog Corky sitting in the rain his ears drooping with water. "Dumb mutt," Bev said. In the letters they wrote to one another, they bitched about work. *Yep that old hen gave me heck again. She always knows everything. I was there till after six, dum old hen doesn't know when to stop.* Such innocent dialogue was the first in a series of steps that led to romance, an ordinary dating ritual for many young people, but complicated and extraordinary for Gina and Bev.

Imagine a sizzling summer day in 1959 when the temperature climbed to one-hundred degrees and people complained the air felt thick as muddy creeks in pastures. Imagine Bev stopping by Gina's desk. "Let's go to the Bridgette, pick up a couple of burgers, and drive to the park at the river for lunch." Suppose this time, Gina said yes. Maybe she agreed because Bev's sexuality and gender were becoming more of a mystery to Gina, a puzzle many teenage girls might want to solve. Bev's cousin Larry thought the relationship between the two women was a consequence of many factors. "Gina couldn't spend much time with Myron that summer because he worked long hours on the construction of Big Bend Dam, ya know just up the river from Chamberlain."

Work on the dam paid well and Myron needed the money for college. "Myron had a strong work ethic," Larry said. "And you know how important that was growing up in a time and place where work defined a man." He suspected that with Myron gone so much, Gina craved attention and companionship. Bev filled that need.

On summer days on the river bottom, the breeze drifts lightly off the river and leaves goose bumps on damp skin. Despite the heat, the grass along the river banks smells mossy. I have felt a sense of freedom on such a day when the waves lap the shores and birds call overhead, a freedom that emboldened me to skinny dip in midday with my friends even at the risk of being caught and having to face my mother's shock and disapproval. It may have been on such a day that Gina and Bev sat at a picnic table under a canopy of tree branches, sipping fountain cokes and sucking ketchup off their fingers. KOMA blared from Bev's car radio while. Gina chattered about school plays and family gatherings or the success of the Pukwana Wildcats sports teams. Bev admired how Gina's fair cheeks turned pink from the sun's rays. Or was she blushing at the way Bev looked at her?

Maybe without knowing it, Gina needed that attention from another woman, something she hadn't experienced before, feelings she perhaps didn't understand. It may be that under an open sky and away from curious eyes, Gina felt emboldened enough to reach across the table and wipe away a blotch of ketchup in the corner of Bev's mouth. Gina later wrote *I love your tiny nose and your giggle. You're very sweet.*

Gina was often given to romantic phrases in her letters. She testified that she was an avid reader. Perhaps these tender words came from the books like *A Summer Place* or *Gone with the Wind,* books popular among many girls at the time.

Did Bev feel affection wash over her at Gina's touch? Did even her bones seem to soften? That day the women wrote rituals for a love that broke the rules. If heartbreak was my initiation into adolescence, their rite of passage into love was whispering coded words into telephones, tucking love notes in the pockets of coats hanging on hooks at the laundry, glancing at one another with knowing smiles at work, and finally, Gina creeping out the back door, running down the street to Bev's car, then snuggling as they drove to Lovers' Lane.

~~~

In their many long conversations, Gina hadn't told Bev about Myron, the boy whose class ring she had accepted. She didn't admit that she planned to marry this boy one day. Maybe she had no reason for this omission. She may have kept him a secret because she was curious where this flirtation with Bev might lead. Perhaps she hesitated to speak of Myron because he was an enrolled member of the Rosebud Tribe, and she knew Bev would hate him even more because he was a native.

Helara and Norma testified that they were puzzled by Gina's comments about Bev's hatred of Indians. "I don't know where that statement came from," Helara said. "All she associated with was Indians. She has got a book full of those girls. She never expressed any bitterness toward Indians."

Yet Bev often used the word "half breed" when she referred to Myron. Because Myron was everything Bev was not—handsome, athletic, masculine, and educated, she may have been searching for something that gave her power over him and so latched on to his native blood. She may not have known that many in the community believed the Waugh family were of mixed blood. We believed this based on their dark skin and the fact that they lived north of Highway 16. For those who judged race by wealth, the Waugh's poverty was testament to their Indian blood. Further proof, some claimed, was that the Waugh family attended mass at Our Lady of the Sioux Chapel on the campus of St. Joseph's Indian school. We made many assumptions based on appearances or behavior, especially regarding native people. We didn't apply these stereotypes to those in our social circles. The well-dressed man who bent over the pew at mass, rosary threaded through his fingers, wouldn't be unfaithful to his wife. The woman who baked cookies for neighbors and kept her children neatly dressed couldn't possibly be wearing long sleeves to cover bruises on her arms. Nobody would believe that the woman who came to church with a fox stole around her neck and diamonds on her wrists lived with tattered furniture and worn draperies.

If Bev didn't know what others said about her family's ethnicity, she did know that Myron was a threat and blamed his race. *Stay away from that half-breed. And that half-breed better stay out of my way to hon. You're mine and only mine. If he doesn't stay away from you he's going to get hurt.*

Half-breed, a word that takes me back to a day I hung by my knees on the crossbars of a neighbor's windmill. My long, blonde hair fell over my face as I swung back and forth. The metal bar cut into the backs of my legs. Still, I was happy and opened my little-girl hands to the wide sky. I felt as if I could fly off that bar and into the clouds. Today was a good day because I was waiting for the older boy who had promised to take me riding that afternoon on the black horse with the white star on his forehead.

In a shed nearby, young men laughed, their voices rising with an urgency to be heard above the others. They used words never spoken in my house—squaw, buck, half-breed, and redskin. My tummy ached with the sense they were bad words like shit and fuck I'd heard on the playground, filthy words that dirtied me somehow. Even in the fresh air of spring, I felt soiled. I dropped off the bar and walked into the house where my mother drank coffee at the kitchen table. "I don't feel well. Can we please go home?" She hustled me out of the house as I knew she would and sped home to put me to bed.

I lay in bed thinking of what I had heard that day. What to make of the conversation? Those men were our friends and neighbors. They wouldn't say those words if they were really nasty, would they? A boy that would take me horseback riding couldn't be cruel to others. My stomach churned at the memory of his language. Over time, however, the words were spoken so often by people I knew and respected, they lost their power to sicken me. That's how it works. Repetition breeds unawareness and ultimately indifference.

Hanging by my knees listening to men talk about Indians, I developed an upside-down understanding of racism. I thought the color of a person's skin, their bone structure, and their behavior and life style were markers of race. Ta-Nehisi Coates offered a better understanding of race when he wrote that Americans "believe in the reality of race as a defined, indubitable feature of the natural world. . . we ascribe bone deep features to people and then humiliate, reduce and destroy them. . . race is the child of racism, not the father."

I assumed that if I didn't used racist words, then I wasn't a racist, lazy thinking that reassured me of my tolerance, which I recognize now as white privilege. Martin Luther King shattered my arrogance when he wrote, ". . . the shallow understanding from people of good will is more frustrating than absolute misunderstanding from people of ill will." He was speaking of me.

Although I lived within a few miles of two reservations, I knew nothing about the diversity of tribes and bands that lived in my state. All native people were simply Sioux. All rituals that weren't Christian were suspect. Their poverty was self-imposed. I never asked why I believed these things. I'm ashamed of the questions I didn't ask. Why didn't Indian children come to our pool, the public library, or the movies? Why were the signs "No Indians Allowed" still posted outside a few businesses across the state? Why was dating native boys a taboo?

Years later, I asked what should have been my first question: What happened to those people who once hunted and roamed on this land I loved? Who left arrow heads and chips of stone tools in the soil of our farm? What responsibility did I bear in making my native neighbors invisible? If rites of passage mark the transition from childhood into adulthood, from unconsciousness to awareness, I hovered in the limbo of knowing and not knowing, never challenging what I was taught to believe. The questions I didn't ask about race, gender, and sexuality would span the Missouri river; the assumptions I held were burrowed deep in the mud of my ignorance.

DREAMS AND DISASTERS

This world is made by man, for man alone. . .
In the future centuries it is probable that a woman
will be the owner of her own body
and the custodian of her own soul.
But until that time,
you can expect that the statutes (concerning) women
will be all wrong.
Do you blame me for wanting to be a man?
Ralph Kerwinieo (nee Cora Anderson)
Gay American History: Lesbian and Gay Men in the U.S.A

I wish honey we were at the drive-in like last summer,
don't you,
a cool breeze blowing in your partly rolled down window
but it was never too cold we sat too close. Well close but
not too close.
Letter from Gina to Bev

Bev kissed Gina for the first time in July, 1959 as Gina lay in a hospital bed recovering from an accident that sent Myron's car spinning over the highway and into the ditch. They were among the lucky ones who survived, unlike many who died on the stretch of highway that led to the Paragon Ballroom. For teens of my generation rock and roll was the road we traveled, and the Paragon in Kimball our Mecca, a holy shrine where on Saturday nights kids worshipped at the altar of youth. It was a square, wooden building with small windows, sagging roof, and a tall pole with light bulbs running vertically down the side spelling "Paragon." The glittering letters served as a beacon for miles in the dark nights on Highway 16, the road that connected the east and west coasts of mid-century America. Caravans of trucks and carloads of tourists drove the highway in a steady stream like kids looping Main on Saturday night prompting South Dakotans to dub it "America's Main Street."

Mine was the first generation to have easy access to cars and the mobility they offered. On Saturday nights, a parade of cars drove to the Paragon—Ford Victorias with chrome grills and leather hard tops, station wagons with wood paneled sides and white wall tires (for kids stuck driving their parents' vehicles), and for my brothers, a 1957 yellow-and-black Chevy Bel Aire with tail fins and a metallic strip down the sides. Teens danced feverishly to The Fabulous Flippers, Myron Lee and the Caddies, Buddy Knox, and the Talismen, bands who covered artists like James Brown and Elvis. Our parents' complaints about the rock stars' swiveling hips and pelvic thrusts made the music sweeter and our adolescent rebellion more dangerous.

Only once did I speed over Highway 16 on my way to the Paragon. Tucked in the front seat between two boys, I twitched with pleasure when the driver, a boy with squinty eyes and a sweet smile, touched my knee as he shifted gears. I leaned into his shoulder hoping he meant the touch as a signal, hoping this night was a beginning for us. We drove recklessly with no fear that a deer might dart in front of us or a tire blow and send us careening into the ditch. Cars weren't equipped with seat belts then. But even if they had been, we wouldn't have used them. Only children and fearful old fogies would strap themselves in a vehicle. We couldn't imagine landing broken and crooked on the grass or crushed beneath the vehicle.

Broken beer bottles scattered shards of glass over the gravel parking lot of the Paragon. They sparkled in the moonlight. The smell of tobacco and beer hung in the air. Teenagers wrapped around one another in the back seats of cars, the windows steamy. Boys staggered down the alley, purple bruises on their faces and blood on their hands, cowboy hats and baseball caps knocked askew in a brawl between jocks and cowboys. In the dance hall, girls in pleated skirts, white bobby socks, and saddle shoes skittered around the dance floor, their pony tails swirling. Boys with slicked-back hair and smoky eyes, wearing jeans with cuffs and white shirts, the collars turned up, twirled the girls around their backs. They grabbed them before they sailed across the floor and pulled them back into their arms. The beat of the bass was rhythmic and sensual. Lust and booze and freedom hung in the air. I dreamed of spending every Saturday night there unfettered by the guilt of tempting disaster.

If a car and the highway represented freedom for many teens, for others the road with its dips and the sudden, hairpin turn at Paragon Curve was a dead end. "They must have been drinking," parents whispered after every car accident, accusation beneath the sorrow in their voices. Bev blamed Myron for the accident, convinced he had been drinking. "It was just a accident, honey," Gina said. "Nobody was to blame." But her words did not change Bev's mind.

We attached blame to tragedies. If a farmer lost life or limb in a power takeoff, people said that he had been careless about getting his pants legs too close to the spinning parts. If he reached his hand through the brush without thinking of rattlesnakes, he was at fault for the black arm swollen three times its size. If a woman crushed the tiny bones in her fingers in the washing machine's wringer "she hadn't paid attention to the task at hand." We assigned blame because we needed to believe such accidents would never happen to us. Unlike city slickers, we were Westerners whose common sense and practical skills, in my case the useless skill of gathering and washing eggs, would keep us safe. We believed this although we all knew somebody who had died on that road.

In early May of 1962, Smokey, my friend Leanne's brother, was killed when his car spun out of control and rolled over, his body flying out of the car. A year before he died, Leanne became my friend when she asked me to accompany her on the piano at regional vocal competitions. Although she was a senior and I a freshman, she treated me like her equal when we stayed late at school to rehearse. I idolized her for that. We spent hours in the choir room in the basement of the high school. I tapped my fingers—ta, tata, ta, tata, ta—on the piano top while she crooned into a hairbrush, her sultry alto sliding over the words "Life can never be exactly as we want it to be." The words meant little to me until that Sunday morning my mother woke me to say that Smokey had died. I was fifteen years old and for the first time I understood that life was filled with unexpected curves and I wasn't in the driver's seat.

Leanne's mother, Helen, was my mother's hair dresser, her beauty shop housed in the basement of Casey's Drugstore. In those days, hair salons were to women what the bars were to men. A place to escape from often dreary or hectic lives at home, a chance to gossip under hair driers or read magazines like *Cosmopolitan* or *Modern Screen*. Mother and Helen spent every Friday afternoon chatting while Helen brushed black dye into Mother's gray hair and rolled it in curlers. So of course, Mother baked a coffee cake and dumped a can of fruit cocktail into her favorite depression-glass bowl. She asked me to go with her to Leanne's home. Terrified at the thought of seeing Leanne, I complained I had a stomach ache, might even throw up. Mother's paranoia about her children's health often led her to keep me home on the day of a big test for which I hadn't studied. This time she saw through me. "It doesn't matter how afraid you are to talk to Leanne," Mother said. "She needs you."

In my mind's eye, Leanne lies in a scrim of smoke among school yearbooks scattered over the chenille bedspread. Her arms wrap around her brother's letter jacket; her curled body shapes a perfect capital 'S." Perhaps these images come from faulty memory or from emotions raised by seeing her so distraught. I am certain, however, that her apple cheeks were chapped from tears and her eyes swollen, that the curtains fluttered in the breeze, and the room smelled of stale cigarette butts spilling over a pumpkin-orange ashtray. Angry at Smokey for dying and leaving my friend to mourn, I wanted to throw the ashtray through the window just to shatter something. But that would be assigning fault to a fellow teen. How could I do that? I took a deep breath and whispered, "Leanne, I'm here. Do you want to talk?" She moaned softly but didn't turn over.

I began to sob and backed away begging my mother to take me home. As we walked back to the car, she clumsily patted my shoulder. She could heal festering boils or slivers from old fence posts with Epson Salts or poultices of baking soda and water. But she had no salve for emotional wounds. She was a woman uncomfortable with expressing emotions and that light touch of her fingers on my shoulders spoke volumes. Later that day, Mother called me into the kitchen to say, her voice firm, "You are not allowed to go to dances at the Paragon. I don't want you driving on that highway at night. That road takes too many lives." If she couldn't heal my sorrow, she could prevent a catastrophe.

That afternoon, my friends and I drove past the body shop staring at Smokey's car crumpled in accordion pleats, the front seat in the back, the windshield a spider web of shattered glass. We didn't speak as we drove to the scene of the accident and parked. We could see the ruts dug into the ground from wheels spinning. Bits of glass glittered in the sunlight. Beneath the fragrance of a freshly-mown hayfield was an odor of something like tractor tires burning in garbage dumps; beneath the music from car radios, the screech of tires and our weeping.

Staring at the wreckage I contemplated for the

first time the cause of tragedies. Some would say that his death was part of God's plan. "God needed Smokey's grin to brighten the days in Heaven," one woman said. Less religious people might call it fate or destiny. On the one hand, it seemed to me, fatalities on the highways were accidents, something that just happened for no reason. On the other hand, some teens chose to drive too fast even when they were drunk. There was a clear cause and effect to their deaths. How to reconcile those views? I didn't want to see God as a puppet master pulling strings that destroyed lives. Nor did I want to believe I had no control over my destiny. I decided to think of Smokey's death and by extension the deaths of all teens in a way that freed him from fault. Perhaps another driver forced him off the road and fled the scene. Maybe he swerved to miss a deer darting across the highway. He was sober. These thoughts comforted me.

~~~

A car accident may have been the catalyst that sparked the kiss that ultimately ended with Myron's tragic death. Gina had planned to work at Kulm's Laundry the summer after she graduated high school and then attend the Stewarts School of Hairstyling in the fall. Her plans were snarled in the wreckage of the car Myron flipped into the ditch that July. Gina and Myron were hospitalized for three weeks at Community Bailey Hospital, a new building just off River Road where cottonwood trees grew tall and blizzards of cotton settled into the window screens.

Bev had already acted on her yearnings to kiss and touch other girls. "You played with girls in school, right? There was nothing in your relationship with other girls that made it different than being friends, was there?" the attorney asked Bev during the trial.

"From the second year in fifth grade on there was."

"What type of emotional feeling did you have, Bev?"

"You mean as far as this love stuff? No more than necking with them."

After the accident, Bev spent every hour she wasn't working sitting by Gina's hospital bedside and probably fantasizing about kissing her. One night she sent Sadie home early. "You need some sleep. I'll sit with her."

Some believed that Bev spent the year planning for such a moment. She took her time and stayed patient, they said, so she could build a close relationship with Gina the way sexual predators do. Perhaps as Sadie claimed, Bev had manipulated Gina into a close relationship. "She was an impressionable girl who spent time with Bev because she pitied her."

It's also possible Bev reacted impulsively when she heard the clacking of wheels as nurses distributed medication and knew they'd soon be in Gina's room. With Sadie gone, this could be Bev's only opportunity. Did Gina know that Bev was attracted to her? Was she attracted or at least intrigued by Bev? Did she sometimes wonder what it might be like to kiss her?

When I imagine the moment that Bev kissed Gina, the scene unfolds like this: Bev sits in the dim light of Gina's room and watches her sleep. She is enamored by Gina's eyelashes, thick with gold flecks, and infatuated with the curve of her cheekbones and the perfect arch of her eyebrows. She leans over the bed and rubs Gina's hands with lotion. Gina has lost weight, and Bev frets about the skin hanging loosely from her fingers. She holds a straw to Gina's swollen lips urging her to take a sip. Bev brushes back the damp hair from Gina's cheeks and lays her hand on her forehead, relieved that her skin feels cool. Bev bends over and kisses Gina, then lingers for a moment, their breaths mingling.

During the hearing, Masten asked Gina, "Where about did she kiss you—on the lips, the face, or hand or what?" Gina may have been too drugged and exhausted to remember the moment clearly. "I lost the insides of my mouth in the accident, so I think she kissed me on the forehead."

The attorney then asked Gina to clarify what she meant by "the insides of her mouth," but she couldn't or wouldn't.

Bev kissed Gina for the second time on a crisp opening day of pheasant hunting in October. They had driven to Gina's uncle's farm where men in orange vests with shotguns over their shoulders sat in the beds of pickups waiting for noon, the official start of the hunt. Dogs skittered around the wheels, whining and panting, ready to flush birds. A breeze lifted the aroma of Milo fields and the smell of coffee on men's breaths.

Gina leaned against the car, arms crossed over her breasts, and her lower lip turned down. Her hair shone bronze and golden in the bright sun. They had quarreled earlier because Gina felt jealous after seeing Bev and a co-worker chatting in the back room the day before. When Bev denied flirting with another woman, Gina wrote a note to her, "So you weren't flirting with Judy. I'm sorry then. That's how it looked to me."

Although Gina testified that she couldn't remember if Bev had kissed her once or twice that day, Bev probably remembered every detail, if only in her imagination; how she leaned toward Gina and placed her hands on the hood of the car enclosing Gina in her arms, how surprised she was that Gina didn't resist. Had the men left by then? Or were they still sitting in pickups in the farmyard nearby? Was Gina's sister Susie watching from the other car? Bev didn't know or care. Perhaps she had convinced herself that Gina had kissed her back. And perhaps Gina had. When Bev opened her eyes, tears from the glare of the sun off the hood of the car moistened her lashes. On a day when the clouds were clear and the air crisp and the pheasants were cackling in a corn field, love may have seemed like the story of a prince rescuing a princess with a kiss. Bev would soon learn that such fairy tales do not always end happily.

~~~

I had dreamed my first kiss would be like a photograph in *Life Magazine*. World War II had ended, and people spilled out of office buildings to gather at Times Square littered with ticker tape. Among the crowd a sailor and a nurse embraced. He wore a navy suit with white piping and his hair was dark and wavy. She was slender and dressed all in white, even her nylons and clunky-heeled shoes. Her curls fell over his arm as he bent her at the waist. She lifted one leg behind her, a skater beginning a layback spin. In the background of the photo, the Times Building stood alone at the end of the street, the news of victory spiraling around the building. In the same way, the young couple seemed both celebratory and isolate, unaware of the people stopping to watch them or of cameras clicking, bulbs flashing. I was enamored by the sense that time had stopped and the street gone silent for two lovers aware only of one another. I practiced that image in front of the mirror, leaning back, my arms around a pillow, my lips pressed into the stuffing.

My romance with Joe began in Latin Class the fall of my freshman year. Our teacher was Mrs. Adams, a small, chubby woman with hair dyed so black it was as purple as the Julius Caesar robe she wore to the Latin banquet. Joe and I were conversation partners which meant memorizing and repeating the declension of words like agricola, agricolae, agricolarum, sometimes singing them to the tune of "Sioux City Sue." Mrs Adam's double chins wobbled as she bounced to the music. I didn't appreciate the value of learning Latin until I entered college. Joe, however, liked the challenge and learned quickly. He patiently helped me master the list. We were two awkward, lumpy adolescents with bad skin and thick glasses fated to find one another.

We had been dating about a week when Joe beckoned me into the music-room closet, dark and jammed with band instruments and uniforms. The smell of trombone spit splattered on the floor mingled with the odor of mothballs. "I have something to tell you," he said. The school bell rang. Above us kids slammed locker doors and ran down the halls. From the parking lot came the sound of engines gunning and tires burning rubber. He grabbed my hand and tugged me toward him. Startled, I stepped on his toes and stumbled into him. Somehow, he kept us upright, his arms around me, his face bent toward mine. He tilted his head so our glasses wouldn't collide. His lips were rough and tasted of beef jerky. We both smelled of Clearasil. I opened my eyes. He stared back at me. At that close range his eyes behind two pairs of lenses (mine and his) were magnified like goldfish bumping against the glass in aquariums. I ran out of the closet and refused to talk to him for days. We continued to be a couple that year, however, and moved past that awkward kiss to nights necking on the river bluff.

In July of 1961, he and his parents traveled to Yellowstone Park. By now, we had become less enamored with one another, our dating life more routine than romantic. But breaking up didn't seem possible. For me, being unattached meant being undesirable. Perhaps Joe didn't want to hurt my feelings or had found our relationship comfortable if not exciting. He hugged me goodbye. "I promise to send a postcard every day."

Our mailbox was a mile away on dirt and gravel roads. For a week I rode my bike there every day, a bumpy, swerving ride over ruts and potholes and through the ridges of loose pebbles. One day, I couldn't keep the bike in the tracks and turned the wheel quickly over a ridge. The tire spun and I tipped over sliding through the gravel and scraping my knees. I pushed the bike to the mailbox, dropped it, sat in the grass, and sorted through the mail. No card from Jerry. The parched dirt absorbed the blood dripping down my leg. By now my obsession over accidents and fate had ended, and I had begun to obsess over the choices that led to either disaster or to safety. How many times had I ridden my bike on this road and never tipped over? What if I hadn't chosen to jerk the handlebars and twist the wheels in the loose gravel? What if I had slowed down? Could I have ridden safely through the loose ridges? It was an adolescent debate between good and bad choices, choices that would grow more serious with each year.

The next day, my father stopped at the mailbox on his way home from the fields. He came into the bedroom where I lay on the bed, a book in my hands. He handed me a postcard. "I guess Joe doesn't know that every altar boy knows a bit of Latin." He grinned as he left the room. I scanned the card and found this inscription at the bottom, "Ego amo te." I ran out of the house, climbed to the granary roof, and sat cross legged on the rough shingles, the postcard crumpled in my hand.

The words I had dreamed of hearing for the first time now devastated me the way Joe's kiss had. I may have been disappointed because I wasn't expecting either of them and didn't have a choice to say yes or no. It was something done **to** me, not **with** me and that was very different from the picture of the couple kissing on Times Square. But behind the romantic myth of that photo was a disturbing truth. The sailor was on a date with another woman and very drunk. He grabbed the nurse and hooked his arm around her neck to bend her back. Her leg was caught at an awkward not graceful angle and her left hand dangled by her side. "And then I was grabbed," the nurse said years later. "The man was very strong. I wasn't kissing him. He was kissing me."

I lay on my back watching crenulated clouds drifting above me, pulled by the prevailing winds that carried the green smell of our alfalfa field. Against the background of the blue sky, a line of geese flew north on their way to the river, their path timeless and predictable. There was a time I found joy in the freedom of clouds and geese, but now I suspected they were locked in a predetermined pattern controlled by forces beyond them. I pondered how life was a sequence of events that happened without our control. Smokey died either because the events were destiny or God's plan or for no reason whatever. The result was a fiery crash and Leanne's despair so deep I couldn't reach her. As a young girl, my body bled, grew hair in places that shamed me, and my breasts swelled without my permission. My first date was my last because of a boy's choice. Joe grabbed me and kissed me in a dark, smelly closet. Now he said, "I love you" without any consideration of how those words might make me feel.

I faced a future with few choices. I could marry, a man of course, and have children. I could be a spinster. I could be a nurse, teacher, or as a Catholic girl, a nun. Nobody asked about my dreams. Were women destined to be those geese locked in predicable patterns? Was it possible for any woman to be in charge of her life? I tore the postcard in tiny pieces, cupped them in my palm, walked to the edge of the roof, and opened my hand. The pieces fluttered as they drifted across the corral, beyond the pasture, and to the corn field where they would land in the stubble and be mulch for next year's crop.

VIRGIN OR TEMPTRESS

I tell you without hesitation
that although God is almighty,
he cannot restore a virginity that has been lost.
St. Jerome

Girls, boys will go as far as you let them.
Your sin is greater than theirs if you arouse them.
When you go home tonight, you must pray the rosary
asking the Virgin Mary to help you follow her example of
chastity.
Father John

I sat on the ground warming my hands over a campfire. The spring semester of my freshman year in college had ended and this would be the last kegger until fall. I chatted with a senior boy who offered me a ride home. He must have been attractive or charming in some way for me to say yes. But I can't remember. His face, his voice, his mannerisms disappear with the other memories of that night. Only feelings remain.

I didn't worry when he drove me past my dormitory and into the open field near the football stadium. Growing up in a hard place demanded a self-reliance that gave me confidence I could take care of myself. At the same time, I was naïve and innocent in the way of many small-town Catholic girls in the 1960s. I trusted him as I trusted my hometown boys. We'd chat a bit, complaining about coursework or the basketball team's losing season, or fretting over paying for tuition. He might ask me for a date and kiss me once, maybe twice, before taking me back to the dormitory.

But this boy parked the car in a dark spot, turned off the ignition, grabbed me, and pressed me against the car door. He stared out the windshield fumbling with the zipper on my jeans. He didn't kiss me; he didn't even see me. There must have been other cars parked around us. Radios playing. Pebbles of gravel shining in the moonlight. I saw nothing. Heard nothing. I was only sensations, my arm twisted against my back, the door handle digging into my spine. I thrashed under his weight. "No, please take me home." But not to the dormitory. To the house on the grasslands to a time when I was a small girl lying in front of the radio listening to *The Lone Ranger*; to nights when my mother puttered in the kitchen, when my father read in his easy chair, and the breeze coming through the windows smelled of spring and new grass.

I began to sob. He let me go, turned the key in the ignition, and spun out of the lot, scattering gravel. I stuck my head out the window, gulped air the way our dog Nipper hung over the side of the truck's bed, eyes wild. In the distance a white beam radiated from the campanile in the center of campus, a beacon seen in all directions. Senior boys joked that a brick fell from the campanile every time a freshman girl lost her virginity. If this boy had chosen, if he had persevered, one of those bricks would have been mine. He stopped the car a block from the dorm and muttered "Get the hell out." I ran down the sidewalk, up three flights of steps to my room, slammed the door, and fumbled to turn the deadbolt lock. I curled up in the corner of the closet trembling and sick to my stomach at the thought of what might have happened. But I wasn't angry at him, but at myself for being a girl who drank beer at parties, who slide into a car with someone she'd just met, a girl worth nothing more to a boy than a notch on his belt.

My understanding of sex as fierce and shameful might be traced not only to that night in the parking lot, but to a day when I was perhaps six-years-old and I heard my mother yelling, "Get off her. Get off her."

I ran to the front yard and stood in horror watching a black lab straddle our cocker spaniel Trixie while my mother whacked him with a broom.

"Mommy, why are you hitting that dog? What is he doing to Trixie?"

"Never mind," my mother snapped. "Just go to your room and forget about it."

I didn't go to my room, and clearly, I didn't forget about it.

My mother had never behaved this way before. She pounded his back again and again, her voice growing louder. "Get off her."

A carload of teenage boys drove by, stopped, pointed at Mother, and laughed—hard—their white teeth flashing in the sunlight. I was embarrassed they saw my mother acting crazy. Maybe she was crazy.

"You go to your room," she hollered again. But I couldn't move, couldn't take my eyes off the dog pumping against Trixie who thrashed beneath him. The lab panted and slobbered and shoved hard against her. Then with a shudder, he slid off and staggered down the alley sniffing the bushes, something slick and muscular hanging between his back legs. Mother stomped back in the house, the door slamming behind her. Trixie quivered and crawled on her belly under a bush by the front steps.

Later that day, I crept out of the house and knelt by the bush holding a piece of minced ham. "Here girl, come get this," I whispered, certain that Trixie's keen nose would tempt her to come toward me. She looked at me with feverish eyes and whimpered. Her honey-colored fur was damp from slobber; there was a moist and salty smell about her. I reached my hand through the dappled shadows of the branches hoping she would lick my palm, hoping she could be coaxed out of her hiding place. She didn't move. This image of Trixie, tiny and vulnerable, pinned under the lab haunted me. Is that what made my mother so frantic? I had seen my mother's tight-lipped disapproval when she smelled tobacco on my father's breath and when my aunt criticized her for letting my sister polish her nails. "It is sinful to alter God's handiwork," she said. Once Mother discovered my uncles passing a bottle among them in the garage and stomped into the house, silent with fury. But never physical blows. Perhaps her outrage had something to do with that protrusion between the dog's legs. But what?

Most country girls learn about sex from observing animals. Not me. My father, a cattle breeder, surely understood it was natural if sometimes violent when a dog rode the back of a female or when our bull mounted a heifer. Despite that, he never talked to me about sex the way he did with my brothers. Perhaps this is a flawed memory, but I recall hopping in the back of the pickup and bumping over the ruts in the pasture to check on the cows. I leaned over the side of the truck bed listening to my father talk about heifers "going into heat."

"Watch how she moves—is she restless? Is she

mooing more than usual or trying to mount a steer?" It was not uncommon to see cows ride one another's backs the way dogs sometimes humped my leg. In my mind they were playing leap frog. So, the serious tone in my father's voice puzzled me as he explained how he separated agitated cows from the herd and moved them to the pasture where the bulls grazed.

A few weeks later as we drove past a pasture, I pointed to the double punching bags hanging between a bull's legs. "What are those, Mommy?"

"Get down on the floor," she snapped. I hunched over the floor mat, my stomach rolling with the sway of the car over ruts in the pasture. Or maybe I sensed I was being punished for something. But what? Even at my young age, I could read the tension in my mother's voice that told me not to ask questions. Years later my mother would confess that she had been confined to the house on days when her father brought the bull to the barn to mate with a heifer.

"Did you ask them why you had to stay in the house?"

She shook her head and sighed. "Of course not. We didn't talk about nasty things in our family."

~~~

One year, Dr. Jones, our family physician, talked to my high school Catechism class about anatomy and sex. Dr. Jones was a former military doctor with a blunt bedside manner and the primitive medical remedies of ranchers. Once when I was a teenager, I was chasing Nipper and stumbled over a tree root. I fell and dislocated my elbow. Dr. Jones marched into the emergency room his surgical gown still bloodied, grabbed my arm, popped the bone in place, and kicked a bucket across the floor toward me. "If you need to throw up, use this." He left the room with me leaning over the bucket and my mother holding my head, fuming. "If he weren't Catholic, I'd look for a different doctor."

In my youth, religion divided commerce the way it separated cemeteries. Catholics bought cars, groceries, and pharmaceuticals from Catholic merchants. Protestants from Protestants. Miss Willrodt gave piano lessons to Catholic children. Protestant children studied with Mrs. Stilly, a Methodist. There were hayrides for Lutheran teens, rosary nights for Catholics, and mostly bible studies for Baptist kids. Even dentists, chiropractors, and lawyers relied on members of their church for business. However, I didn't remind Mother that the only other doctor in town was also Catholic. Challenging Mother's logic, no matter how illogical, was never a good strategy.

My father may have been comforted that Father John would attend the sex-education class to lead the discussion from the Church's point of view which meant abstinence. But my mother preferred Father teach the *Baltimore Catechism*, a theology book filled with questions like "Why did God make us?" We memorized and recited the answers in class. "God made us to show forth his goodness and to share with us his everlasting happiness in Heaven."

"For the love of Mike," she griped, stirring the hamburger so vigorously bits of meat fell into the burners causing small flames to erupt. "Church is no place to talk about sex."

Boys did not attend this class with us. Father and the doctor would visit with them the next week while we girls went to the chapel to kneel in front of the statue of The Blessed Virgin and pray for our religious vocation. Entering the convent appealed to me, the mysterious clothing, sisters who lived for years in silence, and the thin, gold bands on their fingers_proof of their virginal marriages to Christ. Nuns were ethereal creatures. Sister Jerome floated as she walked with hands folded behind her cowl, her chipmunk cheeks squished and puffed by her wimple. What lay beneath the habit? Had tight undergarments pressed her flesh into boyish shapelessness? Or was she born without curves because God had determined her life of celibacy didn't require a womanly body? One day, she lifted her arm to write on the blackboard, and the sleeve fell to her shoulder. That stretch of pale flesh shocked me as if I had spied my mother naked which

I never had. That Sister was womanly, human, beneath her garb provoked a question. Had she once been a teenage girl praying for Mary's help, her skin still tingling in places where a boy had touched her? I silently prayed away these impure thoughts. *I earnestly wish to be pure in thought, word, and deed in imitation of your own holy purity Mother of God.*

Images from that night come in clusters, some vague, some vivid, some perhaps born from other experiences that made their way into this scene. We girls sat on folding chairs in a windowless room in the basement of the church. We fidgeted and chatted and watched the clock. A few girls calmly dabbed their lips with gloss and buffed their shiny nails. Their calm demeanor suggested they knew something we didn't. But what? The room went still when the priest and doctor walked in—one whose white collar seemed righteous and pure against his black waistcoat, the other in a green surgical shirt and pants, a black bag in his hand, and a stethoscope around his neck. His attire told us that his would be a clinical discussion; the priest's clerical garb reminded us the Church had a voice in sexual matters.

Dr. Jones wrote several words on the board—vagina, vulva, hymen, and uterus. Boys used words like pussy, snatch, beaver, and another word sprayed in black paint on the piers of the bridge, a word too sinful and crude to be written in daylight. He then drew an illustration of a woman's anatomy and pointed to a piece of folded flesh above the urethra. "This is your clitoris. It's a small button not far from where you pee. It feels good to touch it."

If Dr. Jones came with the intention of teaching the medical language of sexuality, he resorted to using precious euphemisms parents often used— front bottom, giny, cookies, pecker, dingle berries, weenie. My mother fluttered her fingers in the general direction of our genitals and avoiding our eyes said, "Down there." Now "button" was added to the list of slang that meant nothing. About intercourse my parents had no language or perhaps no inclination to explain it, so I relied on lewd words my friends used like "get laid," "screw," "bone her," and "fuck." These words suggested that sex was something done to someone as it had been to Trixie.

My attention strayed from the doctor's lecture to thoughts of Anne Frank's diary. She once asked her mother about the bump she felt in "that place."

"I don't know and don't talk to others about it."

"Why are people so secretive and tiresome when they talk about those things?" Anne asked, a question I often asked myself.

Anne wrote openly of her fascination with her body and its hidden places. Under the blankets in the cover of night, her diary on my pillow, we explored our bodies. "I have a terrible desire to feel my breasts," she wrote. I sometimes lightly brushed the tender swelling of my breasts with my fingers, both taken aback and yet thrilled with the pleasure of touch. She wrote about her fingers fumbling to find "the little hole that I simply can't imagine how a baby can get out." She gave me permission to do the same.

She likely knew that she would die a virgin in that secret loft or perhaps a labor camp somewhere. In touching that tiny piece of flesh, she experienced a rite of passage that most teenagers take for granted. What about Bev? Did she find pleasure in touching herself? Or were her genitals such a painful reminder of who she was or wasn't that she couldn't indulge in the normal exploration of adolescents?

Father John stood up and interrupted Dr. Jones. "Never touch yourself there. Self- gratification is a venial sin that like all venial sins leads to more serious sins."

Venial sins were less serious and committed without full knowledge. They were among the taxonomy of sins I learned in catechism class: original sin—the sin we inherited from Adam and Eve; sins of presumption—assuming forgiveness without repentance; mortal sins—most grievous and committed with knowledge and willfulness. Most confusing was an occasion of sin which Father defined as being the cause of another person's sins.

He used the example of girls tempting boys by the way we dressed or flirted with them.

Did the boys hear a different message from the priest that absolved them from responsibility? Did boys believe that if they fell out of grace with God by having sex that the fault lay with the girl? Being Catholic, Bev must have heard the same lecture from Father John. Because she identified as male did Bev blame Gina for the sins of her "unnatural" desires? Or did she reject Father John's words the way she defied social conventions?

Father John peppered our classes with holy cards that depicted gruesome images of virgin martyrs who refused to relinquish their purity to men. St. Agnes and St. Lucy committed to flames and beheaded. St. Maria Goretti stabbed multiple times to whom we prayed "teach us courage to flee anything that would stain our souls with sin." Most horrifying of all, St. Agatha imprisoned in a brothel and beaten, her breasts severed. What lesson did her suffering teach?? Better for a woman to lose her breasts than give in to sin even if unwillingly?

Those resolute, self-sacrificing saints were impossible models as I battled my boyfriend and my urges in a car parked on the river bluffs. Better to learn of the internal struggles these women waged to make the right choice for themselves, to have power over their own bodies. As it was, in choosing to jump into a car with a boy, I was both perpetrator and victim in a sexual assault.

Who were Bev's martyrs? She probably had no awareness of the harassment transgender men like her suffered in cities like New York City where police patrolled the alleys and pushed them against brick walls, shoved hands down their pants, and probed their folds with rough fingers. "Let's see what ya got down there." Where officers raided gay bars, led by dogs straining against their leashes and snarling at transmen and women huddled in corners. Where officers charged them with disorderly conduct or disturbing the peace, threw them into paddy wagons, and drove them to jail bruised and covered in blood. The next morning, they walked out of jail, went back to work, and that night gathered again in places like Stonewall in defiance of the police and the laws.

In Catechism class that night, Dr. Jones drew something that looked like the head of a ram in Egyptian artwork. He sketched an oval-shaped object inside one of the horns. "Once a month, one of your ovaries produces an egg. Your uterine lining thickens to prepare for a fertilized egg. If the egg is not fertilized, the uterine lining is shed through menstruation." This was the first time someone provided me a clinical explanation for menstruation.

His words sparked images of canning jars with slick, white eggs floating among strings of dill in vinegar. Likely not what he intended.

"If the egg travels up this tube and merges with a fluid a man produces called sperm," he said, "you can get pregnant."

Father John stopped him. "This does not happen outside of marriage. "

Dr. Jones stopped talking and stared at the priest. "If the egg and sperm don't meet," Dr. Jones, said rolling his eyes, "then you will slough off the bloody lining when you menstruate."

Twenty minutes left. My head ached from the damp and from the conflicting messages between the priest and the doctor. Around me, girls shifted in their chairs, the swish of fabric penetrating the silence. Dr. Jones sketched a tad-pole-shaped image of semen, the fluid filled with sperm that the man's body produces. "When a man and a woman have intercourse, blood flows into the man's penis causing it to become rigid, what we call an erection."

I sat up. Finally, somebody would explain the mechanics of sex. I had never dared touch the front of my boyfriend's jeans and had only a vague sense of what my friends meant when they talked about feeling something hard in a boy's pants when they slow danced or necked at the river. "Eventually," Dr. Jones continued, "the man ejaculates which means he releases semen that swims up the woman's fallopian tube. If the sperm in his semen merges with the egg she's released, she can get pregnant."

Father John interrupted again. "You don't need to know about any of this until you're married." He spoke each word deliberately his voice was tinged with impatience.

Dr. Jones crossed his arms over his chest, turned to the priest, and stared at him with narrowed eyes. Finally, he slapped his hands to shake off the chalk dust. It showered over the classroom in shimmering white clouds like the picture of the Holy Spirit's radiant light bestowing the gift of wisdom. Then he stomped out of the room to our chanting, "Hail Mary, full of grace."

In the same way that Father John focused on girls as temptresses, Attorney Masten delved into Gina's sexual behaviors forcing her to divulge the details of intimacy with Bev. This line of questioning about sexual intimacy had drawn many of the spectators to the courtroom.

"Gina, you testified to love acts you performed with Beverly Waugh. Describe those acts."

"What do you mean by that?"

"Gina lift your head up so we can hear you. Did Beverly caress you above the waist? Below the waist?"

"I guess so."

"Gina, look at the jury when you talk. Did she arouse sexual desire in you, Gina?"

"Yes."

During the trial Masten employed every possible strategy that might spare Bev a prison sentence. Perhaps he planned to portray Gina as less of an innocent teenage victim and more of a willing and "sexually active" partner who manipulated an intellectually and socially challenged lover. But was it really necessary to force Gina into revealing such intimate moments? I confessed my sins behind a linen screen with only Father John to hear them. The Church taught that the priest served as a liaison between myself and God who could grant me forgiveness, but God was never with me in that airless booth. Gina confessed in a courtroom to spectators, lawyers, the media, and her parents. She must have felt their eyes boring in on her as she testified, eyes that reflected curiosity or shock. Or perhaps compassion in some. She must have seen the shattered expressions on her parents' faces and the way their shoulders slumped. Did she feel the gift of forgiveness as she recounted her "sins"? Or did she imagine only judgment from what seemed to her to be an unmerciful community? Gina sometimes evaded answering questions about intimacy with Bev saying things like "I can't remember" or "I dunno." She teetered often on the brink of perjuring herself during the trial, but she was never charged with perjury or contempt of court. Perhaps the judge saw no good that could come of charges against her, and he spared her by cautioning the defense attorney, "Remember she's just a girl."

~~~

In her diary, Anne wrote, "I'm sure my mother never touched a man before she met my father." Surely those words were true of my mother. When she spoke of her honeymoon visiting my father's Bohemian family in Omaha, she described her fear of the traffic and of being intimidated by my father's tall relatives. "They spoke Bohemian and ate food with funny smells and isshy flavors," she said. One food she embraced, however, were the kolaches which his aunt taught Mother to bake, filling pillows of dough with stewed apricots and prunes.

She said nothing about that first night, so I am left to imagine my tiny, naïve mother confused and frightened when my broad and vigorous father turned to her; imagine her shocked and unable to breathe and ashamed of the stains on the sheets the next morning. The year she was married, Mother had two babies in twelve months. She confessed that she didn't understand she was fertile only so many days of each month. She thought women could get pregnant every time they had sex. "I was afraid the babies would never quit coming."

Those words came back to me when I met with Father Louis, the priest at the Newman Center on our college campus. A small German man, with a sharp nose and dark hair slick with hair oil, he seemed austere, and when I first saw his outline through the linen screen of the confessional booth, I trembled. "Bless me Father, for I have sinned." I began my litany of sins involving parked cars in open fields and the wandering hands of boys.

He interrupted me. "I don't want to hear about that. Tell me how you treated people this week? Did you ignore a lonely girl in her dorm room? Did you gossip about a friend?"

This was the first priest I knew to focus on compassion and social justice, including feminism, instead of sexual sins. We became friends and often had coffee at the student union. He used the word "scrupulous" to describe phony morality and encouraged me to think for myself. "You're an adult. You can form your own opinions even if they conflict with what I may say from the altar."

In 1968, the year Ken and I married, Pope Paul VI declared birth control "intrinsically evil" and said it was "morally wrong to use artificial contraception with the intention of preventing conception." Ever an obedient Catholic girl, I approached Father Louis for his approval to use birth control pills. He cocked his head; his blue eyes were clear despite thick glasses. "What would happen if you got pregnant before Ken earned his degree? Would that create a financial hardship for you? Would it affect your plans for the future? If the answer is 'yes,' then you just answered your own question."

A few weeks later, I lay on a table, cotton gown tied in the back, my legs raised and bent, my feet pressed against hard, flannel-covered footrests, my knees quivering. Fingers probing and cold metal inside me, a quick, sharp bite of flesh, and the examination was complete. As he worked, the doctor explained in a matter-of-fact and comforting voice that he used the speculum to widen the vaginal walls so he could measure the width. The quick pain was a swipe with a spatula of sorts to take a cell sample. The pressure I felt was his checking my ovaries and uterus for abnormalities. He talked about intercourse, physically and emotionally. He did so clinically, thoroughly, and gently.

My conception of sex was fragmented by my parents' silence and my mother's anger at the dog; by whispered snippets of conversation among my mother and aunts, by the coarse language of fellow teens, and by the teachings of Father John. Was it unpleasant, violent, something to get over with? Was it a woman's sinful burden? Nasty as the words high school boys used?

"If mothers don't tell their daughters about sexual matters, they hear it in bits and pieces, and that can't be right," Anne wrote. Frank and Helara Waugh didn't talk to Bev about her sexuality or gender bending, not even after she cut her hair or when Helara discovered men's aftershave and shaving cream in Bev's drawer. The Lees said nothing when Gina fed pieces of candy to Bev as they leaned against the kitchen counter or when Gina put her head on Bev's lap while they watched television. They remained silent when Gina turned her collar up to cover the splotches of hickeys on her neck. It's possible their silence came from a lack of knowledge. Bev's brother admitted on the witness stand that he had never heard of lesbianism. Most likely Gina's parents as well knew little about homosexuality or gender dysphoria. Perhaps they were in denial or simply hoped the problem would resolve itself.

Mother knew so little about sex because her parents did not talk to her. Given her own experience, it's not surprising that my mother never spoke about my body or about sexual intimacy. The gynecologist took the role that my mother, Helara, and Sadie avoided because they had no models to follow. I tried to be more open with my daughter.

Still, I often dodged her questions. Old patterns are etched deeply in us.

The doctor wrote a prescription for birth control pills, probably Enovid which had been approved by the FDA in 1960. The pills were packaged in a pink plastic case, twenty-one pills for each month. Those pills invited me into a collective of women in control of our own lives and decisions about childbearing. Contraception reminded me that Father John could not dictate my choices. I no longer saw myself as an occasion of sin, but rather a partner in a mutual expression of love and responsibility with an attentive lover.

Did my mother ever enjoy a satisfying intimacy with my father? I don't how she could have. She was raised in a repressive family and religion at a time when sexual satisfaction wasn't expected for most women, not even encouraged. "It's something to be endured," I heard an auntie whisper. Some even reserved a woman's sexual gratifications for tainted women. Furthermore, my mother juggled the challenges of raising four children under the age of six with that of keeping house, doing laundry, and cooking three meals a day. Her only reprieve was stolen moments at the piano. No matter how tender or careful my father might have been, how could sex ever be pleasurable for someone so exhausted and ill prepared, especially when fear of pregnancy loomed over the bedroom? She said to me not long before she died, "I told your father that someday Catholic women will use birth control." Her voice quivered with anger.

A memory emerges of my mother standing at the ironing board when I came home late from basketball games or school dances. her face flushed by the heat and the iron's steam. I tiptoed past the bedroom where my father knelt by the bed whispering the prayers of the rosary. That memory merges with another, and I see women with swollen bellies holding crying babies in one hand and frying bacon and eggs with the other hand as children cling to their legs. That image becomes a terrified girl thrashing under the weight of a man; she morphs into a tiny, furious woman beating a dog over and over each blow more forceful than the last. I hear boys laughing, a dog whimpering, and a woman yelling, "Get off her. Get off her."

Part Two: Unraveling

LOVE'S LONELY OFFICES

They can steal your wallet,
they can steal your car,
they can even take your life. But the one thing they can't
take from you
is an education.
Henry Woster

If I tried to talk to her,
she just snapped
or wouldn't answer the question at all.
I didn't take her to a doctor. I didn't know what to do.
Helara Waugh

I wanted to talk to an official
but I was led to understand that there was nothing
in the state of South Dakota
that would help.
Sadie Lee

My fascination with things unraveling began the day I crept into the barn to climb the steps to the hayloft curious about the place because my mother forbade me to go up there. "Too many loose boards or gaps between them," she said. "You'll fall through and break your fool neck." She always added the word "fool" to her warnings about potential disasters, as if even my body parts had no common sense.

I carried a thin piece of rope and sat on the dirt-caked floor pulling at the frayed edge until one strand untangled from the others. I tugged at another and then another setting off a chain reaction that separated the woven fibers. Every day I crept into the barn and pulled at the strands of rope until the tattered edge was longer than the braided end. Several days later, my father discovered it hidden in a corner near the trap door. "Mary Alice, come in here. I want to show you something." He stood in the front porch near the milk separator and sacks of chicken feed, the rope in his hand. He had tied the end in a knot to stop the rope from fraying. Still the rope was too short to use. "Did you do this Toots?"

I nodded, afraid to look in his eyes. "Look, I know it's fun to pull things apart. But now the rope is useless." His words punished me more than any spanking might have.

In ninth grade, I read a book about a depressed young woman who ingested a slow-acting poison that would kill her in seven days. Each day after that, she saw the world in a different light. The sky was crystal clear, not the dreary gray that had made her desperate and lonely. The trees had leafed out in shades of deep green and lilac blossoms perfumed the air. The handsome man at her office smiled as she walked by and the clicking of typewriters became the rhythm of music. She desperately wanted to live, but there was no antidote for the poison. Sleepless nights followed for me as I thought about how something could be set in motion and never stopped, how moment by moment the thin thread between life and death kept fraying.

My tight relationship with my father wore thin in high school when he disapproved of my boyfriend. My stubborn refusal to admit he was right untangled the woven threads that held us together. In the aftermath of his cancer diagnosis, overcome with grief, I couldn't think straight enough to repair the damage I had done. Images of my father in his last days still haunt me. He sits on the edge of his bed, a bucket near his feet, his limbs clothes-line thin. A single cell had split and prompted the division of more cells that eventually invaded and destroyed his muscles, organs, and bones. His body had broken a trust with him that he couldn't mend the way I had when I damaged the rope as a little girl, the way I frayed our relationship as a rebellious teenage girl.

Shortly after Gina had accepted Myron's engagement ring, Helara and Sadie watched their daughters' lives come undone. It was then that Bev discovered Gina was cheating on her. Her heart was broken. *Yep it looks like it's going to be another lonely night not having you with me hon. Please. If you love me you won't leave me. No matter what happens they won't be able to take away the love I have for you.*

In those last weeks, Bev's sadness became depression. Depression wove itself into anxiety, and anxiety twisted into anger that became violence. Finally, Bev loaded her rifle to go hunting, but instead she followed Myron's car west on Highway 16. Neither Helara nor Sadie could tie a knot to repair the damage once Bev stepped out of her car and aimed her rifle at Myron. Neither mother could stop the bullet once it had been fired.

~~~

I had started "going steady" with Nick my sophomore year in high school when Father John declared from the altar that going steady "was an occasion of sin that leads to greater sins." He defined going steady as dating the same boy more than three times. Numbers mattered in the Church. There was the Holy Trinity. The Ten Commandments. The Seven Deadly Sins. In confession we were required to state the number of times we committed a sin and then the priest assigned a specific number of prayers we must say as our penance, most often five Hail Marys.

He urged Catholic parents to forbid their children to go steady. Although a parish priest wielded great power over his parishioners, I naively assumed my parents would understand that Father

John had unfairly characterized my virginal romance with Nick as sinful. Especially my father who adored me as I idolized him, who trusted me as I trusted him. One night I crept late into the house breathless and rumpled and found my father waiting in the front porch. His long face was in shadows, but the gravity of his voice told me this was serious. "I need to talk to you." I slouched against the door staring at the floor. For the second time in my life, I sensed my father was accusing me of something. This time, I felt his accusations, whatever they were, would be unfair and I would defend myself. "I don't want you to go steady at your young age. I want you to go to college, earn your degree, and date other boys until you find a man to marry who shares your values."

My father came of age during the depression, and poverty kept him from achieving his dream of going to college. He determined that his children would earn the college degree he had been denied. After a blizzard stranded us on the farm for six weeks, he bought a humble home in Chamberlain so we could live in town during the school year and on the farm in the summer. He became a commuter. For twenty winters, he got out of bed, pulled his bulky coveralls over his slim body, and drove through the dark to daily mass before commuting twenty miles to the farm. While his children settled into school activities and my mother joined a coffee group and

Altar Society, he spent his days working in the fields and tending cattle. In sub-zero temperatures and howling winds, he hauled hay to the pastures and chopped holes in ice of the stock ponds so the cattle could drink. His solitary lunches were often a can of soup and crackers or perhaps a jackrabbit he shot, skinned, and fried in butter. His only company was our Black Lab Nipper. He followed this routine every day except Sundays. He never complained about his solitary sacrifices.

In many ways, Nick was husband material. He was Catholic, essential in the day when mixed marriages were taboo. He was kind to his mother, patient with his younger siblings, and a hard worker. Part of his appeal, I admit, was his motorcycle, something good boys didn't own. Every Saturday night, the rumble of his cycle announced his approach. My heart pounded at the thought of sitting behind him, arms around his waist, thighs butting up against his. I would rest my head on his shoulder, feeling the smooth leather of his jacket against my face, the wind lifting my hair as we roared down Main Street. My friends would hear his cycle above rock music blaring from car radios. They'd watch us drive by, their faces flush with awe and envy. But none of this happened. "Oh, for Pete's sake," my mother griped. "Have you lost your mind? You are NOT riding on a motorcycle." We drove my parents' station wagon instead enduring the jeers of boys. "Cool ride, fag." Fag—the ultimate blow to a boy's masculinity.

By the time my father warned me about going steady, doubts about Nick were already tiny seeds in my consciousness that I refused to let geminate. We had differences. I loved books and solitude; he liked fast motorcycles and drag racing. The high school newspaper and choir practice occupied my after-school hours; he worked at the gas station after school. He listened to country music and watched John Wayne movies. I preferred show tunes and Doris Day comedies. The biggest problem, however, was not my father's worry that Nick didn't plan to pursue a post-high school education, but that he lacked curiosity. He had no interest in traveling outside of South Dakota. "Why do you want to travel so far when there's so much to do here?" Thoughts of traveling to England and Ireland distracted me from the teachers' lessons while tinkering with the engine of a racing car fueled his dreams. He lived for the moment; I lay awake imagining all sorts of scenarios for my life. I ignored these differences because it thrilled me to date a bad boy.

"You're not mature enough yet to know what qualities in a husband will be best for you," my father said that night. Beneath his words I heard, "Nick isn't good enough for you because he isn't going to college." My impulse to defend my boyfriend and by extension to assert my independence kicked in. "You're wrong about Nick. He's everything I want in a man." I stomped up to my room, wrapped myself in a comforter, picked up my pink princess phone, and dialed my friend's number. When she answered, I sobbed, "My father doesn't trust me." I blubbered for an hour. "He's being so unfair to Nick. He wants to ruin my life." She listened patiently while my grievances piled up like the wet, crumpled tissues on my pillow. I didn't tell her that on the deepest level my father was right. As kind as Nick might be, he couldn't be the husband I needed. My moment of melodrama would be hilarious if it weren't so sad and ridiculous. I might laugh about it today if I hadn't for so many years stubbornly clung to my self-inflicted resentments.

After our argument, I began to see myself as I thought my father surely saw me—a good-time girl who missed her curfews, a mediocre student with a lazy work ethic, and an indifferent piano student, the very opposite of qualities my sister had in spades. She was valedictorian, an accomplished pianist, and obedient daughter. How could he not love her more than he loved me? My unfounded certainty of his disapproval loomed over my days. I grew sullen and uncommunicative, often not speaking to him as I walked by the recliner where he read; not even saying good night on my way past the bedroom where he knelt, a rosary in his hand. He was a man of words, the parent who sat on my bed and talked me through my nightmares and fears; who told bedtime stories he made up on the spot, and wrote a tender poem to celebrate my rite of passage into teenage life. My pigheadedness made him a silent man. A man of words without a listener is a very lonely man.

I realize now that I had turned my father into an either-or-kind of man, as many Western men were in my imagination. A man either faces life head on and moves forward or languishes in failure. My father never seemed to doubt himself or waver between choices or beliefs, whether it was his faith, his farming practices, or his parenting decisions. I had put him a box with no space for ambiguities. Either he unconditionally and uncritically loved the little girl who worshipped him or he didn't love me at all. His early death denied me the gift of understanding his complexities and contradictions. It denied me the opportunity to love the man not the image.

~~~

On December 1, 1961, Gina accepted an engagement ring from Myron. When Bev saw the ring, she threatened to twist it off Gina's finger and throw it away. Gina fought back. "I took it and I'm going to wear it."

Sadie must have been relieved that Gina had committed to Myron. That relief was short lived. Despite being engaged, Gina continued to see Bev. She often lied to her mother about her plans for the night. Gina grew silent and insolent with Sadie. She blamed her younger sister Linda for leaving the door unlocked when she crept into the house in the early morning. "Dad said something about me coming in so late. I told him it was Linda. He didn't ask again."

Joe may not have further questioned Gina because he didn't want to face the truth or felt helpless to change things.

During her testimony, Sadie recalled the night she found the two women lying under the covers in Gina's bed, their faces so close their noses nearly touched. Sleeping in the same bed on overnights was common among young girls. Most of us shared a bed with our sisters and expected to do the same with our friends. But there was something unsettling about the way they scooted away from one another when Sadie walked in, a glimmer of conspiracy and guilt in their eyes.

A few weeks later, she walked by the bedroom and discovered Bev and Gina's sixteen-year-old sister Susie cuddling on the bed. Sadie was horrified. Their cuddling was likely the natural, sisterly closeness of young girls. But Sadie thought only of something twisted in Bev that threatened her innocent daughter. She yelled, "Bev. Get out of this room."

She stomped to Gina's room where Gina sat at her vanity brushing her hair. "If you allow Bev to come back after tonight, I'll make a scene."

I can hear my own silent indifference in Gina's words and can hear my sharp tone in her voice when she said to her mother, 'So what? We're of age."

That night Gina wrote Bev. *Mom is mad at me its not what she did say it is what she didn't say. Guess she's giving me the no talk treatment.*

Gina began to divide her time between Myron and Bev, a juggling act she performed for nearly five months. After Myron dropped her off, she would sneak out the back door and meet Bev parked in her car down the street. During the trial Masten questioned Gina about her duplicity in dating two people at the same time. He hoped to make Gina complicit in the murder by proving her to be selfish and untrustworthy.

"As a matter of fact, Gina, you spent until 2:30 in the morning out in the car with Beverly Waugh the night before the murder."

"I don't remember."

"Didn't you realize what you were doing to this girl's mind?"

Gina didn't answer.

The prosecuting attorney tried to counter the

depiction of Gina as temptress. "You never saw your daughter make any advances toward Beverly, did you?"

Under oath, Sadie admitted that "Every time Bev passed by Gina, she stroked her hair or touched her shoulder. . . they were just sitting together and they seemed to have to touch one another all the time. Gina would. . . just reach out and feed her something, give her a piece of candy of something."

"Did Gina discuss any of this with you?" the attorney asked Sadie.

"No."

How many mothers have sat at kitchen tables in the smell of tobacco and steamy coffee or the oaky fragrance of amber liquid in a high-ball, the glow from their cigarettes the only light in the dark? How many women have listened to their husbands' snoring rumble from bedrooms and wondered if they should talk to them about their worries? Did they imagine husbands taking charge so they could collapse in bed? Or did they hear husbands saying, "I have a hard week ahead of me. You handle this."

Like Sadie, Helara had struggled to make sense of her daughter's relationship with Gina ever since the night she walked into the house and found the women sitting thigh-to-thigh on the sofa. They jumped up red-faced and stuttering their goodbyes. During his questioning Masten asked Helara, "You realized there was something unnatural about their relationship. Did that alarm you?"

"Yes."

Helara had no language, no definitions or terminology to make meaning of their behavior until the day Darrell said, "Ma, I need to tell you something. Bev is a queer. She's in love with Gina." Her son gave her a word that explained Bev's behavior, but how could such a thing be possible? What mother in the 1950's in Middle America would have known the language to understand Bev, much less talk about the conflict she may have felt over her body?

"Even though it was around 1956 when Beverly began to dress and act like a boy, you just accepted it?" the attorney asked her.

"Yes. I first discovered she was using a man's deodorant. Then I found after-shave lotion and hair oil in Bev's drawer. She had begun to walk and sit like my sons."

I sometimes imagine Helara sitting in the living room, a sewing basket balanced on her lap as she gently tugs a strand of silk from a nest of threads in the bottom of the basket. In the same way, she tries to untangle the snarls in her daughter's life. Where once Bev took pleasure in being with her niece and nephew, in the last weeks before the murder, she quit playing with the children and snapped at them if they were noisy or pestered her. Bev had become so isolated and depressed that Helara worried she might hurt herself. When she asked Bev if she wanted to talk about anything, Bev didn't answer but withdrew to her room as she did more often. "She just looked terrible," Helara testified. "She had always been so jolly. Now she had dark circles under her eyes and they had a kinda glossy look." Helara had a pattern to follow in embroidering tea towels and pillow cases, but no instructions for how to help her daughter.

~~~

My sister got married September, 5, 1964, the weekend before I began my first year of college. The wedding unfolded perfectly from the music, "Ave Marie" and "Our Father," to the salmon-colored bridesmaids' dresses, the white roses my sister carried, and especially my tall, elegant father walking my sister down the aisle, his eyes moist. That tender moment between the two of them made me jealous and sad, and sadness unspooled into resentment.

I further sabotaged myself by refusing my father's offer to drive me to college the next day. "You're too tired from the wedding. I'll catch a ride with a friend." Instead of letting my father help me carry my luggage, typewriter, and stereo to my room, I lugged them up four flights of stairs by myself, wallowing in the misery I created. I denied both of us the privilege of celebrating a rite of passage that had driven my father to work so hard. The punishment for my narcissism would come the day I walked down the aisle on my brother's arm, not my father's.

I had trapped myself in the box of an either-or daughter the way I had trapped my father into a binary figure. On the one hand, I wanted, no I needed, to individuate myself from the most powerful man in my life, to declare my independence. On the other, I still wanted to be that little girl who danced with him in her fantasies. I couldn't find a way to reconcile the two. The intensity of my little-girl admiration for my father made severing our relationship more painful and the possibility of an easy reconciliation seemed as impassable as the deep, brush-covered river gullies. Still, I wrongly assumed I would have years to navigate the ravines of my emotions. At best, this separation from a beloved parent would be a necessary part of my coming of age. At worst, it altered me in ways I can't clearly define but feels like emptiness.

Despite my rebellion, I knew I was lucky to have a father who had engaged himself in my life. Girls who grew up with less interested fathers may long for a man who makes her feel special, who calls her a pet name—maybe Red or Toots. They may long to have fathers who tuck dimes in their purses when they go out at night. "Call if you need me. I'll come get you wherever you are." Sadie never testified to Joe's response to Gina's relationship with Bev. Did he sit up and listen as Sadie talked about her worries? Did they lie in bed holding hands hearing the clock tick its way to daylight? Or did he turn away and go back to sleep? The transcript and Gina's letters suggest that Joe did not involve himself in Gina's life any more than Frank had in Bev's affairs.

At one point in the trial, Masten asked, "Gina, please look up and speak loud enough so the man in the last row of the jury box can hear you. Did your father say anything to you about your relationship with Bev?"

Silence.

"Gina, did your father say anything to you about Beverly?"

"No, he stayed completely out of it."

Would her life have been different if her father had advised her to cut the ties to Bev? Would she have done so? Perhaps at the time, she would have resisted or resented her father's unwelcome advice as I had. In later years, she might have realized that although the connection between father and daughter had loosened, their history would keep their relationship from tearing. Or she may have waited too long to repair the damage and lived with regret the rest of her life.

What would Henry Woster have said if I had been dating a girl? Would he have found it inconceivable that he had fathered a lesbian? A devout Catholic, would he have considered my behavior sinful and would he have waited in the shadows of the front porch, his eyes dark with disgust? "What you're doing is sick." Would he be Gary Cooper in *High Noon* never doubting his convictions even if it meant losing a daughter? He loved me. But sometimes I imagine him walking out of the room and never again tousling my hair or calling me Toots. Other times, and this is more likely, I picture him opening his arms and wrapping them around me as I lean against his chest, the worn flannel soft under my cheek, the smell of cigarettes on his breath. His words are warm against my skin. "It's ok, Toots. We'll figure this out."

INEVITABLE ENDINGS

I wish things could be the way they were before hon
always together and happy.
I love and care for you
and this is coming deep from my heart.
Bev's letter to Gina

Hon, everything we had together was good
but now Things can never be good for us
it's just not meant to be and we both know it.
No more hurts, ok Hon?
Just forget about me. I'm not what you want.
I'm sorry for everything.
It doesn't do any good but I'm sorry
Love, love, love, that's all I have time for now.
Gina's letter to Bev

After Sadie banished Bev from the house, Bev
drove to Pukwana most nights, sometimes circling
the house and peering through the windows relieved
whenever she spotted Gina at home. *Yep my girl was
in the kitchen doing the dishes.* Today such behavior
would be considered stalking, a crime of power and
control. But girls tended to be flattered by a boy's
persistence when I was a teen. I had a friend whose
boyfriend followed her as she walked around town
or sat right behind her at the movie, sometimes

leaning over to whisper in her ear. I interpreted his relentless presence as a profession of love for her. "He wouldn't give up," some girls said, a bit of envy in their voices.

Bev's nightly visits concerned Sadie. "Sometimes she parked in front of the house, and sometimes behind the house, and sometimes over by the Lutheran Church. There wasn't anything a person could do," Sadie testified. "It was a public highway."

The women began to write one another every night. Sometimes they mailed the letters; often they slipped them to one another at work—in the back pocket of Bev's jeans or under the calendar on Gina's desk. Were they as giddy as I had been passing folded sheets of paper to Nick in study hall? Did they feel thrilled and nervous about flaunting society's taboos as teenagers did about breaking school rules? Did they find something sexy or erotic in their rebellion?

Scenes from 1960's teenage movies like *Gidget* prompt my imagination in describing Gina writing her notes. She lies on the bed in baby-doll pajamas and little-girl furry slippers, her freshly-washed hair in pin curls, her face scrubbed. A candle on her vanity stand infuses the room with a fragrance, perhaps Enchanted Sugar Plum, sold by the Avon lady. In the mirror, the flames are stars sparkling outside her window. She holds the pencil gingerly between her fingers to keep the nail polish from smudging. She illustrates her letters with flowers trailing a fence line and babies in bassinettes. Inspired by the night sky, she draws a crescent moon and planets at the top of the page with an arrow that points to a heart below and the note *I can't even have a kiss good night even if it's only over the phone?*

What I see now is that those movies, and others to follow like *Grease,* presented binary images of girls in the same way that western movies had for men. Girls could be either chaste like Sandy or slutty like Rizzo. Girls who blurred the line between virginal and seductive mirrored how I felt about myself after the boy accosted me in a car. Perhaps that's why I wanted the security of boundaries, a model to follow in defining myself as a good girl. At the same time, I pushed back against those boundaries drawn by the Church and family expectations.

The way I imagine Bev writing letters to Gina comes directly from words she scrawled on stationery she sometimes snitched from the laundry. She writes of taking a break now and then to stand in front of the mirror picking at blackheads sprinkled across her nose, of stepping outside and smoking a cigarette, or grabbing an apple from the refrigerator. She frets on the many nights that she can't get KOMA on her radio "only static" and speaks of her favorite songs: "She Lost Her Keys," "It's a Lover's Question," "Slow Twisting," and "If I cry every time you hurt me."

She often writes of happiness:

I saw my girl coming. So sweet and warm with a big smile on her face. Yes hon were really happy together and it is a wonderful felling hon. I found a wonderful gal I really love and care so much about. Gina I really love you. I like to have a lifetime with you hon. The more time we have together the stronger our love gets for each other it is really great hon. Darling we have the whole world together and its going to be a happy one.

As winter melts into the spring, Gina begins to pull away from Bev, breaking dates and refusing phone calls. Bev's words become more tentative and bewildered. *I want to know if you really love me. I'm lonely tonight and I wish you'd write me. We never seem to have much time to talk together I have always been true to you haven't I hon and I hope my gal is being true to me. I'm not going to let you go for nobody.*

Bev writes of hurt that evolves into anger. *Yes hon I was hurt Sunday when you told me you were going to clean your room and then I saw you with him. I love you hon and nobody is going to take the one I love and care for.*

~~~

Sometime in May of 1962, Helara discovered a packet of letters buried beneath a jumble of Bev's underwear. At the top of one letter was a picture drawn in a childish hand of a pie that had been cut in eight pieces. *To my sweetie pie. So you started whistling when you were three and you've been flirting ever since huh? Is this true Stinker?*

"Who's writing letters like this?" Helara wondered. She pulled more letters from the pile and sat on the edge of the bed reading them. *I soaked my hickey but it only made it brighter—darn you honey, you're bad.*

"It made me sick to read them," Helara later said in the courtroom.

Helara decided that Sadie needed to read the letters. What courage it must have taken for this timid woman to overcome her anxiety and pick up the receiver, hands shaking, and ask the operator to dial the Lee home. The next day, Helara drove up the hill from their house and down another toward Main. She pulled into the alley behind Joe's Super Value, parked the car, and waited for Sadie. I envision two mothers in a car, one as delicate as a gardenia and emotionally as fragile, the other broad-shouldered with ropey forearms and thick biceps, both women surely devastated and perplexed by their daughters' behavior.

Helara handed the packet of letters to Sadie.

"Did you know about this?" Helara asked. "We should be doing something."

Sadie may have been too weary for this conversation, too tired to help this confused and frightened mother when she herself couldn't see a straight line to a solution. What lay ahead were only gnarled links of Gina's bad decisions leading from one disaster to another. "Well, as Gina says, they're of age. If they want to live together like this, it's up to them."

Later during her testimony, she denied saying these words. "Mostly we talked about what we could do to help our daughters, maybe take them to the doctor or something." Sadie's waffling is not surprising. The way we perceive events, especially during traumatic times, often differs not only between people but within ourselves. Did I really see it that way? Did I actually utter those words? Most of us, however, do not have to worry about perjury when we question our memories.

During his questioning, Masten asked Sadie, "You did recognize that this was an unnatural sex relationship, didn't you? You understand that her relationship with Bev was a 'form of sickness' on Gina's part as well. And you knew that it was an illness and that possibly she needed help, but you didn't go anybody for help?"

"No."

Sadie did call Dr. Jones twice to make an appointment for Gina, but he never returned her call. In a town where doctors still made house calls, failing to respond was unusual. He may have believed that being a general practitioner he needed to focus on "womanly" problems he could treat with a pat on the shoulder and valium. Likely he knew nothing to prescribe for sexual or gender "disorders." If he couldn't cure Gina, why see her? Or perhaps he was uneasy as most of us were with such sexual "perversion." Whatever the reason, he left the mothers to deal with this problem by themselves.

~~~

Although Helara hadn't been to mass for years, she still believed that a priest was his parishioners' spiritual father and therefore entrusted with helping his children. She took the letters to Father George who served at St Joseph's Indian School, a boarding school on the Missouri River bluffs. Every fall when I was growing up, yellow busses, bright as sunshine, rumbled into my hometown delivering children from the nearby reservations to St. Joes. I accepted that these children should be taken from their parents because they needed to be assimilated into the majority culture which, of course, was my culture. In the same way I thought that Bev needed to be more feminine so she could fit into my gender, the way I believed that love could exist only between a man and a woman.

Helara took Gina's letters to Father George who then asked Bev to come to his office. From Bev's letter and testimony, I have imagined the moment the two met. The priest sits at his desk, his black waistcoat unbuttoned, and the white collar glowing in the lamplight. He glances up from the sermon he's writing to see Bev standing in the doorway, hollow-eyed and shaky. Despite the boots and western shirt, the greasy hair and the cigarette pack in her shirt pocket, she looks small and vulnerable. He invites her into the room and offers her coffee. He knows she doesn't attend mass anymore and feels obliged to bring her back to the fold.

"Beverly. Why have you walked away from the church?"

Bev shakes her head, puzzled by his assumption. "I really didn't. I still have love in my heart for my church."

When she pulls a cigarette out of the pocket, he hands her an ashtray and watches her cup her hands around the flames as she lights it. He is troubled by the sexual innuendoes in the letters. *Are you tired today? I am again now. Come put mama to sleep. Mama loves Daddy.*

He takes a deep breath and begins, "Beverly, every human being is called to receive a gift of divine sonship, to become a child of God by grace. To receive this gift you must reject sin, including anything that arouses a sexual response in someone of the same sex. Do you understand what I'm saying?"

The concept of a priest serving his congregation as a father rests upon people having experienced a father who protects, guides, and loves them. Frank was a man too troubled perhaps to fill the role of father, at least in a way that Bev may have needed. She had no reason to trust Father George. Besides, Bev was tired of people telling her what to do. Even this priest wanted to "tear her and Gina apart."

"Beverly, you must quit seeing Gina and come back to Mother Church."

Is it the light of compassion in his eyes that makes her weep? Pure exhaustion? Loneliness? Is it the panic men often experience when a woman cries or the tenderness a father feels toward a troubled child that prompts the priest to reach out and pat her shoulder? She surprises them both when she stands, crawls up on his lap, rests her head on his chest, and sobs. *Yep, hon I cry in Father George lap last night. I guess he think I have trouble. I didn't think I would cry in a priest's lap. Hon what you said Saturday night isn't true is it hon. If my angel love me she wont leave me will you hon. If so Father George won't have to help me. You know how it will end up hon.*

I imagine the priest in this moment. Ill at ease but too kind to push her away, he wraps one arm around her shoulders feeling his waistcoat dampen with her tears. In the silence, only the hiss of the radiator and the ticking of a clock, the smell of Brylcream tangling with the fragrance of damp wool, and the taste of cold coffee lingering on the tongue. Across the wide yard, the dorm lights flicker one-by-one like fingers moving over a rosary until the campus is cloaked in darkness.

~~~

That spring of 1962, Nick and I parked on the bluffs overlooking the river where the night air smelled of spring in the shoots of grass pushing through the sod. Beneath the music on the radio, crickets chirped and cigarette wrappers scattered in the short grass rustled in the breeze. "Close your eyes and give me your hand," he whispered. He put something in my palm and wrapped my fingers around it. The hard edges of metal cut into my clenched fist. I opened my fingers and studied the red stone set in a gold band with Nick's initials embossed in the side. Nick looked at me, his eyebrows lifted. I didn't respond. "Will you wear my class ring? I love you and want you to be my girl. I'll replace this ring with a diamond once you graduate from high school."

At first his professions of love and his desire to marry me seemed sweet. Over time our relationship became strained. He complained that my school activities were taking time away from him. "Do you really need to be in Latin Club? How is Latin going to help you be a mother?"

When he spotted college catalogs in my hands, he sighed. "You know if you go to college that will delay our getting married by four more years." When I didn't answer him, he turned up the volume on the radio, lit a cigarette, and peered through the smoke. Although we had planned to spend the afternoon together, he drove me home, stopped, and left the car running. He didn't walk me to the door as he usually did.

I began to question if what he really feared was not losing me, but rather the security of our relationship. Those fears nibbled at the edges of my mind as well. Starting over seemed too daunting. Then his pleas became demands. "You can't do this to us. We belong together." The more he begged, the more I felt as if he were picking me apart bit by bit like crows feeding on roadkill. Although I couldn't articulate it at the time, I sensed that if he won this battle, I would forfeit an essential part of myself that I had not yet discovered.

I didn't know what my dreams might be or even what I wanted beyond college. I didn't have a career in mind; few of us girls did in the 1960's. But I knew there was more than marriage at eighteen. A string of lights on the bridge reflecting on the water was a satiny ribbon unraveling over the waves, but I felt a noose tightening around me at the prospect of being committed to this boy, to any boy at this young age.

The smooth stone on his ring glowed in the light of the crescent moon that floated above the river. The moon sparked memories of the night an astronaut circled the globe three times, the tenuous thread of communication with the ground crew snipped for thirty suspenseful minutes. Finally, he dropped into the ocean miles from the planned site. I didn't understand what Walter Cronkite said about thrusters and mission control or the spaceship's retrorockets. But I understood the feeling of landing somewhere I didn't plan to be. That place was being a woman dependent upon a man, a fate my father encouraged me to avoid. "If you have a college education, you'll always be able to provide for yourself." My father's words gave me the courage to give the ring back to Nick. "No. I'm sorry if I'm hurting you, but I'm not ready to be serious with anyone right now, especially if I have to give up going to college."

He grabbed the ring, turned the ignition, and pushed hard on the accelerator, pebbles spinning under the tires as he pulled onto the highway. He said nothing on the drive home. I never saw him again. If I told my parents that Nick and I weren't dating any longer, I am quite certain I gave them no explanation. That would be admitting my father was right.

~~~

It was most likely on Lovers' Lane that Bev stopped the car and pulled Gina close. Lover's Lane north of Pukwana was a familiar spot for teenage lovers. The Pukwana grain elevators rising through the night were castles towering over the store fronts. Something about those shapes in the mist made a cow path in a pasture mysterious and eerie and brought to mind the story of death masquerading as a plague victim wandering through an abbey spreading the disease. The nuns said that we would never know when Death would ride a pale horse toward us. In my imagination, a milky-colored steed galloped across the prairie, ribbons of dust spiraling under its hooves, the rider wearing a mask. Perhaps Gina knew the same stories. If so, she, like me, would soon learn that the rider was not coming for us.

Bev lit a cigarette, fumbled in her jeans pocket, and brought out a small box. Gina had seen the box before and knew it contained a diamond chip on a gold band, a ring Bev claimed she bought at a jewelry store in Mitchell. Later Bev admitted she purchased it through the Aldens' Catalog for thirty-five dollars.

179

It was among several white lies that Bev told that year—that she was born in a car, that her parents named her Charles, and that she had applied for a marriage license. Unnecessary lies told for reasons not explained but that made her less credible on the witness stand.

Gina had refused to accept the ring several times, but that night despite the promise she had made to her mother to break up with Bev, she accepted it. "Bev told me she didn't have no use for it so I might as well keep it. I took it as an act for friendship," she told the jury.

Sadie testified that she "figured Gina was trying to break away from Bev but didn't how to do it." Masten argued that Gina had accepted the ring because she was greedy. It's more likely that Gina took the ring because she was afraid of Bev who was becoming more volatile and was making several threats toward Myron.

I seen you with him. Honey I don't want to see it again. I suppose you don't think I'll do it. Well hon your wrong. I want to know if you really love me. You say you do hon and when I hold you in my arms I feel that you love me. But hon if you do why do you see him?

Rejecting Bev again might trigger a violent response.

When my friends reported that Gina had accepted Bev's ring, I called her a "cock tease," the insult a boy used for me when I refused to have sex with him. That phrase somehow diminished me and yet suggested I had an unhealthy power over a boy. Although I wasn't sure how the term applied in the case of Gina and Bev, I used it in a mean-spirited, spiteful way toward Gina that made me feel for the moment as powerful as boys.

The prosecuting attorney argued that Bev controlled Gina. "Do you think Beverly was able to dominate Gina and get her to do pretty much what she wanted her to do?" he asked Sadie.

"Yes."

"Did your daughter have much willpower?"

"She doesn't have much, no."

The possibility that Gina fantasized about a future with Bev was never raised by the prosecutor.

Masten often tried to establish greed as Gina's motive for dating Bev. He pointed to the extravagant gifts she bought Gina —steak dinners at Al's Oasis, a popular tourist destination just west of town; the most expensive box of Whitman candy off the top shelf of Casey's Drug for Valentine's Day, and clothing from Baron Brothers, an upscale department store on the corner of Third and Main in Mitchell.

I remember on rare trips to Mitchell staring at Baron's window displays that changed with the seasons—jack-o-lanterns, turkeys, snowmen, red hearts, and once an egg in white enamel, trimmed in gold filigree and set with glittering red stones. The interior was spacious and softly lit with plush carpeting and labels like Mary Quant, Peter Max, and Pappagallo, labels I saw in the *Seventeen Magazine* advertisements for clothes I could only dream of wearing. My family shopped at Kramer's Store in Chamberlain where boxes stuffed with underwear, socks, and sweaters were stacked on shelves that reached the ceiling. Shoes in the dusty store windows were oxfords with black laces and clunky heels or rubber-soled sneakers.

In the spring of 1962, not long before the murder, Bev and Gina skipped work to drive to Barons. Likely Bev felt out of place and yet pleased to see Gina smiling as she thumbed through racks of blouses and skirts and dresses with pearl buttons. That night she wrote Bev, *I could tell you the special occasion but I won't. It's quite a ways away and I don't want you to get me anything.*

Helara and Mr. Kulm scolded the women for missing a work day. Gina felt repentant. *I wish we hadn't skipped work. As your mom says it was a kind of a kyd's trick.* But Bev, once dependable at the work place, didn't care. She was too obsessed with losing Gina. Her reputation as a good worker and pleasant colleague began to fray. Mr. Kulm would testify that she grew "less attentive" and less likely to follow orders. "It seemed like she was in daze or a stupor or whatever you could call it."

Mrs. Carey, a co-worker, testified that Bev seemed distracted and unresponsive. "I was on the wrapping end of the job and needed more clothes to package. I asked Bev where the handpieces were. She didn't respond to what I said so I asked her again and she didn't seem to be hearing me. Finally, I took her arm and said, 'Bev where is the hand wash?' She looked at me in kind of a daze and told me where it was. Later I thought to myself, 'Well that was kinda funny.'"

"Do you remember the occasion when Mrs. Carey was trying to get your attention?" Masten asked Bev during his direct examination.

"Well, there was always somebody griping about something," Bev answered.

The next week, Bev drove back to Barons and bought a pair of slacks, a jacket, and a knee-length coat for Gina. In her next letter Gina gushed, *All the pretty new clothes and slax suit and a spring coat from Barons you dummy, the most expensive shop in the whole town. You sure have exquisite taste in clothing. Thank you. Thank you.*

Bev also feared her rattletrap car would cause Gina to break up with her. *That poor boom boom of yours just about died today, huh? No I don't think you will lose me because of you're having no car.* The hesitancy in the words, "I don't think," probably burned in Bev's brain. Girls didn't date boys who didn't have cars. Bev had already sold her radio, luggage, camera, and rifle (Bev borrowed the murder weapon from a friend.) to pay for Gina's gifts. Now she hoped to get a loan to buy a 1957 Olds, but Helara urged her to wait. "You're already in too much debt."

When Bev ignored her, Helara asked Gina to "talk some sense into Bev" about her spending. Gina wrote, *I know you owed some bills, but hon I never knew you owed so many. Pay them all something soon. I didn't especially want to say something to you. It was none of my business and I wish I had no part of this.* Bev ignored Gina as well.

~~~

On the Saturday night before the murder, Bev drove east on Highway Sixteen drawn by a hunch she'd find Gina and Myron at the Paragon. The spring of 1962 had been an unusually rainy one and the women mentioned the weather often in their correspondence. They worried about a lightning strike that set a hayloft ablaze and winds that leveled a neighbor's barn. Yet Gina found beauty in the storm. When high winds knocked down electrical poles and cut off power in Pukwana, Gina wrote by the light of a kerosene lamp her father found in the garage. *A dim glow is coming from the lamp, pretty. See you in the morning sunlight.*

On such nights, clouds cover the moon and the sky is inky black except for a few yard lights scattered across the rolling hills. Rain puddles glisten in the headlights. Myron sped toward Pukwana, water splattering beneath the tires. His shift at the dam gave him only two free nights a week. He didn't want to miss a Saturday night with Gina even if it meant he couldn't watch his brother William compete in the saddle bronc competition that weekend, even if the cowboys chided him for being "pussy whipped."

He picked up Gina and drove to the Paragon. They were parked there when they heard the rumble of the broken muffler on Bev's car. She parked, walked over to Myron's car, and slid into the back seat. "Please, Gina, just five minutes. I just need talk to you that long." During the trial, Gina testified how confused and trapped she felt those last weeks. "I didn't know what to do. I couldn't go and I couldn't stay. And I couldn't turn to anyone for help."

Desperate to placate Bev, Gina looked at Myron. "Please?"

"Ok, five minutes."

Gina followed Bev to her car and hopped in the front seat. She scooted close to the door on the passenger side. Bev's face was ashen, the oil in her hair shiny. Her shirt was wrinkled and her boots muddy. She looked as if she hadn't taken a bath or shampooed her hair for days. Her disheveled appearance must have devastated Gina. Bev had always been so particular about her appearance. Helara testified, "She used to be so awfully clean and she always wanted a clean shirt. . . done just so. But in the last month she didn't care how her clothes looked, her shirts were always dirty at the collar and she didn't care, she just wore them."

"Please, let me hold you, Angel," Bev begged.

When Gina moved further away from Bev, she felt something hard beneath her shoes. She leaned over, ran her hand over polished wood and metal, and brushed the trigger with her fingers. At the trial, the lawyer asked Gina, "Was it a pistol or a long gun, would you recognize the difference?"

"I'd know the difference," Gina said, likely annoyed at the question. Like me, she grew up with guns and was comfortable with them racked in the back windows of pickups. We thought nothing of empty shotgun shells rolling around the floor of the car or pistols in the glove compartment. We may not have known the make and model of the guns our fathers and boyfriends carried, but we could distinguish between a handgun and a rifle or shotgun. "It was a rifle."

Bev usually didn't carry a gun in her car in the front seat unless she was going hunting. It's possible that Gina had driven Bev's car over rutty pastures while Bev hunted rabbits. Most of us did this for our boyfriends. Because she hunted in the dark, Bev attached a spotlight to her car so she could to see a rabbit pouncing through the grass. Now Gina looked for a spotlight in Bev's car. There wasn't one. Gina remembered Bev's words. *I seen him tonight hon. One of these times he isn't going to get out of town. Stay away from that half breed, Gina, and nobody will get hurt.*

Bev was hunting something other than rabbits.

Gina asked, "Bev, what are you going to do with this gun?"

Bev ignored the question. "How come you didn't wait for me hon? I told you I would get off at five."

"I couldn't get out of this date tonight. Don't get shook up baby. I'm sorry."

Bev grabbed Gina's hand and tugged at the diamond ring. "If you don't give this ring back to him, I'm going to kill myself."

In her letters, Bev had threatened to commit suicide, but she'd never spoken the words aloud before. Her words must have terrified Gina who later wrote, *I want you to forget about hurting yourself. That's silly. Mama loves daddy.*

"I'll kill myself if you leave me," Bev said again.

Myron honked the horn. Gina jumped out of her car and ran over to Myron's, trying not to hear Bev's pleas. "Gina please don't leave me. Don't leave me."

Myron spun out of the parking lot and drove toward Pukwana. Perhaps Gina watched in the rearview mirror, holding her breath until the headlights of Bev's car faded into the dark. Gina must have been exhausted with fear and indecision. Loving Bev was a round-about with no exit, a never-ending circle from hope to despair, from trust to fear. Myron may have driven so fast they didn't notice the yellow warning signs—no outlet, road closed, blind crossing, slippery when wet. With each mile, Myron pushed harder on the gas pedal, the dial on the speedometer inching higher and higher.

~~~

Memorial Day 1962. It was late morning when Bev was startled awake by someone banging on her car window. The night before, she had parked her car in the church lot down the block from the Lee house waiting for Gina to come home from her date with Myron. About midnight Myron's car pulled up. He walked Gina to the door and leaned over to kiss her. Shortly after Myron drove away, Gina crept out the back door and darted down the street to Bev. They drove to the country and parked on Lovers' Lane for the last time.

Bev was still sleeping in her car when the policeman found her the next morning just before noon. I think of him cupping his hands against the window, his face so close Bev could see the stubble of beard on his chin. A badge on his shirt glittered. His white Stetson perched at an awkward angle on the back of his head. "What are you hanging around for?" the officer asked. "I had complaints about your loud muffler."

Bev grumbled, "Can't a person get some sleep around here?"

She glanced in the side mirror and saw churchgoers watching the policeman lean his hip against the hood of her car as he wrote a warning ticket in his notebook. Bev was weary of people staring at her, weary of "wonderful old buzzards" calling her "pervert" and "sicko." She longed to find a place somewhere in the west where nobody knew their story, a place where she and Gina might have a fresh start with fewer rules and laws that controlled them.

The police officer handed Bev the ticket. "Now get out of here and go home."

The officer shut off the red lights as he drove away, and the curious walked back to their houses. Bev lit a cigarette deciding what to do that day. She tossed the butt out the window, turned the key in the ignition, and drove to the gas station to buy a bottle

189

of pop and a candy bar. She called Gina from a pay phone. A few minutes later, Gina drove up in her father's truck. Bev asked, "Is it true what people around here are saying about you moving to Iowa?"

"No. I told you. I'm not moving."

This was a lie. By now Gina had come to fear the threats in Bev's letters and couldn't admit to her that she was in fact moving out of state to live with relatives.

"Can I see you tonight?" Bev asked.

"No. I have to visit the cemetery with Mom and Dad to put wreaths on my grandparents' graves. Then we'll have a picnic with family."

Bev suspected that Gina often lied when she said she was staying home to clean her room or wax the kitchen floor. She believed that Gina was with Myron, perhaps eating burgers at the truck stop or parking on Lovers' Lane. *Are you going to be with him? If you do Gina I will know about it. One of these times he isn't going to get out of town. Don't see him anymore and there won't be any trouble.*

Don't do anything, hon, Gina wrote back to Bev. *It might lead to a big trial; none of us could take it right?"*

Bev stomped back to her car, revved the engine, and spun away. Gina left the gas station, went home, and wrote her last letter to Bev. Her words may have been sincere or they may have been meant to keep

Bev calm until Gina left town. *When we are together nothing else in the world matters but when we aren't which is most of the time, what then? Just what goes?*

Later that afternoon, Bev called the Lee house several times until finally one of Gina's sisters admitted that Gina was with Myron. Bev ran to her car parked at the top of the hill, jumped behind the steering wheel, and sped east on Highway 16 past Frank and Helara coming home from the Chamberlain cemetery. "She always honks and waves," Helara testified, "but this time she just stared straight ahead and she was going as fast as she could up the hill."

She circled the Lee house but didn't see Gina. She'd never been as nervous, angry, and frightened as she was that day. "I was kinda mad at Gina and wanted to talk to her," Bev testified.

"Were you angry because she hadn't told you she was going out with him and had told you she wouldn't?" Masten asked.

"Well, some lies she told me."

As long as the day "was ruined," Bev decided to go hunting. She loaded the rifle, put it barrel down in the front seat, then drove back to Pukwana. But she was too nervous to hunt. She thought she might hang around Pukwana "to cool off" and maybe talk to Gina again. She was parked on a gravel road just north of town when Myron and Gina drove by. Myron spotted

Bev's car. He knew he had the faster vehicle and decided to drive to Chamberlain so he could ditch her there. Bev put the car in gear and followed Myron, almost without will or awareness of what she was doing as if her car were being towed by an invisible rope toward Sanborn Street.

After the crash, Gina stared ahead, gripping the door handle afraid to turn around and see Bev framed in the rear window. Bev had often threatened to harm Myron. *One day he won't make it out of town.* Gina had dreaded this confrontation, this moment when Bev followed through on her warnings of violence. She had once written *If you're going to shoot Myron, you will have to shoot me first because I will always stand in your way.* Now she was frozen with fear. She hollered into the stillness. "Bev, move your car so we can back up."

Bev didn't answer. She got out of the car, knelt by the door, and propped the rifle on the window frame pointing the gun first at Gina and then Myron. "Get out. Get out." Myron said nothing. Did nothing.

Bev stood up and walked toward Myron's car. In the light of the setting sun, her duck's ass was slick and shiny. The studs on the plackets of her western shirt gleamed with polish. A rolled-up sock bulged in the crotch of her jeans. She carried a .22 caliber rifle. Bev walked to Myron's car and opened the door. Gina

192

put her arm over her eyes to shield them from the glint of the gun's barrel in the slant of the fading sun. She took a breath. "Bev, move your car so we can back up. Get out of the way, please."

Bev held the rifle against her thigh and glared at Myron. "Come on. Get out." Myron didn't move.

"Are you going to get out or am I going to shoot you right here?" Bev's voice echoed low and hollow as if she were standing in a culvert.

"Well, I want to know what for?" Myron asked.

"Because you're with her."

"I ought to be with her. I'm engaged to her."

"You mean you were engaged to her."

Myron didn't fear Bev. He had read her threats of violence toward him in the letters she wrote to Gina. *You think I won't do it, but I will.* Nothing had come of them.

Bev squeezed the trigger until she felt resistance just shy of the point where the gun would discharge.

Gina whispered, "We still are engaged."

In a swift, fluid motion, Bev brought the gun to her hip and pulled the trigger.

Bev looked at the gun in her hand as if noticing it for the first time. Myron didn't groan or even flinch. Gina felt woozy, her limbs weightless as if she were sinking to the bottom of the river. Then Bev lowered the gun and tossed it to the gutter. She stood by the car door watching a tiny, crimson stain bloom over

Myron's shirt. Myron reached toward Gina, made a gurgling sound, and fell across her lap. Gina gasped, pushed his body off hers, and bolted from the car. She ran down the street. Her screams mingled with the shrieks of starlings crashing through tree branches, fleeing by instinct from the sound of danger.

THE AFTERMATH

I don't know how to say this hon but I'm sorry, I didn't mean to do it Gina. I suppose you never forgive me for it or no one else will. I been asking them to let me see you. Yes I'm behind bars now and so far away from you. All I have been doing is praying and looking for you to come. Please Gina come down and see me. I suppose after Wednesday or today I won't be able to see you or anyone else. Yes hon I give up hope for the rest of my life it look like it done for. I want you to forgive me. I do want you to come down and see me. Will you Gina? Pray for me Gina and God Bless you always. I've been asking the Lord to forgive me but I guess he can't hear me. Your tiny one Bev.

Last known letter that Bev wrote to Gina, June 1, 1962

There must have been a second of silence on Sanborn Street after the crack of the rifle, then Gina's screams and a faint smell of gunpowder. Men in front yards put down their beers and looked in the direction where the shot was fired, holding their hands to their foreheads to shield their eyes from the angle of the sun. Small children playing tag in yards spotted their fathers staring at cars smashed against the curb. They stopped short their arms and legs turned to stone. Mothers looking out kitchen windows saw the puzzled and frightened expressions on their children's faces. They dashed

195

out of houses and stood on their front stoops watching Gina race down the street toward Main, her shrieks piercing the stillness.

At City Hall Gina ran up the stairs to the police station. The door was unlocked, but the lights were off and the office vacant. She dashed back to the street and grabbed the arm of a man walking by. "Help—Bev—rifle—couldn't stop her." He led her to the Blue Moon Café, settled her into a booth, gave her a glass of water, and phoned the police department.

A policeman screeched to a halt outside the bar, rushed in, escorted Gina to his car, and drove her to the hospital where presumably she was sedated. She may have been there while Myron's body lay on a gurney in the morgue down the hall. The steel table gleamed in the fluorescent lights as the coroner Ben Pankonin tracked the path of the bullet from the entry point on the left side above the sixth rib, through the lung, the heart, and lay loose to the right of the liver. The end point for a tragedy that began years ago.

Lowell Foltz, the local grocer on a holiday drive with his wife, Florence, arrived first on the scene. His memories were clear. "I was driving real slow because the street was rough." He spotted two cars parked at an angle, tires smashed against the curb. The front fender of one car crinkled the front fender of the other. Then he noticed the gun in Bev's hand.

"It didn't look good when you seen somebody pointing a gun at somebody."

He pulled over and stepped out of his vehicle just as Bev pulled the trigger. POP. Lowell ducked. Florence jumped, looked up, and saw Myron "twitch and kick some, and when Gina got out, he fell down clear out of sight in the car."

Many questioned Bev's mental state after the shooting. Some people claimed that she was stunned, but Florence disagreed. "I wouldn't say she appeared to be dazed. It didn't seem like it bothered her until she heard he might be dead. Then she cried."

Sherriff Virgil Haley later testified that Bev did not know Myron had died for three days. Maybe Florence's description of Bev was accurate. Maybe not. Bev claimed to remember little about the moment, not the feel of cold metal under her trigger finger or her surprise at the gun's recoil so powerful she staggered and nearly lost her balance. The rarity of murder in our little town likely scrambled the memories of those who were there that night. Or perhaps terror shades the details in fuzzy shapes and images. Either way, events of such proportion prompt contradictory accounts that make the truth elusive and slanted by the teller. Perhaps truth is never possible.

Bev testified she wasn't aware of anything but "Gina running down the street. That's when I noticed the gun in my hand." She threw the rifle to the curb, walked to her car, and leaned against the hood. When she was asked later if she remembered seeing Myron fall over, she said, "Sort of, in a way. I kinda seen him fall down."

Although Bev no longer had the gun in her hands, Lowell testified that he approached her cautiously. He stood beside her, said nothing, then took a chance she wouldn't run. "Bev, you better stay right here until the law comes." She didn't move.

He sprinted to the Blue Moon Café where the regulars were lined up at the bar like birds on a telephone wire. "Give me the phone," Lowell hollered. The men turned, cocked their heads, and watched with shot glasses to their lips while Lowell asked the operator to ring Sheriff Haley's number. "What the hell's goin' on?" one man asked. The others shrugged and turned back to their drinking and talk of cattle prices. In days to come, each man would tell the story of what he had witnessed in the Blue Moon the night that Bev Waugh shot Myron Menzie.

Officer Dale Krog was on night patrol and strolling past Fuller's Drug Store when he turned east at the American Legion Hall. He didn't hear the shot, but if he had, he may have assumed that it was teenagers setting off a stink bomb or maybe a bottle rocket. Both were illegal in May but harmless. He didn't consider murder in a town where the crimes he investigated were vandalism, public intoxication, petty theft, and speeding. Although he probably appreciated the safe monotony of small-town crimes, he may have sometimes wished for more excitement. He would likely learn that monotony had its virtues.

A stranger dashed up to him, bent over to catch his breath, and pointed to Sanborn Street. "Go up to the corner."

"What's up there?"

"Go find out," the man yelled. He ran away and was never seen again. Few strangers wandered around our small town, and I recall no murders in my childhood. The two events were inseparable in my mind, both equally astonishing. Some said he was the scraggly-haired man in soiled work clothes seen walking the streets earlier that night. Others speculated he was the man in suit and tie with a bible and brochures in his hands. Such a man had come to our house smiling broadly when Mother opened the door. "Have you been saved?"

"I have my own religion," she snapped and slammed the door just as he extended the pamphlet in his hand. He managed to get his fingers out of the doorway in time, but the pamphlet was caught. It dangled in the screen door for most of the afternoon.

Whether the stranger was a criminal or evangelist, news of his presence quickly spread through the town, his description more threatening and the details more sensational with each telling. For the first time in my memory, my father locked the doors that night.

Krog bolted up the hill past two little boys jumping up and down and hollering, "Oh shit, oh shit."

"What's the trouble?"

"There's been a shooting down on the next corner," one of them yelled. The other stared at the crashed cars, his mouth open.

Krog sprinted to Sanborn Street in the clumsy, bowlegged stride of cowboys, his boots thumping on the pavement. He spotted a gun lying in the curb and made a mental note that it was .22 caliber rifle. Bev stood by her car. He had seen her earlier that night turning the corner at the bakery. "I thought she took the corner a little too fast and I motioned to her. She waved and just went on." He thought of no reason to follow her.

He took off his cowboy hat, twisted his body between the steering wheel and the front seat, and pressed two fingers against the hollow beneath Myron's jaw line. He could detect no pulse. "I didn't notice anything unusual on the man except for a little spot of blood about the size of the eraser end of a pencil on his stomach, consistent with an entry wound from a rifle," he later testified.

He hustled to his squad car and called for an ambulance and the coroner. Then he walked over to Bev. "Who shot this man?"

"I did." She seemed "plumb normal" to the policeman.

It must have been about the time Krog approached Bev that a boy skidded into the parking lot of the Dairy Queen where my friends and I had gathered. "It's a gunshot coming from somewhere down the hill. A block or so off Main."

We ran to a car, I don't remember whose, and sped to Sanborn Street where beacons of red flashed above police cars and the ambulance. The sirens were silent. The ambulance's back doors were open, and men lifted a sheet-covered gurney into the ambulance box. Dr. Clifford Binder and Officer Krog leaned against the vehicle their heads close. Edwin Buckingham, the newspaper editor, circled the cars snapping photos. We turned onto the street but Office Krog waved us away. "Get out of here. Go home now." He looked both angry and frightened. His hand rested on the butt of a pistol in his holster. My throat tightened. Maybe the killer was still on the loose.

We didn't go home. We drove over the river to the gas station in Oacoma where we bought bottles of Coke and bags of salted peanuts that we dumped into the soda, the sweet, salty bubbles stinging our tongues. We chattered as we drove, interrupting one another, our voices high-pitched and shaky. I tried to make sense of the look on Krog's face as he ordered us to leave. I had seen that stunned and panicked expression on a policeman's face years before when an elderly man hit a little boy riding his bicycle. He dragged the boy and the bike for several blocks before someone stopped him on a street across the gully from our house. The ambulance, siren wailing, pulled up and two men jumped out running over to the boy. They knelt by him taking his pulse, wrapping straps around his torso, and inserting tubes in his nose. They carried the stretcher to the ambulance and sped away. The little boy was hospitalized with broken limbs and head injuries. It was years before he rode his bike again. Something equally serious had happened on Sanborn Street.

A classmate drove up and motioned for us to pull over to the curb. "Bev Waugh murdered a man tonight. Her girlfriend's in the hospital."

We sped south on Main toward the hospital. Despite the warm evening we kept the windows rolled up, certain we were in real danger. We drove slowly past the emergency room entrance. Light from one window spilled over the dark and lit the hospital doors with eerie shadows the way the car's headlights lit dark, country roads and turned ditch weeds into creepy figures. "There's nothing there. It's just thistle," my father always assured me. I hoped he could reassure me tonight that I was safe.

Questions came like bullets. "Do you think she's going to be electrocuted?"

"What did he mean by 'her' girlfriend?"

I had my own questions. Why did she murder someone over a girl? What did any of this mean? And why were we all so curious and a bit excited about such dreadful news? In the weeks to come, we would repeat the stories we heard from the trial, would add questions and possible answers to all we heard. We would be both as titillated and unnerved by the revelations of two girls in love as we were by the story of murder.

Around 7:30 that night Sheriff Haley arrived at the crime scene where a crowd had gathered. He drove past two little girls who straddled their bikes and sucked on the ends of their braids as they watched the commotion. He rolled down the window and hollered. "Go home now." They sped up the hill, dropped their bikes in the grass, and ran into the house to tell their mothers something had happened on Sanborn Street. Years later, one of the girls would walk by Bev in a dim tunnel under the

State Hospital grounds and feel the same fear she felt that night.

The sheriff got out of his car and strode toward Bev still slouched against her hood, the gun not two feet away. I envision this moment unfolding like scenes from the western movies that dominated my childhood. The sheriff looked calm but his heart was racing. Already, he suspected the motive. He had seen Bev and Gina riding in a car so close "You thought there was only one person in the car, but you knew it was two." He also knew that Gina was engaged to Myron, an inverted love triangle he once couldn't have imagined. Although he knew the answer to the question, he turned to Bev. "Who shot that man?"

"I did," she said, her voice flat.

Haley leaned against the car next to Bev, cowboy hat in his hands, one tooled leather boot crossed over the other. He didn't handcuff her. Perhaps he was so nonchalant because he didn't want Bev to flee, didn't want to risk a chase through the crowd or the possibility he'd have to fire his weapon. With one hand, he slipped a pack of cigarettes out of his shirt pocket, pulled a loose one out with his teeth, lit it, and handed it to Bev. When Bev tossed the butt on the street and ground it out with the toe of her boot, Haley asked, "Beverly had you ever made any plan to kill the Menzie boy? You were angry at both of them, right?

"Not planned it, no, but maybe things I said kinda scared him."

"You're under arrest. Now get in your car and stay there."

He led Bev to her car, the motor still running. She didn't resist. She slid in and slumped behind the steering wheel staring out the windshield, disoriented but calm. A stream of cars flowed past the crime scene. In the glow of the streetlights, the passengers' faces were pale moons floating in a glass sky, their eyes cratered with shock and fear. For a while, Krog directed traffic away from the scene, but cars kept coming. He told the sheriff that he would take Bev to the city jail. She was still so docile he didn't feel the need to cuff her. She trailed behind him and without a word slid into the back seat of his squad car. She spoke for the first time. "Can I see Gina?" He didn't answer but thought it odd she didn't ask about Myron.

She asked again, "Can I see Gina?"

"If the States Attorney lets you." He knew that Bev would never again see Gina outside a courtroom. He drove past the Five and Dime and turned down the alley behind City Hall to the back entrance of the police station. He helped Bev out of the car and gripped her elbow as he escorted her down the stairs to the cell, slammed the door, and locked it.

~~~

Now a one-level brick community center on Main Street, City Hall in my youth was a two-story structure with a neo-classical symmetry in the columns and windows. The main floor housed the police department, the mayor's office, and the gymnasium where the high school boys' basketball team practiced and played their games. The top floor housed the library. The jail was in the basement of the building across from the hastily-constructed classroom where I attended first grade. Construction of Big Bend Dam on the Missouri River brought hundreds of men to Chamberlain as well as other river towns in the early 1950's. With the workers came their children. The old elementary school my siblings attended became too crowded to accommodate all those children. The school board decided to move the first-grade students to a room with unpainted plywood walls, concrete walls, and small windows in the basement of the City Hall.

Even today my stomach knots at the memory of sitting in my father's idling pickup in the alley behind City Hall, fear and the smell of gasoline fumes nauseating me. My father was patient, but anxious to drive to the farm to begin his day. He reached over and rubbed my shoulder, his blue eyes asking a question I couldn't answer. Why did that basement classroom terrify me? Why did my heart stutter and my breath stop with a sense of the walls closing in on me? Why couldn't I go to the same school as my siblings?

"Why are you afraid to go to school, Toots? Are your classmates mean to you? Does Miss Scott frighten you?"

I gripped the handle on the lunchbox my mother had packed that morning—a thermos of tomato soup tucked inside the lid, crackers, an apple, and peanut-butter cookies. I shook my head. Nobody teased me, the farm girl who had just moved to "town." Miss Scott was lovely. She had red hair and her nylons swished when she walked through the rows of desks, leaving a trace of Chanel No. 5 behind her. She gave me no reason to dread school.

Eventually my father persuaded me to get out of the pickup. I held my lunch box in one hand, clutched his index finger in the other, and walked down the staircase. Perhaps my school phobia colors my memories of that basement. But I remember that a span of concrete between the classroom and the jail served as our playground, although a temporary wall kept the jail from view. Bare bulbs dangled on thin wires from the ceiling, and shadows loomed on the walls. Beneath the chants of little girls jumping rope *Down in the valley where the green grass grows, there sat Janey sweet as a rose* was the clanging of bars as men in handcuffs were locked in the cells.

I realize now that the dark classroom with its locked door offered refuge from danger the way our damp and dingy storm cellar carved into a small hill sheltered us during tornadoes. Yet the cellar also housed rattlesnakes coiled under the shelves of canning jars and spiders scuttling up the dirt walls. Danger and safety wove themselves into my subconscious, and I sometimes couldn't distinguish between them. Ultimately, my desire to learn to read outweighed my fear of the classroom. I found safety that year in discovering the connection between sounds and letters and the way they shaped words on the pages of the Dick and Jane books. In uncertain times, I still find refuge in books.

Chief of Police George Winchester had been entertaining friends at a Memorial Day barbeque when he was called to City Hall by States Attorney H.L. Holmann to interview Bev. At nine o'clock that evening, he walked down the back stairs and crossed the open space between the classroom and jail to find Bev slumped on a cot. When he asked her to empty her pockets, she fumbled in her jeans and pulled out a couple of shotgun shells, a cigarette lighter, a jackknife, and a coin purse with two centavos. (Bev was friends with a young woman who came with her family from Mexico to live in town for a few years. Likely that girl gave the coins to Bev.) Bev stuffed the pocket lining back in place and asked for a cigarette.

Winchester explained her constitutional rights and told Bev she didn't have to talk to them without an attorney. She didn't respond.

Krog wrote the first sentence of her confession on legal paper. *I Beverly Waugh say that I know that the person to whom I make this statement is George Winchester and H.L. Holmann. I make the following statement of my own free will without any threats or duress and without promise or hope of any reward.* He then asked her to write the rest in her own words, but she said she didn't feel like writing anything. Winchester asked, "If I write it down, will you sign it?" She nodded. He scribbled her words verbatim on the paper.

I followed Chuck Menzie from Pukwana to Chamberlain. He was trying to lose me, but he didn't. I caught up to him by the Post Office and didn't let him go by. I told him to get out of the car, he wouldn't. I went over to the car and talked, but he wouldn't get out so I raised the gun up from my hip and pulled the trigger and Gina run down the street. I walked around the car and threw the gun down. Then Lawrence Foltz walked over. I don't remember what he said, then Dale came over.

A few weeks after her arrest, Samuel Masten, chosen by Judge Fred Nichol to defend Bev, drove to the Davison County Jail in Mitchell where Bev waited on her cot. Masten didn't anticipate that Bev would be so fragile-looking, more vulnerable than violent, more pathetic child than cold-blooded killer. "Why that mind wasn't capable of intent," he said in his closing argument. "That mind making these childish threats is no different than the threats of my own children."

His first question to Bev was, "Did you mean to kill Myron?"

"I only wanted to scare him a little bit."

"Do you remember killing Myron Menzie?"

She shook her head.

"Did you understand your Miranda rights when the sheriff read them to you?" She shook her head again.

Masten hoped to prove that Bev had confessed under duress and without an understanding of her legal rights. "Bev, did they inform you that you were entitled to an attorney or a lawyer?"

"Well, I suppose they tried to explain it to me but I didn't understand."

"Bev, do you know what the word "duress" means?"

"Duress? No."

Masten later discovered that nobody was called to advocate for Bev when she signed a confession. That Bev signed this statement without any legal representation to help her understand the legal terminology was among several errors Masten would later cite in his appeal of her verdict.

At some point that evening, Krog brought her coffee and a hamburger she didn't remember eating, although Krog testified she wolfed it down. She did remember they "asked some pretty dumb questions like Bev, are you a good shot? Can you shoot jackrabbits on the run?"

"Yes. I can."

"Why did you shoot him? Have you been drinking? Are you insane?" Krog asked.

"No. I knew what I was doing. I don't like Indians, especially half breeds, and I don't want Gina to go with Myron."

Her statement about half breeds must have complicated Masten's defense strategies.

Although the Waugh family lived just over the bluffs from Sanborn Street, Frank didn't hear the report of the rifle. Perhaps the sound was muffled by the dense woods that covered the hills between the murder scene and their home. Maybe Frank was fishing at the river bottom or tinkering with the engine of an old car perched on concrete blocks in the yard, too preoccupied to hear the gunshot.

Whatever the reason, he didn't learn of the shooting until James called around nine pm to tell his father that Bev had murdered Myron. He likely knew what he had to do but was unsure how to begin. Would he say "Helara, I have something awful to tell you"? Or "Helara, you need to sit down."? Why do we always encourage people to sit down before hearing bad news? What difference does it make whether standing or sitting? The news is always a blow to the gut and the tragedy never averted. Frank did the only thing he could do. He walked slowly into the house through the dark living room and into the kitchen. "Helara."

By the time Frank arrived at the jail, Bev had been questioned for two hours. She looked exhausted. Frank had laid bricks all his life and must have known how to construct walls and even how to demolish them with satisfying whacks of a sledgehammer against brick, the blow vibrating through his wrists, elbows, and shoulders. He knew about patterns in bricks, knew how to mix mortar that sealed the irregular gaps and held the wall together, knew how to repair the wall when the gaps weakened. But in the last years as Bev transformed from his daughter into a stranger in jeans and cowboy boots, as she retreated more frequently to her room, he likely had no instincts to follow in being the father of a transgender man and ultimately a murderer. No aggregate could hold his family together or repair the damage his daughter had done.

~~~

Bev spent the summer of 1962 either in psychiatric wards or a jail cell in Mitchell. Meanwhile, the four lawyers who would argue the case met with Judge Fred Nichol in his chambers in the Brule County Courthouse. At that time, Nichol was a judge of the Fourth Judicial Circuit Court of South Dakota. Three years after the trial, President Lyndon Johnson appointed Nichol as a federal judge to the United States District Court for the District of South Dakota. In 1974, Nichol presided over the controversial trial of American Indian Movement members who in 1973 had occupied the village of Wounded Knee on the Pine Ridge reservation. The most notorious defendants in that trial were the flamboyant Russell Means who went on to star in movies and the reserved but passionate Dennis Banks who returned to the reservation to continue the fight for his tribe. Nichol threw out the Wounded Knee case because of insufficient evidence and misconduct on the part of the government. His decision angered many South Dakotans who felt justice had not been served.

The community knew that Nichol had the power to determine Bev's fate. Nobody considered that the verdict would be not guilty. They speculated instead whether Nichol would commit her to the state hospital or send her to jail for the rest of her life. A few argued for the death penalty despite the rarity of public executions in the state. Since 1877 the state of South Dakota has executed twenty people. The methods ranged from hanging to the electric chair to lethal injections. The first and most famous to die was Jack McCall who in 1877 shot Wild Bill Hickock in the back of the head while he sat at the poker table. The last person was Charles Russell Line who in 2019 was accused of murdering Donnivan Schaeffer, a co-worker at a Rapid City donut shop. Of the twenty that died, five were native. No women have been executed.

H.L. Holmann, the States Attorney for Brule County, would prosecute the case. Jack Morgan from Mitchell would represent Gina and advise her throughout the trial as well as obtain immunity for her. George Wuest, also from Mitchell, was hired by Bill Menzie to assist Holmann. Bill sold his fat cattle to raise the twenty-five-hundred-dollar fee Wuest charged, an exorbitant amount of money and a supreme sacrifice for a cattle man.

In capital cases the court chooses a talented public defender with impeccable qualifications. Sloppy work on the part of the defense could result in an appeal, and Nichol wanted a solid verdict by early fall. For that reason, he appointed Samuel Masten, States Attorney for Lincoln County in Eastern South Dakota. Masten earned his Juris Prudence degree from the University of South Dakota in 1946. He had an illustrious career that included serving as president of the state bar association and founding the South Dakota Trial Lawyers Association. At the time of Beverly's trial, his work as states attorney kept him busy and as did the drives from his home in Canton to Chamberlain, a three-hundred-thirty-mile round trip. Masten spent weeks crisscrossing the state.

During the trial, the opposing attorneys acknowledged Masten's skills. "He is considered one of the great and most able attorneys in the eastern part of the state," Holmann said. "I feel honored that he would appear in the same courtroom with me."

Masten proved their assessment of his talents in the first meeting with the judge. "I would like to lay a little foundation here. I have never called a judge before and I'm not sure of my grounds, but I am going to ask for oral testimony from you."

Oral testimony is the oldest kind of evidence and is used to put additional information on record. It was an unusual tactic to ask the judge to testify. Judge Nichol must have lifted his eyebrows at the young lawyer's effrontery. An astute legal scholar himself he likely suspected that Masten was already planning to appeal an almost certain conviction. He may have wondered what angle the young lawyer was using toward that goal. "I suppose I could refuse, but I am inclined to think that if you want to call me, you have that right."

"Has Bill Menzie at any time appeared in front of you? Did he indicate in any way or threaten that he wanted the girl taken care of or else he would do it?"

Masten knew that shortly after the murder, Bill had staggered past the judge's secretary, his eyes bloodshot, his breath smelling of whiskey. He barged into the judge's office without knocking. "Fred, if the jury don't do something about her I goddamn will."

Judge Nichol remembered how he had walked over and put his hand on Bill's shoulder. 'Now, Bill, you wouldn't do something like that, would you.'"

"Goddamn right I would."

I can imagine a hint of stridency and defensiveness in Nichol's voice when he told Masten, "I didn't take it seriously as a threat or a danger that he would actually go through with it."

Masten probably asked about this encounter in hopes of winning a dismissal on the grounds that the judge and the victim's father had met before the trial which may have prejudiced the judge. Or he might have believed he could get a change of venue citing the difficulty of an acquittal in a case where Judge Nichol and Bill Menzie were on a first-name basis.

Asking for oral testimony from Nichol was a nifty legal strategy. Masten was able to get two significant pieces of information on the record. The first being Bill's threats in the judge's office to harm Bev. The second was Nichol's allowing Bill Menzie to hire an attorney over Masten's objections. This appointment, Masten had argued, was neither requested by the court nor necessary to the prosecution. Both motions were denied. Now Masten could argue that Bill Menzie was not interested in justice but in vengeance, and yet the judge allowed it. Still the defense attorney knew that despite his highly-regarded legal talents, the odds were stacked against him.

~~~

While the lawyers and judge deliberated on how to proceed with the trial, curiosity about the murder spread like prairie fires through neighboring counties. Great numbers of boys from nearby towns drove rumbling cars down Chamberlain's Main Street, flicking cigarette ashes out the windows. The red embers drifted through the dark in tiny meteor showers. The boys were drawn to my hometown by curiosity over the woman who had become a man and the lurid crime that had become legend.

"Hey," a boy yelled one night as I drove Main. "You're from Chamberlain, where men are men and so are women."

They howled when I furrowed my brows not sure what their words meant. My stomach tightened. I was a little girl once again running out of a barbershop through the laughter of men. The driver popped the clutch as he drove by. A bang and then gasoline fumes stinging my eyes.

I parked in front of the marquis of the State Theater and studied my reflection in the rearview mirror to see what provoked their taunts. Chapped lips, short, pale eyelashes, patches of acne blooming on my cheeks, a dishwater blonde ponytail, and rough unpolished nails chewed to the quick. Behind me a neon rainbow arced over the Rainbow Café. The vivid colors washed over the faces of girls sitting with boys in booths sipping coffee or chocolate sodas. Their bouffant hairdos shone with lacquer and their lips gleamed with pink gloss. I knew that they wore circle skirts and cardigans and charm bracelets that jingled when they waved their fingers. My attire was cut-off jeans and a sweatshirt, clothing meant to hide my chunky frame. On the next block, the pole outside Elmer's Barbershop was a ribbon of red, white, and blue spiraling upside down in a continuous loop but going nowhere. The colors were as stuck and hopeless in that cylinder of glass as I felt in this awkward and unlovely body.

The next day, I went to Helen's Beauty Shop to have my hair cut in the "Bubble" style made famous by Sandra Dee. That night, I bleached my hair with a kit called Summer Blonde, rolled the strands in stiff plastic curlers, and crawled into bed. I studied how the models in *Seventeen Magazine* applied shadow above their eyes and painted their lips in shades of apricot and watermelon pink. My sleep was restless from the anticipation of my metamorphosis, but mostly from the curlers pressing into my scalp leaving it a dimpled orange peel. The next morning, I back-combed the curls and sprayed them with Aqua Net. I put my jeans and sweatshirts in the drawer and donned a cardigan and a starched parachute of netting under a circle skirt. Then I slipped on a pair of black patent-leather pumps and sprayed White Shoulders in the hollow between my collar bones. When I wobbled into the kitchen, my mother looked up from the dishes, her eyebrows raised. She bit her bottom lip. "You look very nice, Mary Alice." She was lying. She always chewed her lip when she said something that wasn't true. That day, I limped down the school halls, a girl with a thick middle and stocky calves, blisters pooling on her heels. The stiff fabric of my petticoat scratched my legs and made my hips look even wider. I squinted to see without my glasses. If Bev was a sad imitation of James Dean, I was a pathetic Sandra Dee impersonator.

CARNIVALS AND VOYEURS

So, let's not handle this case on the basis of revenge.
It's not a matter of revenge.
That's not what we're here for.
We are here for understanding.
I suppose you always wonder what you forgot,
what you should have said,
or how you could have made them understand.
Samuel Masten, closing argument

September 24, 1962. Imagine the flurry of activity in a small town on the opening day of a murder trial. Farmers took baths in the morning. "The corn isn't quite dry enough to pick, so I won't be going to the fields today. Might as well go to the trial," they told their wives, looking in mirrors as they shaved, sheepish expressions on their faces. Mothers packed lunch buckets with thermoses of chicken noodle soup and peanut butter sandwiches, avoiding their children's questions as they hustled them out the door for school. "Why did that woman kill that man?" They dashed down the street to the supermarket to buy slices of bologna and loaves of bread, maybe a package of Lorna Doone or Oreo cookies, plucked tomatoes off the vines in their gardens, sliced cucumbers in bowls of vinegar, and

221

left the breakfast dishes in the sink. They planned to spend the day in the courtroom, if they could get in, so supper would be light that night.

Business owners juggled schedules to allow employees chunks of time to attend the hearing. Those employees scurried down the sidewalk to the courthouse a few blocks south of Main. Each person returned with a different story. A clerk from the hardware store claimed she was standing on the corner when the Davison County sheriff drove his squad car into town with Bev handcuffed in the back seat. Bev looked helpless behind the meshed screen that trapped her, still the clerk said she felt a chill when Bev turned to stare at her as the car drove by. "She just kept looking at me with those dark, dark eyes." A waitress at the Hilltop Café spotted a caravan of cars driven by newspaper reporters with press badges strung on cords around their necks. The banker noticed the Lincoln County license plate on a car and knew the driver was Samuel Masten.

Was the first day of the trial as beautiful as I remember? Sunny with a hint of gold in the cottonwood trees and a faint chill on bare skin? A season when the air smells of autumn and of burning leaves? Or was it hot and muggy, a day when the oppressive air zaps the energy out of living things and children trudge to school, quiet and sluggish? Sparrows and mice take refuge in the shade of cottonwood trees, and the lawyers pack extra handkerchiefs to wipe away the sweat that collects on their brows.

On my way to school that morning, I drove by the courthouse where people gathered on the lawn. Samuel Masten pushed through the crowd, a briefcase in his hand, a folded newspaper under his arm. He was tall and lanky, his arms long and thin. His Navy sports jacket hung loosely from his narrow shoulders. His white shirt was starched and pressed and gold cuff links gleamed in the cuffs. With blonde hair cut in a buzz and youthful skin, he looked wholesome and bright, a high school basketball player or debate champion, and far too young for the task ahead of him. But when a seam in the crowd opened, he walked confidently through it.

During the trial he would address the complaints of some in the community that he, an outsider, had come in to defend Bev for the money or to enhance his reputation. "There have been some comments about myself which are a matter of indifference to me. On occasion, we make considerable money. On occasion we don't. Generally public defenders are not paid much but they take the case anyway. Attorneys do not refuse when a judge asks them to represent a client."

Women in printed housedresses swayed in the muscle-memory motion of mothers soothing their babies. Ruddy-faced men in plaid shirts and dark jeans held Stetsons in their calloused fingers. They studied the ground when they spoke. High school girls giggled and tugged at their skirts. Some took pictures with their Brownie cameras, flashbulbs popping and chemicals storing images on silver crystals of film the way memories were being embedded in the hippocampus of their brains. A few boys clumped together jostling with the hungry energy of baby chicks around a feeder. The senior boys mostly slouched against their cars pretending to be bored but unable to conceal the nervous shuffling of their feet against the grass. In a town that often seemed dull, the trial was homecoming, the rodeo, and the carnival wrapped into one week.

The excitement in the crowd made my stomach swoop with the memory of the night my father and I strolled down a carnival midway. We came upon a tent with posters advertising the freak shows—the pygmy and the giant, the fat lady and the midget. One poster showed photographs of The Wild Boy from Borneo crouched in the corner of a cage. He wore tiger-striped fur and his hair was ragged and dirty. He extended his hand, or claws, toward me, his eyes narrowed like a cat ready to pounce. Looking at him, I felt the same flop in my stomach, the same rapid heartbeat I felt on the Tilt-A-Whirl and the roller coaster. This boy with his unruly hair and yellow eyes terrified me. But it was his very frightening, freakish nature that made me desperate to see him in the same way I couldn't resist the carnival rides. "Oh, please Dad. Can we go see the wild boy? Puleezzze?"

He shook his head. "Paying money to stare at unfortunate people is cruel. That's not how good people behave. Now how 'bout I buy some cotton candy instead?"

I pulled on the sticky threads as we strolled past the Merry-Go-Round and the Ferris Wheel. I felt accosted by and nauseous from the jumble of senses—flashes of neon lighting the sky; barkers calling us to shooting booths, their voices rising above the squeak of swings on the Chair-O-Planes; the discordant melody of the calliope screeching beneath the clanking of wheels as the roller coaster ascended the steep tracks.

My father talked about riding the rails with the hobos to the Chicago World's Fair. "I slept in a flophouse, Toots, along with the bums. The next couple days I toured all the exhibits. It was all so exciting for a farm boy."

He had told me this story before, so I thought he was distracting me from my disappointment over missing the wild boy. But the sideshows that year included two Filipino men described as "dog-eating missing links" and the "Live Two-Headed Baby," in reality conjoined infants preserved in formaldehyde. Perhaps my curious father had memories, shameful memories, of buying a ticket and walking past the "freaks" trapped in their grotesque shapes like ammonites in Badlands shale.

Did those who stood in line to grab a seat at Bev's trial come with the same flutter in their stomachs as those who walked past the wild boy or the missing links? Would the photos of a splotch of blood on Myron's shirt or the details of sex between women cause a spike of dopamine in the brains of the spectators as the carnival rides did? Or did some leave the trial feeling dirtied and sick to their stomach as my father may have in Chicago? Did they, too, leave with compassion for others' suffering?

Nobody under the age of eighteen could attend the trial without permission from their parents, so all the kids clutched slips of white paper. I didn't ask my parents for permission. Rumors spread that the trial would reveal saucy (my mother's word) details of sex. Growing up Catholic, I was surrounded by pregnant women, but my mother was tight-lipped about those bulging bellies, even her own. When I was five-years old and she came home with my baby brother, I asked her where he came from. "Don't worry about that. He's here, isn't he?" I pictured someone delivering Kevin the way Santa Claus crept into the house and tucked presents under the

Christmas tree. As for my father, he probably saw this trial as a carnival sideshow that only the cruel people would attend. So, unless my parents woke up one morning in a freakish transformation of their characters, they would never agree to sign such a slip.

When the doors to the courthouse opened, people prodded and shuffled like cattle in chutes up the stairs and into the courtroom. I had never been in the courtroom, but as a teenager my little brother Kevin went to court often mostly for curfew violations. The last time he appeared in this room, he had been caught bagging more than his limit of pheasants. Kevin stood below the raised platform where the judge swiveled in his enormous, black chair looking over his glasses at a teenage boy trembling and sputtering apologies. Finally, the game warden said, "He's not a bad kid, your honor. He's just damn stupid."

Kevin escaped with a stern warning from the judge. "I don't want to see you here again."

In the 1960's, going to court was something like being sent to the principal's office for a lecture and detention. People stopped for speeding, public intoxication, or drunken driving often left the courtroom with only a fine and a stern warning. Our neighbors from nearby reservations, however, were routinely tossed in jail for the same crimes. They remained there until family and friends could raise bail often set higher for them than most folks. The lady with the scales was not always blindfolded when justice was dispensed for Native Americans in our state. But I didn't wonder why that might be so. I just accepted that drunkenness was different for white people than for native people. Years later, my brother Terry admitted himself into a treatment program for alcohol dependency. I then understood that while I mindlessly accepted discrimination against one group of people, alcohol didn't.

~~~

The men and women of the jury chosen after a lengthy process took their seats in the jury box. *Voir dire,* the process of selecting the best jury members, often includes asking leading questions that may give the attorneys insight into the biases of potential jurors. Questions might include "Is there anything in your own life that reminds you of this case?" Or "If you were my client, would you be comfortable having yourself as a juror?" For Masten, finding a juror with no preconceptions about Bev proved difficult. Bev was already notorious in the community—a menacing oddity to some who saw her leaning against her car parked on Main Street, a cigarette in her mouth, her thumbs hooked in the loops of her jeans as she watched traffic. The biggest obstacle in defending her, however, was that she shot Myron in daylight in front of reliable witnesses. Masten likely posed questions that revealed the prospective jurors' compassion and open-mindedness. Or lack of those qualities. The prosecution probably assessed jurors based on the opposite qualities. More than a hundred people were questioned and then dismissed before the twelve jurors were finally seated. In his closing statement, Masten alluded to the process. "I am sure we even had to smile about the examination of the jury, the repetition of questions. But a tremendous responsibility will rest upon your shoulders. . and you have accepted it under oath."

For five days, the prosecutors and the defense attorney would construct their narratives of the murder. The prosecution held the winning hand in this trial. They had witnesses, the weapon, and a motive. Bev, the prosecutor argued, was a desperate lover who in her own words hated half-breeds. Layered beneath the evidence was the perception in the community that Bev was weird and possibly dangerous.

"She scared the heck out of me," my brother Terry said.

Brother Jim agreed that she frightened him but now he wonders why. "I don't remember her ever doing anything to me or anyone else that warranted fear."

In defending Bev, Masten presented her as a wounded animal, manipulated by Gina and ostracized by the community. "It is society that is being tried here," he told the jury, "not Beverly Waugh. Beverly Waugh didn't shoot somebody, she shot back at society."

But implicating the community would not be sufficient to overcome their perception of Bev, even if those perceptions were false. Defending her would still be a game of chance like the milk bottle challenge my father played at the carnival. "Should I win a stuffed animal for you Toots?" he asked, his eyebrows raised as if he didn't know the answer. A former baseball player, he mimicked the pitcher's stance on the mound and juggled the ball between throws. Three times he brought his arm back and hurled a ball at the bottles. Three times the bottles jiggled but held firm. He didn't know that the bottles were filled with lead and the balls with cork. The law, too, can be stacked against the competitors and sometimes the outcome determined before the contest begins.

SEX AND SCANDALS

I came here to expose the truth as best I could.
The things I heard in the town from people
who seemed to know so much
but knew so little.
You had impressions, but isn't reality different?
Samuel Masten

Scandal is gossip made tedious by morality.
Oscar Wilde
Lady Windermere's Fan

In the fall of 1962, rumors from the trial wafted through the Rainbow Café like cigarette smoke from plastic ashtrays. Owned by my mother's cousin Babe and his wife, Irene, the Rainbow Café served as the gathering spot for the community. Businessmen ate eggs and ham there before heading to work. Housewives came in mid-afternoon when the laundry was done, the furniture dusted, and the children still in school. Teenagers filled the booths after basketball games going from table to table celebrating a big win or mourning a loss. Babe and Irene scurried from the kitchen to the dining room bringing malts and burgers and bottles of ketchup.

Every afternoon women gathered around tables at the Rainbow. Their hands flittered around their faces, eyes wide, lips pursed as they repeated testimony from that day's hearing. Gina had often griped about the gossips, "the nosey poopheads" she called them. I complained that the women at the Rainbow were busybodies, yet I grudgingly respected their pipeline. They seemingly knew before the after-school-bell rang which kid was in trouble with the principal for talking back to a teacher or for smoking in the john. They knew my friend Leslie was pregnant, probably before her parents did, and knew that the police caught Judy and Kenny down by the river, their hair mussed, and jeans around their ankles.

Rows of booths upholstered in an orange-tinted vinyl ran along the front windows and the back wall. Metal napkin holders and salt and pepper shakers lined up on a counter that stretched the length of the room. The style seemed vaguely art deco with multicolored neon signs on the wall, plenty of stainless steel, and sparse decorating except for heavy drapes in a floral pattern that framed the windows.

Beige accordion doors separated the café from a large, wood-paneled room with a jukebox where Babe and Irene hosted Friday night sock hops. I remember my brother Jim dressing for the sock hop.

232

He wore white socks and black loafers and jeans, the cuffs rolled. I had puffed up with pride when a senior girl told me that Jim was best dancer in high school. The scene at the Rainbow might have been Arnolds in *Happy Days*, an endless adolescence with Buddy Holly, jitterbugging, and French fries dipped in ketchup.

It was here my friends and I spent hours trying to make sense of the testimony the psychiatrists gave concerning lesbianism and what one called "a third sex," by which he meant transgender. It was here we first began to contemplate the reality of the complicated, sometimes sordid, lives in our small town.

~~~

It was her eavesdropping on the women's telephone conversations that prompted Masten to call Frances Dutro to testify. "Rubbernecking" we called listening to other's conversations on the party lines shared by several homes. My mother often took a break from baking cookies or frying chicken to plop on a chair near the curio cabinet in a sunny corner of our kitchen. Her face glistened with sweat. Her swollen ankles were rounds of dough falling over the tops of her shoes. She sighed, wiped her face with the hem of her dress, and tucked her bangs away from her eyes with a bobby pin. On the shelf near her elbow sat a black rotary dial phone as big as a bread loaf. She slowly lifted the receiver off the hook, covered the mouthpiece with one hand, and held the receiver to her ear with the other. If I happened to run into the room, she snapped her fingers and pointed to the door. I grabbed a cookie from the counter, the chocolate chips warm and gooey against my teeth, and crept past the canary cage covered with a flour sack so the bird wouldn't sing while she listened. But such precautions were unnecessary. Our neighbors knew she was on the line because they were rubbernecking as well.

Although many in the community engaged in gossip, nearly everyone denied repeating or even listening to gossip. When Masten questioned Lawrence Folz he asked, "Hadn't you heard about their relationship in town? You recognized as a resident here that there was something going on there of a rather strange nature?"

"From gossip, just gossip."

Officer Krog waffled as well when he was asked if he had been told that the women were caught "necking by the river."

"Well, no, I wasn't exactly told."

At the time of the trial, Frances worked as a secretary for States Attorney H.L. Holmann taking dictation and transcribing notes and depositions. I remember Frances as matronly, although she was probably in her forties, pleasant but reserved, and rather plain and unremarkable in her appearance. I assumed she was unhappy because she was a "spinster." It never occurred to me she might have preferred being single. She testified that she and Bev attended grade school together and played during recess and that she often went to the Waugh home after school. Bev was a nice girl, Frances said, "perfectly all right."

Masten's line of questioning focused on how often Frances eavesdropped on the women's conversations. "Miss Dutro, have you had any past knowledge there was this unusual relationship between Gina Lee and Beverly Waugh?"

"Just common gossip I heard around town."

"Now Miss Dutro, what is your telephone number? That is an awful question to ask a young single woman, isn't it? Seriously, what is your telephone number? Because you share a party line with the Waugh family, you did have the occasion to hear the conversation between the two women, isn't that right?"

"Yes, but only for a minute. I never heard them all. I didn't realize who it was."

"You knew the women called each other every night, sometimes more than once and talked for twenty-five minutes, right? And those conversations you heard on the telephone were rather shocking to you?"

"I don't recall because all I ever heard them say was "hon" and "darling" because I never listened only for a few minutes, and then I hung up."

The lawyer likely paused to let her answer, her lie, settle in the jury's mind.

"You recognize that you are under oath here?"

"Yes, I do."

Darrell Waugh, the only male in any of the families to testify, took the witness stand shortly after Frances. A swarthy man, his hands rough from hard work, he swaggered to the witness chair the way he did when he walked down the street intimidating young boys like my brothers. Masten likely wanted to establish the contradictions or possible lies in the testimonies of the prosecution's witnesses because in his summation, Masten reminded the jury that "if a witness has testified falsely you can disregard that testimony."

Darrell refuted Miss Dutro's claims during his testimony. Masten asked him, "Did you hear of the affliction or illness that your sister had from Frances Dutro?"

"I went to Mr. Holmann's office on May 16th to pay some bills and Frances asked, 'What are you going to do about your sister? They're driving up and down the street almost sitting on one another's lap. The whole town is talking about it. Are you going to do something about it?'"

"I said I might if I have time, but I believe you. I asked what we could do and she said there was nothing to be done unless a family member signed a complaint. Then she said, 'One night they were talking and one of them said—I don't know which one it was—I will get on the bottom and you get on the top tonight and the other one said 'Oh, goody.' If you don't believe me, come down any night around that time and just pick up the phone and listen in. Mr. Farnsworth seen them over west of the river necking up a storm.'"

Most likely Bev and Gina knew people were listening to their chatting on the phone. It's easy to imagine that they embellished their conversations with sexual innuendoes just to shock the listeners, a way to get back at the busybodies. I might have done the same thing.

In his summation, Masten argued that gossip isolated Bev from the community and made her freakish and lonely even though she was often the center of conversations. "You have a community here where everyone knew about Beverly and nobody did anything. Who was the one person who couldn't help herself? Beverly could not help herself and nobody helped her. She was the loneliest, sickest human being alive."

Because I wasn't allowed to attend the trial, I often needed the women at the Rainbow for the news of the trial. I sat in a booth with my friends eavesdropping as best I could despite the fizz of the soda fountain and the clatter of the cash register. The smell of Lysol on the silky Formica surface of tables rose in the steam from coffee cups as the ladies pushed up against the table to hear another woman's report of that day's testimony. Although the smoke burned their eyes, they didn't lean back until the saga was told. No doubt the story changed with each teller. But slippery facts didn't deter them from repeating these tales. Gossip was their escape in a place where little happened but many things were reported.

Those women seemed to take pleasure in recounting the pain or shame of the Waugh and the Lee families. But there may be another way to consider their gossip. The word gossip derives from the words for God and sibling. Its antecedents include *sabha,* a village community notoriously interrelated. Citizens of small towns weave an intricate tapestry of stories. One family's story of tragedy may help the others in the community to identify with the target of that gossip and through that connection feel empathy. Masten alluded to such compassion in his summation ". . . being in this community has been a fine experience for me. I have been stopped in the stores to buy cigarettes and stopped in the stores to buy coffee, and people have even stopped me on the streets and they have said, 'I hope you can help Beverly.' They understand her."

~~~

The way I had once pondered what lay beneath the nun's habit, we girls pored over pictures of Bev and Gina in *The Mitchell Daily Republic* we spread over the table in the cafe. We couldn't imagine any woman being lesbian, even those like Bev who wore cowboy boots and western shirts or who went hunting and fishing but never drank coffee with women at the Rainbow. But after the trial we began to wonder about girls like Patty, who sometimes hunted deer with her father or Judy who never walked but always ran, faster than some boys. Were they lesbians? Were their bodies different from ours? How were lesbians different from tomboys, the only word we knew for boyish girls or even for Bev?

We especially puzzled over how they "did it." Even today, such questions underlie much of the prurient speculation and bias against LGBTQ+ people. Many prefer to keep the focus away from our common humanity to what some call sinful deviance from that ordained by God. Knowing more about the "other" may lead to understanding and understanding to acceptance. Fear of a shift in the social order motivates many to discriminate against those who are "different."

For me, the most shocking news from the trial was that Bev had fashioned a dildo from a bubble-gum cigar. Mother fretted her cousin Babe would be called to testify that he had indeed sold the cigar that Bev used, an unfounded rumor. Still, I like to imagine Mother and the other women glancing under their eyelashes at the case beneath the cash register where boxes of cigars with shiny bands lined up on shelves. One slumps in her chair and picks a piece of tobacco from the corner of her mouth with her pinkie finger. She looks bored, but her mind races with questions she wouldn't dare ask. What kind of cigar? A Tiparillo? A Roi-Tan? The exotically named Monte Cristo?

The women scoot their chairs even closer to the table, smoke coiled around their faces, as the woman whispers that the lawyer asked Bev, "Did you strap the gadget to your body?"

"How could she strap a cigar to herself?"

"Maybe she didn't," one woman says. "Maybe she held it in her hand."

What on earth did that mean? Why was she holding it? And where did she put it? A pause, then eyes widen as the women grasp the answer. They sit back in their chairs, silent.

At one point in his cross examination, Masten picked up a plastic bag and took it to the judge's bench. "Your Honor, I want to enter this as exhibit fifteen. Do you recognize this, Gina?"

Inside the bag was a cigar made of pink bubble gum, wrapped with strips of white tape and covered in Vaseline, the home-made dildo Bev had crafted. "Isn't it a matter of fact she used this instrument on you? Did she use it below the waist?"

"I don't know."

Masten walked back to the defense table and picked up the folder of letters Gina had written. He read this passage from one letter. "Weren't you kinda sticky with that "stuff" you put on. Like glue. Maybe it was anyway. You got stuck. Oh. Oh."

Tittering surely rippled through the crowd, especially from high school kids who leaned forward in the benches, their eyes bright. It was for this moment they had begged their parents to write permission slips to get them into the courtroom. This was the testimony they had hoped to hear. Most of the girls had never seen a dildo before; in fact, I had never heard that word until the trial. The girls squinted to get a better look at the cigar, puzzled. Some whispered to boys, "What is that?"

"I'll tell you later." The dildo might become a teaching tool for girls that night. What words would the boys use to define the object—broom handle, corn cob, strap-on, potato digger? What language to explain sex between women? They are likely nervous about educating the girls in sexual slang. At the same time the language may have excited them, and they anticipated where such a conversation in a car parked on the bluffs might lead.

The "gadget" prompted a lesson on sex for me. My textbook was a rolled-up sock like the one Bev wore in her jeans, my classroom a back booth in the Rainbow Café with the clattering of dishes and the smell of hamburgers sizzling on a grill. My teacher was Susie who bragged she "had gone all the way" with her boyfriend. Several girls clustered around the table staring as Susie twisted and rolled a sock into a tight tube. "Now imagine the sock is the cigar Bev used to feel like a boy's dick when he's excited." Then she formed a circle with her fingers. "And this is Gina's pussy." I fidgeted as she tried to push the sock through the hole her fingers shaped. What would it feel like to have someone probe my deepest places? Pleasure? Assault? But she couldn't form something firm enough to slide through her fingers. "Oh damn." She gave up. The deep muscles in my belly loosened and my breathing slowed. At the same time, my feelings appalled me. Was I a girl like Gina and Bev?

By the time the trial had ended, both Masten and Holmann had delved into the sexual intimacy between the women in ways that seemed unnecessary and intrusive. Yet an attorney I interviewed told me that likely "the details were so well-known and so unusual that rumors were flying." Both sides had to discuss sex to clear up misconceptions, she said. Also, the questions may have been needed to establish motive. "So much of the case was related to another relationship or affair so it would hard to keep it out."

Masten agreed that it was difficult to ask a young girl such personal questions. "But a life is at stake," he said.

I can't help thinking that two lives were at stake.

DECEPTION AND DEFENSES

Who was the one person
who was so diseased
as to the condition of her mind,
that she couldn't even know how to get out of it herself?
When we make our decision
let's think about this girl who came out of loneliness.
That's where she lived.
Sam Masten's closing statement

Lesbians are psychopathic, selfish, and self-centered.
They will lie or steal
or deviate sexually without any remorse.
Dr. Lawrence Behan testimony

Think of that September day when the bailiff escorted Gina through the double doors and into the courtroom past her parents and Bev. It may have been about that time, I hustled down the hallway fretting about the first-hour chemistry test that awaited me. I wasn't thinking about the trial. But I wonder now if while Gina placed her hand on a bible and vowed to "solemnly swear to tell the truth and nothing but the truth," I sat at a school desk a few blocks away puzzling over the periodic table hanging on the wall of the chemistry room. While I reached back in memory to answer the quiz question "What orbits the nucleus of an atom?" Gina tried to recall what her lawyer said when he prepped her for the testimony. "Look at the jury when you answer and stick to the topic. Don't volunteer information."

Later when my friends reported that she was much prettier in person than in the newspaper, I pondered over her makeup and wardrobe choices. What is appropriate attire for a murder trial? A dress? Neatly-pressed slacks and blouse? What shade of lip gloss would be suitable or more importantly would not smudge or cake on her lips? I imagined my parents sitting in the front row listening to me confess to my intimate moments with another woman. Did Gina feel ashamed as I would have? Defiant? Terrified? I don't recall feeling sympathy for Gina, however. "She made her own bed and now she can sleep in it," people said. I'm sure I agreed.

Exaggeration came easily in teenagers' reports on the trial. Friends who attended it told me that Gina wept softly when Mr. Holmann opened with the question, "Where do you live?" A hush fell over the room they said. Some even claimed to hear Gina's sniffling under the sound of leaves rattling on tree branches outside. Perhaps for Gina sound wasn't diminished but intensified. The clicking of the keys as the court reporter typed became wheels clattering on railroad tracks; the scratching of pencils in reporter's notebooks, chalk on a blackboard. Was she terrified by the sounds? Or did sound hollow out and the faces in the room ripple as if she were looking at them from the bottom of a swimming pool? Maybe her grip on the arms of the chair loosened and the room swirled as if a whirlpool were sucking her into the river.

A major line of questioning for the defense and the prosecution involved the extent to which Bev had tricked Gina into believing she was a man. The prosecutor aggressively questioned Bev about the day the women drove to a photographer's studio in Mitchell. In the days before the interstate dissected South Dakota, Highway 16 dipped and twisted through the main streets of a string of small towns—Pukwana, Kimball, White Lake, Plankinton, Mount Vernon—towns with tourist cabins called Shady Rest or Pine Tree Place. Stucco gas stations shaped like gingerbread houses butted up against the highway alongside cafes named Earl's or Diner 16. The pace on the highway, fifty-five miles per hour, was as slow as life in those small towns.

The photographer must have done a double take when the small man with slicked back hair and a curl over his forehead said, "My name is Bev Waugh."

"Are you a boy or a girl?"

"I'm a boy. I just wear my hair this way."

"Why is your name Bev?"

247

"My parents wanted a girl. My middle name is Charles."

"Beverly," the prosecutor asked, "physically you are a woman are you not? You have the woman's body and a woman's physical parts, isn't that right?"

"Sort of, yes."

"You don't have any male characteristics physically, do you?"

"No."

When I was a teen, I had no term to describe someone like Bev other than tomboy. Scout Finch, the narrator in *To Kill a Mockingbird,* whom I admired a great deal, defined a tomboy. She wore denim overalls, scuffed and muddy shoes, and cut her hair short. She liked boys' games and adventures like climbing trees and spying on the neighbor next door. She was spunky, inquisitive, and bright. Even her name suggested boyishness. But I applied no sexual or gender connotations to the word "tomboy" because I didn't know the words lesbians or transgender.

In the same way, the medical community searched for language to define Bev's gender bending. Dr. Richard Leander the psychiatrist who examined Bev shortly after the murder confirmed that Bev "oriented to male." The official statement of charges included the words "took the male role when out with girls." Even the psychiatrists who testified at the trial struggled with the language to describe Bev, one settling on a category called "a third sex." That term sparks images of extraterrestrial creatures landing in the rolling grasslands surrounding Devil's Tower. In that scenario, LGBTQ+ people are foreigners or outsiders invading the larger human community by which we meant heteronormative. Even today making a diagnosis of gender dysphoria can be tricky. Children may suggest a desire to be the opposite gender by the way they dress and act. Only about a quarter of those children may feel throughout their lives that their inner selves are misaligned with their bodies.

In his questioning, Masten challenged the prosecutor's charges that Bev lied to Gina by not admitting she was a woman. "Bev, did you ever tell Gina you were a boy? Well, you knew you were a girl, didn't you? But you realized you had some of the feelings of a boy, is that right?"

"Yes"

"In which way did you lead Gina to believe you were a boy, if any? Did you say something to her about being a boy or girl? Did you deliberately trick Gina into believing you were a man?"

"Not actually told her no. I never actually right out told her no. But in some ways, she might have believed it. Well, I guess it was after she—well she scratched my back or something and she snapped my bra, or brassiere, or whatever it was."

Bev testified that in one letter she wrote from jail she confessed to Gina for the first time that she was a girl. But that letter was never introduced in court. On the advice of Gina's attorney, her sister burned that letter and five others. "I didn't really read through the letters; I just pulled them out of the drawer and had them burned sometime in June," Gina testified.

Masten asked Gina, "Did you burn them to protect Bev?"

"No."

Although tampering with evidence may have damaged Bev's case, nothing suggests that either the lawyer or Gina suffered legal consequences. For some reason, Masten was not inclined to pursue the matter. "I had no opportunity to know what Gina had in her possession," Masten said of the letters. "Let's not consider what we do not know."

Had the letters been presented as evidence, it might have changed or at least weakened the prosecution's argument that Bev had manipulated Gina through deception about her gender. Bev's words in that lost letter might have proven that Bev wanted to be honest with Gina.

Masten told the jury the burning of the letters was just one more injustice Bev suffered at Gina's hands. ". . . here is this Lee girl twisting this mind (Bev's) and controlling it. How can people do it?"

During his cross examination of Gina, Masten challenged the prosecution's depiction of Gina as an innocent victim of Bev's lies. "Did you consider Beverly a boy or a girl? Just as she sits there now it is quite obvious that she has the breasts of a woman. . . isn't that correct? What is it about her other than her clothes that indicate she is a boy? You and Beverly slept together in the same bed over there in Pukwana, isn't that right? You couldn't undress together in the same bedroom and sleep in the same bed and not recognize that, could you?"

"It wasn't like that. I went into the bathroom and got ready for bed, and when I came back, Bev was in bed but all she took off were her boots."

"Now Gina, I don't want to embarrass you, but a man has an entirely different construction than a girl, and you recognize that fact, don't you? There were various times you engaged in some sort of sexual intercourse, she certainly took some clothing off, didn't she?"

"No."

In his novel *Stone Butch Blues*, Leslie Feinberg defines stone butch lesbians as those who adopt the male role in their relationship. They want to give pleasure to their lovers, but they avoid being touched or being seen naked. Some are unwilling to reveal bodies scarred by police brutality, which might be interpreted as a sign of weakness for not protecting themselves. Often, transgender men or butch lesbians want to cover their genitals for fear of being rejected by a woman.

Whatever Bev's motive, her refusal to undress in front of Gina likely intensified Gina's confusion over Bev's gender. Or maybe Gina didn't want to see Bev naked because then she would have to admit that she was attracted to a woman. Maybe she was simply a small-town girl in 1962 who didn't know how to deal with such complexities of sexuality because she had no access to information to explain her feelings. As she said in court, she felt she had nowhere to turn and nobody to help her.

I knew little about the ways even straight people expressed themselves sexually. Few of us girls did. I imagine some of my friends leaning forward as Masten questioned Gina during the trial. ". .. you have read a lot Gina. . . have you read anything about sexual deviation or lesbianism?"

"No."

"You never ran into that before?"

"No."

"But you know... of the normal acts between a man and a woman?"

"Yes."

How much did Gina really know about sex? Masten may have assumed that reading materials on sexuality were available to teenagers in our small town. I'm certain he was wrong. The school offered no sex education classes. In biology when we dissected frogs during our unit on reproduction, I gingerly lifted the slimy ovaries out of the frog wondering if my ovaries were tiny grapes like these. But I didn't ask the teacher. If books on sexuality existed in the public library, they were well hidden. Besides, none of the girls or boys for that matter would have the courage to approach Miss Arp with her intense blue eyes and prim cardigans about such books. Mostly we relied on questionable information from older girls and lewd innuendoes from the guys.

Masten further hoped to challenge the image of Gina as a frightened girl who had been duped by her lover. He used language that might sway the jury to see Bev as mentally ill, childlike, and more a victim than Gina. "Gina pulled the trigger," said Masten, "not actually, but by teasing this poor pervert with a subhuman mind. She dominated two people, Myron and Bev. She was the guilty one who twisted and controlled Beverly's mind, playing both ends against the middle by dating Beverly and Myron at the same time."

~~~

The question of Bev's sanity at the time of the murder was also critical to the case. The prosecution called Dr. Lawrence Behan, an administrator at the state hospital in Yankton where Bev spent much of the summer after the murder undergoing blood and urine analysis, x-rays, and psychiatric examinations. Behan testified that Bev was a twenty-four-year-old female with the emotional capabilities of an eight-year-old child. The psychiatrist measured her IQ between seventy and seventy-two, the line between low normal and "imbecile" he said. But later in another IQ test she scored between eighty-two and eighty-four. Stress undoubtedly explained the discrepancy in the scores.

He also ordered a serum test for congenital syphilis. Something about the structure of her nose and her teeth and her intellectual deficiencies made him suspicious. The results must have been negative or inconclusive because syphilis is never mentioned in the trial. Surely Masten who built his defense around her intellectual and emotional limitations would have used a congenital syphilis diagnosis as further proof of Bev's limited mental capacities. He could then strengthen his plea that she be hospitalized rather than jailed.

The prosecutor focused on lesbianism as an explanation but not a defense of Bev's actions. "Are lesbians generally quite jealous people?" the prosecutor asked Behan.

"In their love situations, yes."

"And it's a rather frustrating situation, isn't it?"

"It is because it has to be subversive and secretive because of social objections. They are basically lonely, unhappy, and afraid to admit it. Homosexuality must be eliminated for the sake of happiness."

His comments were supported by the psychiatric profession at that time. *The 1962 Diagnostic and Statistical Manual of Mental Disorders* defined homosexuality as a "sociopathic disorder." The language used in the manual and throughout the trial reflects the lack of knowledge within the medical and psychiatric professions concerning sexuality and gender. In fact, no language for gender dysphoria existed within the psychiatric field at that time. However, few people would have challenged Behan's words. He was the professional.

According to Masten's son, Jeff, his father felt squeamish using lesbianism as a defense, but he determined that his best chance of keeping Bev out of prison was a verdict of not guilty by reason of insanity. "I came here for treatment," Masten said in his closing argument. "She needs treatment and there is a place for her."

That possible verdict required that he use words

like "sexual deviant" and "compulsive neurotic confused by her own gender." In a community that valued conformity, such language might convince the jury that Bev was so psychologically impaired that she could not be responsible for her actions. Or it could further sway the jury that she was dangerous and must be incarcerated. He walked a thin line between showing Bev as a sexual deviant given to violence or a victim of circumstances. It was a risk he would have to take.

Masten called Dr. Richard Leander to testify for the defense. Leander had also examined Bev that summer of 1962. He began by defining Bev's condition as a mental illness. "Most people go through a phase of same-sex attraction. But for some reason, which is entirely background, their development arrests, and they remain immature and do not develop into normal adults sexually."

At the time of the trial many in the medical profession debated the cause of homosexuality. Some studies argued that homosexuality resulted from genetic alteration. One doctor even suggested that homosexuals were more likely to be born to parents of the "degenerative class. . . who lacked strong sex characteristics." Was Dr. Leander placing responsibility for "aberrant sexual behavior" on the parents? Was he using the argument that environment altered sexual development—the smothering mother, the detached father?

Leander continued, "Immature people react to stress in an animalistic manner. They (lesbians) react more violently." Masten used the doctor's words to argue that Bev had not planned the murder but responded instinctively with the violence of a trapped animal.

"Do you think Beverly over a long period of time could be channeled back to a normal girl?" Masten asked.

"The prognosis is guarded. It depends a lot on the desires of the person being treated. Some live their lives in a rather frustrated fashion. Satisfactory to them, but rather disturbing to us from a society standpoint. I think Beverly was happy and didn't want to change."

Bev's cousin Larry questioned the doctor's opinion. "She was always so angry and I didn't understand why. Now I know. Being a lesbian was shocking and sinful in those days. Her family didn't understand her and we didn't help her." What happiness did the psychiatrist observe in Bev that her family hadn't seen?

The belief that homosexuality might be cured is a misconception and inaccuracy that can be traced to the early twentieth century when psychiatrists wrote of their success in converting gays and lesbians to heterosexuality. It's a fallacy that promotes today's gay-conversion camps, despite the great harm done to young men and women subjected to a treatment that teaches among other things that homosexuality is a sinful, perverse choice that displeases God. Many who have experienced "reparative therapy" struggle with addiction, depression, and thoughts of suicide. Many have acted on those thoughts.

For five days, Bev and Gina sat in a courtroom listening to the attorneys draw their version of the story from the witnesses. The police chief, the sheriff, the women's matron, doctors, and the coroner all told of their interactions with either Bev or Gina. Other witnesses described the women with words that reflected different facets of their personalities. Bev, testified her boss, was a good worker, reliable, and friendly with the other employers at the laundry. "She had a good reputation as far as I know," he said. But a woman who worked closely with Bev testified that she would consider Bev an acquaintance, but certainly not a friend.

"She was a kind person and an awfully nice girl at home," Helera testified.

"She was a "cold blooded and calculated killer" the prosecutor argued, with a "depraved disregard for human life. A sexual deviant who should not be running loose in our society."

Many things were said about Gina as well. One reporter described her as "an all-American girl"—a cheerleader and honor student who didn't smoke or drink.

Sadie called her as an innocent girl who had been "manipulated by Bev out of pity. She had no will power and could be dominated by a stronger personality." Two stories were told; two interpretations of those stories presented. The jury would choose which version would be recorded as history, which version would determine Bev's future.

In his summation, Masten admitted to the jury that like many people he was initially repulsed by Bev's odd appearance and switch in gender. But over time, as he heard her story, he began to understand and care about her. He was the first person to whom Bev spoke of her love for Gina and her sense of isolation and despair as a man in woman's body. "How could I not be moved by her story?" he asked the jury.

Masten reminded the jurors of the judge's instructions that the jury must determine Bev's sanity at the time of the murder. He pointed out that Bev placed the gun in car because she had planned to go jackrabbit hunting. When she fired the rifle, she was holding the gun to her hip not at her shoulder. In a fatal and tragic but unplanned series of events, the gun went off and pierced Myron's chest. These facts suggested that Bev's actions were impulsive, not premeditated. "There is a presumption of innocence in our trial system. The burden of proof lies with the state. Reasonable doubt decides the case," Masten argued.

Bev's attorney didn't question the events of the murder but having spent time with his client he believed that prison was not where Bev belonged. "There is nothing more important to me than finding help for her," he told the jury. He asked them to contemplate their verdict not only with their minds focused on justice but also on the best facility to serve her needs. "All of the psychiatrists who testified here believe that the worst thing we can do to Beverly is put her in prison where there are problems with homosexuality."

"If I have done nothing in this case but bring on the light of understanding, it would be worth it. We contribute money to mental health; we contribute to heart disease, but what do we really do with our hearts and minds? It's like dropping a dime in a blind man's hat. You're not giving him a dime; you're buying ten cents of relief that he was born different from you. It is society that is being tried here, not

Beverly Waugh that girl who came out of loneliness. Loneliness is where she lived."

Masten acknowledged that the jury faced a challenging responsibility in deciding the verdict, a responsibility for another person's life that he had accepted months before. "But at this time, I want you to know that I have carried the burden for some time and that burden is shifting off my shoulders, and I feel a lot lighter but it's shifting on to your shoulders, and your hearts must be heavy... so do this for me."

"Beverly and I will be waiting for you. When you come back, we will be waiting for you." He sat down while the bailiff led Bev from the courtroom to the jail where she would wait during jury deliberations.

After five days of hearing testimony and without lengthy deliberation, the jury convicted Bev of manslaughter in the first degree.

October 3, 1962. Bev returned to the courtroom for the sentencing. Masten hoped he could encourage the judge to consider placing Bev in the Yankton facility instead of prison. "Dr. Behan said that God made her that way," he told Judge Nichol. "She couldn't help it. She needs treatment and there is a place for her. By your verdict of not guilty by reason of insanity, the law sends her to that place. She goes to the hospital where she belongs."

Masten revealed a private conversation he had with Dr. Behan in which the doctor admitted he did not believe that Bev intended to kill Myron. Because this was an unrecorded conversation, Masten could not introduce it during the trial, but he could do so as part of the sentencing. "Sam, we can accept her down here," Behan had said. "We will be glad to have her. She is a good worker. Her treatment will be difficult. It is long. But we can help her. Homosexuality occurs whenever groups of the same sex live together, boarding schools, military barracks, prisons. The worst place they can put her is prison because of the homosexual nature. She is an amateur now at this time, but she will be a professional when they get done with her in the penitentiary."

Holmann challenged Masten's contention that Gina played a part in the murder. "I want you to consider only the facts. There is only one person on trial and that is the defendant. She has not denied it. You will recall who the psychiatrist said was the aggressor. Beverly Waugh. She is responsible. The State has presented to you a clear-cut case of murder. We have done our job. Now you do yours."

The prosecutor argued for life in prison. "If you deal softly with this person, then in the future more people are going to be inclined to kill if they feel or find that they can get out of it without suffering the full extent of the punishment."

Finally, Judge Nichol asked Bev to stand. "Do you have anything you wish to say Bev?"

Bev said nothing.

"Bev, you have had a fair trial. You didn't give Myron Menzie a fair trial on that night last May 30 when you took the law into your own hands and shot him in cold blood and your sexual aberrations are no excuse for the taking of a life of another person."

Calling her a menace to society, Judge Nichol accepted the verdict of first-degree manslaughter defined as "causing the death of a person with culpable negligence and with wanton disregard for life." He sentenced her to life in prison.

Think of the moment when Bev heard her sentence. Surely Helara wept. Or called out "No. Please. No." Norma may have held her mother or turned to her husband, her face stricken. Or maybe she was stone-faced and silent, tears being useless. Bev may have responded to her mother's tears. "Please don't cry, Ma." Or maybe Bev wept as well. She might have heard whispers sweeping through the courtroom or perhaps only stillness when the sheriff approached her with handcuffs and leg chains. She rose, spread her feet, and put her hands behind her back. A snap of metal against metal vibrated through dead air as the sheriff clasped the cuffs around her wrists and the chains circling her ankles. Then he wrapped his thick fingers around her elbow and nodded toward the open door. Bev Waugh, who once swaggered down the street in boots and bulging jeans, shuffled in baby steps out of the courtroom and down the long hallway, the clatter of chains echoing behind her.

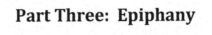

Part Three: Epiphany

CHOOSING LOVE

If I get that farm job I was telling you about today
honey will you go with me?
Hon, we can start a new life together
and I'll make you real happy.
I know we'll be happy together
away from the dum people around here.
If you care for me honey will you go with me?
I know you really love me.
When I hold you in my arm you really care and when I
kiss you.
Bev's letter to Gina

I hope you destroy all these letters
or someday you'll say
and to think I married her this kyd so silly.
Gina's letter to Bev

June 22, 1968, six years after Myron Menzie was
murdered, I stood in the foyer of St. James Catholic
Church watching Ken handsome and understated in
a black tux and starched white shirt take his place on
the altar. I met Ken at South Dakota State University
in the fall of 1965, but we didn't begin to date until
1967. While Bev languished in jail mourning the loss
of her love, I had just met mine. He was handsome
with a gap-toothed grin, thick hair, and dark
complexion. His eyes, blue as my father's, folded me

into their warmth. Five months after our first date, he proposed. There had been other boys in my life, but he is the only man I've ever loved, a man like my father—steady, tender, and intelligent who on my wedding day lay in a hospital bed in Minneapolis recovering from surgery for stomach cancer.

Six days before my wedding, my family first heard the words Henry Woster and terminal cancer in the same sentence. Our days fluctuated between celebration and grief. I felt both immersed into and yet removed from the confusion around me. Lips moved, but made no sound. Hands wiped away tears, but those hands were detached from bodies. I was alone; I was surrounded by family. I was a bride-to-be; I was a grieving daughter. I planned to cancel the ceremony until my father could walk me down the aisle. But he surprised me by saying that he would stay in the hospital that week and the rest of the family would be in Chamberlain until after the wedding. "You and Ken are going to need each other in the days to come, Toots."

Those days blur except for a few distinct memories. My mother sits in a chair looking out the window, shoulders sagging, her cheek in the palm of her hand. If she had an opinion about what we should do, she didn't say, or at least I don't remember her doing so. My father had always been the decision maker and like many women of her generation she deferred to him. Likely she couldn't think clearly for the shock of the news and the realization that life had taken a turn for which she wasn't prepared. None of us were. Who were we without Henry Woster? In the days to come, my mother would find the strength to answer that question and through her example we found that we, too, could carry on. But I, for one, was never the same.

I honored his wishes to go on with the wedding in part because it's impossible to argue with a dying man. Another part of me wanted to get married as planned. I busied myself making place cards for the bride's table, printing the wedding programs, and buying candles for the unity service. Had I dwelled on his unselfish love for me, I wouldn't have made it through those long days.

The week of my wedding the grace of family and neighbors was made manifest in tater tot casseroles, goulash, and sloppy Joes; in salads, wilted spinach and Jello, and in toffee bars and peanut butter cookies. My cousins moved silently through the house mopping the floors and making beds for guests. Aunt Evelyn arrived early as she always did in times of crisis, bringing her steam iron. An excellent seamstress, she didn't trust anyone else to iron my wedding gown. Standing on swollen feet, she pressed the tip of the iron around the embroidered daisies and pearls on the bodice, her face glistening from steam, her hazel eyes moist. Keeping their hands busy was the way my Irish aunties dealt with grief. In the same way, keeping her fingers on the piano keys helped Mother cope. My father once said, "Look at your mother. Everything she feels is coming through her fingers." After that, I heard her music with a different appreciation. The sad Irish tunes she played brought memories of my grandmother who died when I was only five. Jigs and ragtime reminded me of lively family gatherings. Her music underlay our days that stressful, sorrowful week. But not maudlin music. Muscle memory of ragtime was embedded in her fingers and the songs came unbidden. "Toot, Toot, Tootsie" and "Twelfth Street Rag" incongruous melodies perhaps in other families' grief but comforting in ours because her music was and still is the soundtrack of our childhood.

"Your father always put his family ahead of himself," Aunt Evelyn said. "You need to honor his unselfishness by being happy."

Then this stoic Irish woman grabbed me and held me. "He was a good man." She wiped her eyes and turned back to her ironing.

Devastated by her unintentional use of the past tense "was," I dashed out of the room and drove across the bridge to seek the solace of the river bluffs. I parked the car, dialed the radio to a rock station, and smoked until the taste of tobacco was bitter on my tongue and the car hazy. Small rainbows glistened on the water. They sparked memories of a sunset when I was a little girl.

Several pheasants spread over the yard, their wings tucked under their bodies and their heads listing to the side. I knelt and touched the down on the birds' breasts marveling at how soft they were and how still in death. Earlier my father had tromped through a field in air so crisp it sparkled. There must have been the hard, fluttering sound of a pheasant flushing, a bang, and a thud. We would feast that night on pheasant breasts coated in flour and fried in butter. "Look at this, Toots," my father said. He held a fan of feathers in his grease-stained fingers— feathers of gold and rust with patches of blue and red, colors as radiant as stained glass in cathedrals. "Toots, have you ever seen anything more beautiful?"

In my memory, the slant of the sun that day filtered through the feathers and bathed my father in a rainbow. That image is not possible. The angle of the sun would have lit the scene differently. Still, it was a moment as mystical as the rainbow that follows a storm. He didn't say anything, but I want to believe that he was telling me that we must honor the offering of one life for another, that love demands hard sacrifices. He plucked a feather from a wing and gave to me. I used the feather as a bookmark until it was dry and dusty and crumbled between the pages.

~~~

There was the feel of August that June day when the temperature spiked to one-hundred-and-thirteen degrees. On the way into the church, my heels sank into the tar of the parking lot. With each step, I heard the sucking sound of the sinkhole of deep loss for which my generally happy youth had not prepared me. Inside the foyer, the wind hissed through the open door carrying the smell of dusty grass. Waves of heat seared the stained-glass windows. My impulse always is to touch a beautiful object, to feel the lines and textures of a painting, a sculpture, a wildflower. I reached out and traced the pattern in the window, the lead panes burning my fingertips. The pain felt good somehow.

My brother Terry played a guitar and sang "For Bobbie" as three bridesmaids processed down the aisle. They wore different colored dresses—pink, yellow, green—the colors of the bouquets of daisies they carried. Daisies were everywhere that day—scattered among pearls on the bodice of my dress and on the brims of the picture hats the bridesmaids wore, tucked in the netting of a small corsage on my mother's breast, and arranged in tall vases at the feet of the Blessed Mother's statue. Daisies are the flower of love and simplicity, beautiful whether a single blossom on a sturdy stem or clustered together. Each flower made lovelier by the other. They symbolized what I wanted in my marriage to Ken—two independent lovers enhanced by one another's presence. But in the heat, the daisy-laced hats drooped over the bridesmaids' faces and the flowers shed petals on the floor the way my girlish dreams of a perfect wedding were strewn over a week of shock and sorrow.

Perhaps my adolescent vision of my wedding came from my parents having married on Valentine's Day, a date that captured my childish imagination. In their wedding picture, they stand on the front stoop of St. Mary's Catholic Church in Reliance, South Dakota. My father looks dashing in a top coat with a scarf tucked into the lapels. He holds a Fedora neatly creased with a feather in the band and smiles at the camera, head tilted slightly, his shoulders relaxed. Even in high heels, my mother's head barely reaches his shoulder. Her coat is buttoned at her slim waist; its wide lapels expose the scoop-necked collar on her blouse. She scowls at the camera. She never smiled with an open mouth, in part because her sharp front teeth which she called her "fangs" embarrassed her. But I suspect that she was nervous that day about leaving the security of home and the large family that had always sheltered her, nervous perhaps about what to expect on her wedding night.

My mother first noticed Henry when she was senior at Reliance High School and he drove the bus for the school district, spending most of his day reading in the small library of the rectory of St. Mary's Church. One winter day, she looked out the window and saw him twirling across the Reliance Dam tracing figure eights in the ice. She admired his grace and skill but never dreamed that one day she'd spin and twist through life with him. I like to imagine she drew a heart in the frosty window, the cold burning her fingertip, a blush creeping over this shy girl's cheeks. She wiped away the heart with the sleeve of her sweater and went back to class still flustered by what she'd done. This didn't happen. She was not given to romantic gestures.

My father spotted Marie McManus in the choir loft at St. Mary's. He must have appreciated that she was delicate yet sturdy, that her hazel eyes gleamed when she played. He probably was attracted to her shyness which masked a spunkiness that would later frustrate him. He must have imagined their home filled with music, which it was. They owned two accordions, a trap set, a saxophone, an organ, and always a piano. Nearly every night my father stood next to the upright he bought his young bride, his lyrical tenor blending with my mother's harmonic alto as they sang, *We'll build a sweet little nest, somewhere in the west.*

Her family watched in horror as the courtship unfolded. They huddled in the kitchen whispering about his character flaws. He liked to talk, too much in their estimation. He was too cocky. Both were often true. One day he rode his bicycle from his farm to theirs, a round trip of more than twenty miles. I like to imagine him spending the day in the living room, long legs stretched across the linoleum floor, talking books, politics, and theology. Knowing my father, he would have been oblivious to the hostile circle of bandy-legged Irishmen that drew tighter around Mother. He couldn't imagine someone might not find him interesting and likeable. Although I think now some of this was family lore, perhaps even of my own creation, I still think of my father pedaling over dirt roads, singing perhaps, the wind lifting his thin hair and his spirits in knowing he'd win the heart of this Irish lass.

The biggest strike against him in her family's eyes, however, was that he was Bohemian, not Irish. Lyman County was still populated by little clusters of ethnic clans. Marrying outside one's heritage was nearly as taboo as marrying outside one's faith. My aunt refused to attend her son's wedding in a Congregational Church. My cousin's father-in-law chose not to witness his grandchild's baptism in a Catholic Church. Given the rigidity of some family members, I shouldn't have been shocked to learn that my grandparents did not attend my parents' wedding. When I asked my mother why, she dismissed the question with a wave of her hand. "Oh, nobody went to weddings in those days."

Sometime later, we were having coffee at my aunt's house. A large picture of her wedding day hung in the living room. She wore a long, satin dress and veil and held a lush bouquet of flowers. She and my uncle stood on the altar surrounded by family and the wedding party. On the drive home I asked, "Mom, why did you tell me that nobody went to weddings back in the day?"

She kept her eyes ahead as she maneuvered our Nash over the gravel road. "I didn't say that. I might have said people didn't drive a long distance to go to weddings. I think you heard me wrong."

I heard her right. But there was nothing to gain by asking more questions.

I had always assumed that my mother was the special girl my father had serenaded when he sang "The way you look tonight." Then I discovered a faded photo of my father in the days when he wasn't my father. He sits on the hood of an old truck, his legs crossed at the knees, toes of his laced boots pointing up. He leans back against the windshield and clasps his hands behind his head. It must have been a summer day because he wears a short-sleeved shirt under striped overalls. His biceps strain against the sleeves. The open collar exposes a neck of ropey muscles. A petite woman in a flowered dress, black slippers, and bare legs drapes her body over his thighs, her hands folded on his knees. It appears the day was breezy because her Marcel waves lift away from her forehead and the hem of her dress ripples over her calves. There is an intimate physicality between them that I never saw between my parents. On the back of the picture, written in my mother's handwriting, were the names Hank and Noreen. Who was Noreen? What motivated my mother to keep this photograph? Did she not see how comfortable this young couple seemed with one another? Of course, I didn't make the connection at the time, but likely Noreen was not a Catholic and so their romance was doomed.

"I never did anything to disappoint my parents," my mother often said particularly when I challenged her about curfews or my choice of clothes. She took pride in being a compliant daughter. Despite that she chose to marry my father. Why? She often said that she wanted a "house full of babies." For that she needed a man who would be a solid and caring father. She wisely chose the strong, dependable man with a sweet tenor who would provide for his family through hard work and broad hands.

If my parents had concerns about my marrying a Protestant, they didn't tell me. Perhaps they knew their objections wouldn't have mattered. I was going to marry Ken regardless of what they thought. Maybe my father remembered days when young Catholics didn't have the option to choose a "mixed marriage." When I told him Ken was a Methodist, he said, "If he's a good man, that's all that matters."

That my father may have loved another woman does not bother me. Nor does it upset me to think my parents may have married as much because of religion as love. Love is a choice. I once said of Ken, "I could marry him even if I didn't love him because I know he'd never try to change or control me." Pragmatism served me as well as passion in choosing a husband. In the same way, my parents' faith sustained them during hectic days of raising five children and worrying about cattle and crops, hail storms and blizzards, bank loans and machinery repairs. Their commitment to the Church and to their family gave my siblings and me a solid foundation for our lives and mostly gratifying days for them.

I didn't think of my parents' wedding the day I married, however. Woozy from heat and lack of sleep, I gripped my brother Jim's arm as he escorted me down the aisle. I could smell English Leather and cigarette smoke on his wool suit and feel the sleeve scratchy and damp beneath my fingers. His biceps trembled a bit, and he chewed on his bottom lip, a nervous habit he shared with my mother. He had walked into the church a son and now, although he was only twenty-eight-years old, he left the head of the family. None of us asked if he wanted that responsibility. He never faltered that day, or in years to come, matching his stride to mine. When we reached the altar, he took my hand and wrapped my fingers around Ken's arm. In my memory, he walked back down the aisle to sit in the pew with Mother who looked tiny despite her now heavy breasts and fleshy hips. The veil on her pillbox hat didn't hide the way her face crumpled when she saw me. But she didn't cry. But parts of that memory, too, are faulty. In fact, Jim left the altar and ascended the stairs to the choir loft to sing with Terry. Why this false memory? Science suggests that under emotional distress memories can be distorted. Perhaps in clinging to the image of Jim with my mother, I'm substituting a brother for my father as a way of avoiding the pain of that fatherless day. Possibly I revised the moment so I wouldn't think of my stunned, emotionally fragile mother sitting by herself in a long pew.

I do recall standing at the altar and regretting the hours I had spent planning for this day. Years later when our daughter, Maura, chose a destination wedding to Jamaica, I was relieved. "Aren't you disappointed you can't plan a wedding for your only daughter?" people asked. I joked about the luxury of soaking in a pool and sipping a Pina Colada an hour before the wedding. The truth is I no longer trusted plans. I had no plans for the heat of June that made the church an oven or for how I wilted at eyes that tracked me when I walked down the aisle. I had no way to prepare for a father's dying young, for a day when sorrow overshadowed joy.

I can't remember saying the vows or feeling a ring slipping on my finger. I can't hear the kneelers creaking at Communion or the priest's monotone voice as he placed a host on my tongue. As I recall, my mouth was so dry I couldn't swallow the wafer and had to dig it off the roof of my mouth with my finger, a venial sin one nun had taught. I can, however, see the crease of worry between Ken's eyebrows and feel his hand wrapped around mine, the warm knot of his knuckles, his ragged nails, and the slight pressure of his fingers when he felt me sway.

After the ceremony, we posed for pictures, a moment as cloudy as the sanctuary filled with candle smoke, as ephemeral as the fragrance of daisies and incense. One memory, however, still haunts me with the clarity of a photo. The photographer adjusted the train on my dress, straightened my bouquet, and brushed a loose strand of hair off my cheek. College friends stood at the back of the church watching, and for some reason I began to giggle, a giddiness that still shames me. As he stood behind the camera, a black cloth covering his head, the photographer muttered, "Selfish girl." A pop and a flash blinded me, but I saw the truth in his words. My father was dying while his daughter was eating chicken timbales and kissing when people clicked their forks on their goblets. People whispered behind their hands and shook their heads. Maybe pity darkened their eyes, not condemnation of a girl who celebrated her marriage without her father. But even today when people say, "This is what your father wanted for you. You were simply honoring his request," I nod and thank them. But I don't believe them.

Back at the house, we opened gifts and packed the top layer of the wedding cake in a freezer container. We planned to eat the cake on our first anniversary. But we didn't do that. The cake remained in the freezer for several years growing stale and hard as a brick. My mother finally threw it in the garbage. I changed into a brown linen dress with white piping, part of my trousseau that included lacy underwear and a white nightgown trimmed in daisies. Mother pinned a corsage on me and patted my shoulder. "Have a good time and don't worry about things at home." In the rearview mirror I saw her standing in the yard watching us drive east toward Highway 16. She wrapped her arms around her waist as if to steady herself in the stiff wind.

~~~

If Myron and Gina had married, theirs would have been a racially-mixed marriage, disapproved of socially but not legally. Despite the pervasive racism in South Dakota, anti-miscegenation laws did not apply to native people. It was, however, illegal for people of European origin to marry Blacks, Asians, and Filipinos. That law passed in 1909 was likely in response to the Black Hills Gold Rush which brought men and women from many ethnic backgrounds to work in the mines, laundries, or brothels. Whatever the reason, the law remained on the books until 1957.

If Gina and Bev had married, their union would have been complicated by many factors. It would have been a mixed marriage. Gina was Lutheran and Bev, Catholic. They had very different social backgrounds and educational levels, the same differences my father worried about in my dating Nick. They might have overcome those challenges as Nick and I might have, but they could not get around the law in 1962 which prohibited same-sex marriage. Still the two women talked of marriage and family.

"Gina, look directly at the jury so they can hear your answer. Had you and Bev discussed marriage?" Masten asked her.

"Not really."

The attorney picked up a letter. "What did you mean by these words? 'Yes, it can be kinda western. But don't overdo it. I don't want guns in the living room like Dad. Issh.' Were you already decorating a house for the two of you?"

Gina didn't answer.

Masten read another letter. "'Karen will probably have her baby in early August. Yes, sugar they will beat us. Oh well you'll get your fill of washing dirty diapers. Oh yes this is your job. I don't want to. Have fun Daddy. You sound like you could be disappointed if our son turned out to be a girl. Maybe we shouldn't have children. I may let you down.'"

"Do you want the jury to believe that you thought perhaps Beverly had gotten you pregnant?"

"Yes. That's what Bev wanted."

"You were still having menstrual cycles, weren't you Gina?

"Yes."

"You hadn't gone to a doctor about this pregnancy. Did you talk to your mother or the

Menzie boy about this problem? Did you talk to your minister?"

"No."

Did Gina really dream of someday sharing a home and raising a family with Bev, perhaps on that ranch in Nebraska where Bev had begged her to go? Or did she write these fantasies to reassure Bev who was becoming more paranoid and aggressive each day? Bev stalked Gina and Myron. Her letters became more threatening. She sometimes shouted insults at Gina and shoved her around. What a trap for a teenage girl lying to her parents, her fiancé, and her lover. Gina must have been terrified that harm would come to Myron or to herself if something didn't change. But what and how? Her future was scrambled with bleak possibilities and she believed that nobody could help her, that nobody could understand her dilemma.

For her part, Bev had found unexpected happiness with Gina. *I don't think two people could be happier than we are together. Darling we have the whole world together and it's going to be a wonderful future.*

Fear of losing Gina her psychiatrist said made Bev mentally unbalanced, citing the difficulty in a rural state for "sexual deviates" to find someone to respond to their needs. "Lesbians are few and far between out here." His statement reveals how little even the medical profession understood about gender and sexuality in 1962. The first misconception was that lesbianism was a perverted deviation from the norm. The assumption that few lesbians lived in the state was equally misleading. This might have been accurate if it applied only to openly gay women, not to those many women who lived on and operated ranches and farms or were closeted in marriages or convents. If living in a rural area may have isolated women like Bev and Gina, if it potentially denied them the companionship of other lesbians, living in the west paradoxically protected them. The libertarian spirit that exists in the Great Plains sheltered them from the police brutality or harassment that lesbians and transgender men in cities endured. When Sherriff Haley was asked why he didn't arrest the women, he said, "They weren't breaking no law as far as I could tell."

Gina and Bev's affair may have been a temporary romance, fierce and fleeting, and ill advised. We have all had such relationships. Gina may have come to believe that the obstacles to marriage were too daunting to overcome even if the state would grant them a license. Perhaps Gina worried about being ostracized by her family or friends. Perhaps her affair with Bev was simply experimentation prompted by curiosity. Over time, Bev may have grown weary of Gina's duplicity and lost trust in her. She may have fallen in love with another woman. For any number of reasons their affair may have failed. Severing their relationship would have been their decision. But had they stayed in love, marriage by law was not a choice they could make.

On June 26, 2015, the United States Supreme Court lifted the ban against same sex- marriage citing the constitutional rights of all people, rights denied Bev and Gina. That day, two women from Rapid City became the first lesbian couple to legally marry in South Dakota. Nobody protested their marriage. Codified law once stated that consent to marriage was not enough but must include solemnization or a ceremony performed by a state or church official. The women's union was solemnized not by a priest as mine had been, but by all those who had for years lobbied legislators, marched down city streets, and stood outside courtrooms holding placards. Their union was celebrated by the explosion of fireworks that lit the skies across the nation that night. Neon rainbows glittered on the windows of the White House and lit the spans of bridges crossing the Potomac River. Their marriage was sanctified by this statement from President Obama. "Tonight the White House was lit to demonstrate our unwavering commitment to progress and equality, here in America, and around the world."

Ken and I celebrated our marriage by driving east for a honeymoon in a northern Minnesota cabin we had chosen for its rustic appeal with knotty pine walls, plaid bedspread and ruffled curtains, and a fire pit by the lake. We had imagined a week hiking the woods, roasting marshmallows over a wood fire we'd built, and lying on blankets looking for the North Star and Big Dipper. It would be perfect. What did we say to one another during the trip? Maybe nothing. I do remember the radio played Frankie Valli singing our song "You're just too good to be true." But we didn't turn up the radio and sing along as we usually did. When we reached the cabin, I crawled into bed, sobbed myself to sleep, and slept for twenty-four hours while Ken rowed a boat around the lake and played solitaire in the lobby.

GRIEVING LESSONS

I want you to forgive me hon.
No matter what happens
they'll never take the love I have for you away
never.
I do want you to come down and see me.
Will you. Pray for me and god bless you always.
I love you always.
Last known letter Bev wrote to Gina, June 2, 1962

Women who had fathers for only a short time
never give up the search....
we look for some trace of the lost father
sometimes in the forward tilt of a tall man's head.
Alice Steinbach
Without Reservations: The Travels of an Independent Woman

When someone dies,
you don't get over it by forgetting;
you get over it by remembering,
and you are aware that no person is ever truly lost or
gone
once they have been in our life and loved.
Leslie Marmon Silko
The Delicacy and Strength of Lace

In my dream I furiously pedal a unicycle, my
knees pumping like pistons, the wheel spinning
backward and forward. The cycle lurches to a stop,
and I jiggle my body to keep my balance before

pedaling again. My arms stretched overhead are rail thin and trembling. The world is cupped in my hands, its weight pressing on my shoulders. The dream presents itself in vivid colors—the blues of oceans, browns of buttes and deserts, and the greens of forests. The background is midnight blue, the unicycle white with silver wheels. My face in the shadows is gray and ghostly. The cycle turns this way and that in a topsy-turvy ride of fear that I will drop the world and it will shatter at my feet.

My unicycle dream came to me for the first time on the night before my father's surgery revealed stomach cancer. The same dream came again when my mother battled a staph infection that offered her only a ten percent chance of survival. It haunted me the night before Ken's first bone marrow biopsy that diagnosed Chronic Lymphocytic Leukemia. Each time, I woke up drenched in sweat, heart pounding, and legs quivering and weak. I fell back to sleep, but the dream came again and again. The sensation of thirst overwhelmed me. I threw off the blankets, hobbled into the kitchen, and stood at the sink in the dark drinking a glass of water, then another, and another.

Denial became my ally. I refused to speak the word "cancer" when people asked about my father's diagnosis, irrationally believing that if a word weren't said aloud, it wouldn't be true. In the terrifying days of Ken's diagnosis and treatment, I rarely left the house and often wouldn't answer the phone. I didn't have the energy for questions from concerned friends and family. I didn't have the courage. My mother had been no better at facing bad news. She never wanted to break her children's hearts with painful truths. She even lied when she told us as small children that we were going to town for ice cream, when in fact, we were going to the doctor's office for vaccinations. She justified the lie by saying, "I didn't want you to be afraid." When I asked her about my father's prognosis, she fell back on her need to tell protective lies. "He'll be fine." She didn't look at me. Mother's evasion about his illness terrified me more than the truth and may have set me up for a lifetime of coping by avoiding.

My friend Leanne walked down the aisle in the shadow of her brother Smokey's casket, her long hair covering her face, her sobs echoing over the hymn we sang. Myron's father, Bill Menzie, turned to drink and anger in his grief. He was often seen stumbling out of bars yelling, "If I get a hold of her, I'll take care of her." The Menzie and Waugh brothers apparently channeled their grief into violence. For years after the funeral, according to my cousin Leo, the tension between the families erupted in fights if they chanced upon one another. "It was almost like the Hatfields and the McCoys, but fortunately the dust finally settled without another killing." In the Celtic tradition women keened, a ritual wailing "like banshees." This was likely too primitive for the Catholic Church, which wanted orderly and prayerful observances—the rosary, the funeral mass, and the burial, solemn ceremonies focused on sin and salvation. Keening was among the many customs my ancestors left in the rich soil of Ireland.

In the Lakota grief ceremonies, mourners honor their dead by observing *Nagri Gluhapi*, the Keeping of the Soul ritual. They purify a lock of the deceased's hair with smoke from sweet grass and place the lock in a buckskin pouch or sacred bundle. On the first anniversary of the loved one's death, they take the bundle outside and open it to release the soul. Lakota women who grieved often chopped off their hair, their most sacred possession. At the time, I didn't know about these means of expressing grief. Yet the day after my father's funeral, for reasons I still don't understand, I cut my shoulder length bob into a pixie as short as a boy's. As strands of hair pooled on the floor a weight lifted off my shoulders.

My own experience of grief was shaped by being Irish, Catholic, and a child of the prairie, a place where challenging times required toughness. Or perhaps we'd become immune to death, at least not surprised by it. Roadkill was as common as bird songs; tragedies as predictable as the seasons. I was only a toddler when a horse stepped in a gopher hole, broke his leg, and tossed my cousin Frances into the air. He fell to the ground, his neck snapping with the impact. He died in my Aunt Grace's arms as they raced to the hospital. I have no memory of that time and my family rarely talked about his death and so the details are sketchy. I mostly remember my aunt's smile that wasn't a smile but rather a grimace as if others' happiness pained her.

Nobody prepared me for the grief I felt after the loss of my father. In the years to come, I followed no predictable pattern or time frame in mourning his death. Even today, grief catches me unaware by its timing and ordinary circumstances. A battered straw hat on a farmer in a café or a pheasant flushing from a milo field can still knock me flat and leave me wobbly.

~~~

When Bev realized that Gina was pulling away from her, she took the first step in the process of grieving, a pattern Kubler-Ross described as a passage through tumultuous emotions in a definable series of steps—denial, shock, bargaining, anger, depression, and finally reflection and acceptance. Bev bargained. She would quit smoking if Gina stopped seeing Myron. When that didn't work, Bev smoked more than she ever had. *Once a pack of cigarettes lasted me three days, now a pack doesn't last a day.* She probably needed the spike of nicotine in her brain, the sense of euphoria it sparked. Perhaps smoking made her feel more masculine and in control like the Marlborough Man in Stetson and boots, a pistol on his hip, and a cigarette dangling between his lips, a sense of power that may have prompted her to write *One of these days, he won't get out of town. Don't see him anymore and there won't be any trouble.*

Bev must have detected an odd disconnect in the letters Gina wrote in the days just before the murder. In the first few paragraph of one letter, she writes about her supper (a pear) and Bev driving her brother-in-law's car. Then she abruptly segues into the obstacles that the women faced and couldn't overcome. *Things can never be good for us. We both know it. My mom doesn't care at all for our relationship in any way and I think you mom will always have doubts about me.* Her words may reflect a teenage girl's conflict between wanting her parents' approval at the same time she wants to defy them. She certainly acknowledges family problems their marriage would create.

In next paragraph Gina hints of the grief that she feels at knowing their relationship is doomed. *Hon, it's no good. And is there any hope? When we're together nothing in the world matters. But when we're not, which is most of the time, what then?*

But then as if she had said nothing about the sad dissolution of their relationship, she writes about watching Route 66 on television and anticipating the meatloaf her mother will serve the next night. This abrupt shift in thoughts may simply reflect the flirty, fidgety teenage girl who sketched posies and rainbows on her letters. Or it may suggest she fears being truthful with Bev and tries to bury the bad news beneath trivial topics. Perhaps she is avoiding facing the truth herself.

Once Bev realized that she had lost Gina, she seemed to speed through the steps of grief beginning with depression and physical changes. Helara said that Bev spent most of her days alone in her room and lost so much weight her eyes were protruding from her thin face. Gina, too, noticed Bev's loss of appetite and subsequent drop in pounds. *You didn't even finish your stew. You'll get skinny like a sparrow. Naughty.*

A photo taken of Bev in jail, "some pretty dumb pictures" Bev later complained to her attorney, illustrates Helara's and Gina's worries about Bev's weight. She sits on a cot looking tiny and dazed and alone. The open collar on her denim shirt falls away from her thin neck and exposes a wrinkled t-shirt underneath. She looks to her left, away from the camera, her eyes unfocused. The photo of Bev has faded over time and the images blurred as if Bev were merging into the shadows. Nothing of the fierce woman I once feared remains but only a lost, little girl.

If I needed years to reach the acceptance stage of grief, Bev's words in her last letter written to Gina suggest that she quickly accepted responsibility for her crime and loss of Gina. *Well, hon looks like I'll get life in prison or death. I get it will be over hon. I'm sorry. I met have been better off if I shoot myself. I suppose you never forgive me for it or no one else will.*

~~~

In 1968, that long summer of my father's dying, he spent his last days sitting in a lawn chair in the shade of a tree in our front yard. He used the time to make funeral arrangements choosing men who farmed and hunted with him to be his pallbearers and asking that "Ave Maria" be sung at the Offertory. My brother Jim sat with him listening to his wishes for renting the land we owned just west of the Missouri River. "Take care of your siblings and especially your mother. She'll need help with finances and managing the farm. And be generous in your business dealings with your Uncle Frank. He was a good partner." Jim was attentive to his father, as he always was, and he jotted notes in a small, spiral-bound notebook he kept in his shirt pocket. Just as my Aunt Evelyn and my cousins held back grief with chores, Jim dealt with pain by completing tasks my father assigned to him.

One day, I plopped into a lawn chair close to my father. I had planned to apologize for letting my adolescent pride or insecurities damage our relationship; to tell him that he was a rare father who harbored the same educational aspirations for his daughters he did for his sons. I wanted him to know that the gentleness and respect he showed me inspired me to expect the same from my husband. People drove by our house slowly, gaping at the sight of his thin frame. Nobody stopped to visit with him. Cancer was a word spoken in whispers in the same way people spoke of "alcoholism" or "mental illness" as if the disease were something shameful or contagious.

If my mother steered away from the truth, my father's body didn't. His eyes, once the clear blue of autumn skies, were now wintery gray and unfocused. Hands that once ripped open feed sacks and biceps that pounded fence posts into hard soil were now skeletal. Broad shoulders that carried me high above the ground sagged. He had been unable to keep fluids down and his voice was parched and whispery. "I'm sorry," he said. "I know how hard this is for you."

He was a man who had already died. How could I talk to a ghost? I fled the yard, drove to the river bluffs, parked on a point, and walked down the hill to a small, gravely beach. Despite my resolution to quit smoking, I lit one cigarette with the butt of another and tossed the butts in the river. The sensation of drawing smoke into my lungs intensified the heaviness in my chest. I accepted the weight of it as my punishment. My days became a Dirty Thirties of emotions—the joy of being newly married became billows of dust roiling over arid fields and my belief in the future was the dry, cracked dirt at the bottom of stock ponds.

My father died two months after he was diagnosed with stomach cancer. He was fifty-six-years old. I had expected him to stay on his feet and wrestle the disease the way he wrangled steers, expected him to beat back death with a two-by-four. And if the unimaginable happened, he would be stoic in the face of death, like my bull rider, triumphant in defeat. But those last days he lay in his bed thin and silent. "I thought I would live to hold my grandchildren, Toots" are among the few words I remember him saying to me. His surrendering to death so easily surprised and devastated me.

My mother believed that my father died quickly because the doctors gave him no hope. There were tiny seeds of cancer sprinkled throughout his belly they told him. Perhaps radiation could stop the seeds from spreading in the way that pesticides slowed the proliferation of weeds. But my father knew the weeds always came back. Like many western men of his generation, he believed he was indestructible. He had no health insurance, and his life insurance would not cover the haystacks of medical bills piling up on the kitchen table. He would not leave his family in debt.

~~~

August 22, 1968, two months to the day after my wedding, I stood once more in the foyer of St. James Catholic Church feeling numb as the priest draped a white cloth trimmed in red and gold satin over my father's casket. The priest sprinkled the cloth with holy water saying, "In the waters of baptism Henry died in Christ and rose to him in new life." This ritual reminded mourners of my father's baptism into new life as an infant and now, new life in death, a paradox at the heart of our faith. The pall bearers carried my father's casket to the altar where Ken had waited for me that day in June, an anxious expression in his blue eyes. Where Terry once sang, "I'll be there to kiss away the tears if you cry," now the choir chanted the ancient, solemn words of the funeral rites. "Deliver me Lord from death eternal."

My mother wore the same dress to the funeral she wore to my wedding. My brothers likely wore the same suits. My sister wept quietly. My brothers looked stoic but broken. I felt frozen, stiff, a deer in a snow bank. My head ached from the smell of incense and roses mixed with candle wax dripping on the floor. Faces in the pews were distant as if I were looking through the wrong end of binoculars. I was grateful so many had come to the funeral, but they seemed too remote to comfort me. Father John prayed in a monotone that suggested this funeral was business as usual. "Remember your servant Henry was called to yourself." Father John's days would go on as they always had, but mine would forever be altered by this moment. Why wouldn't he acknowledge that? Why didn't he quit reading from the scripted words, look directly at my family, and say, "I'm sorry. I don't know why good people die. I don't know what I can say to comfort you."

After the funeral mass, we followed the hearse up Highway 16, the same hill Bev drove that Memorial Day. I leaned my face against the window, my warm skin dampening against the cool glass. But tears didn't come. I had learned from prairie people that tears were for people without fortitude or faith, and although I had neither that day, I behaved as if I did. Along the road, men in overalls and scuffed boots stood by their pickups, the headlights on despite the noon hour. They knew my father from Knights of Columbus meetings, from chatting as wheat fell from their trucks at the grain elevator, and from drinking coffee and talking cattle prices at the stock yards. They had removed their hats, and the white bands of skin on their foreheads glared against their weathered faces. Drawn and weary, they nevertheless stood straight, shoulders back, soldiers honoring a fallen comrade. To this day, I do not find the grace of the Holy Spirit in rays of sunlight cleaving the clouds. Rather, grace comes from ruddy-faced men by the side of the road, holding Stetsons or feed caps over their hearts.

Ken threaded my fingers through his as we walked behind my mother over grass brown and shriveled from hot winds and sun. Spirals of dust rising from newly-turned sod were miniature tornadoes whisking in the wind across the cemetery. My father's grave was an open wound surrounded by artificial turf. I wanted to rip to bits that patch of plastic in the dusty grass, as if the undertaker were trying to deny the cycle of life and death that had defined the man who had tilled the soil. In truth, I was angry at everything. At the doctor who waited too long to refer him to a specialist, at daughters whose fathers still lived, and at God for deserting my father in his last days. This man had knelt by his bedside every night, a rosary in his hand, and attended mass every morning before driving to the fields. But that summer he lay in his bed sullen and angry at God for abandoning him. A man of the West to the end, he responded to pain with anger, anger being a show of strength demanded of men in a landscape determined to defeat them.

Father sprinkled holy water on the casket and on the ground of the burial site. The drops plinked against the plastic. Pools of water glistened on the dry shale. The ground and artificial turf were not receptive to water in the way that I was not receptive to the platitudes uttered at the funeral. What did God's will have to do with this man's death? How could my yoke be both heavy and light? Below the cemetery, the undulating river, caterpillar brown, flowed in a timeless cycle joined by countless rivers and creeks on its path to the Gulf. Life, too, is a sequence of events that merge and lead eventually to death. My father was born. He married and raised children, cattle, and crops, and then he died. Always the farmer, the caretaker of land and family and a man of the seasons, that spring of 1968, fragile and exhausted with pain, he planted seeds in straight rows knowing he would not live to see the harvest.

After the funeral, I wandered around the house thumbing through the pages of books he especially loved—*Riders of the Purple Sage* and *Girl of the Limberlost.* I ran my fingers over the keys of his accordion, slipped his worn, grease-stained gloves over my hands, the smell of gasoline still embedded in the fibers. His scuffed and mud-caked boots sat in the corner of the back porch, the leather uppers worn and droopy. Images came to me—my father's boots planted in the dirt, a board in his hand as he beat a stubborn steer, his boots on the wide tines of the hay stacker he used to lift hay into piles or stacks. I plopped down on the floor and picked up the boot twisting a lace around my fingers and tracing the road map of nicks in old leather looking for clues into a father I sometimes didn't understand. An image came to me. I was leaning against my father's legs, my sneakers planted on the toes of his boots, my tiny body swaddled in his arms. He nodded to my older brother who pushed down on a lever that lifted the tines several feet above the ground. The earth fell away. The house and barn grew smaller as we rose higher and higher. He took my hands and lifted my arms above my head. "Let's fly high, Toots." In that moment, I understood that Henry Woster was not only defined by the day he beat the steer with a board but by the day he encouraged his little girl to fly.

~~~

For years after my father died, I dreamed that I was driving the back road to our farm searching for him. I knew he would be standing in green alfalfa fields or golden wheat, his long legs spread, and his boots planted deep in the soil, as if the land had woven him to itself in the way that the prairie roots were anchored and intertwined beneath the ground.

303

The dream never varied. It begins on Highway 47 and runs north out of Reliance. Ahead lies Medicine Butte, a site of healing power and wisdom for the Lakota, for me, a reassuring landmark which measures the distance from home. At one point, it appears that the road will lead me into the butte's womb, a tempting and comforting thought. But something compels me to complete my journey, and so I turn east at the cemetery, moving past the graves of my ancestors buried on the Catholic side, separated in death as in life from Protestants. Crumbling tombstones mark the graves, and scraggly cedar trees are scattered here and there, stubborn survivors of erratic prairie weather.

Further on is Reliance Dam where my father took us fishing on Sunday afternoons. Gathering his five children around him on the grassy banks, he baited squirming earthworms on hooks, snapped red and white bobbers on the lines, and helped us cast over the cattails and rushes. We watched the bobbers bob and dip as bullheads nibbled on the worms. The dream continues, and I turn left at the wheat field where I took bologna sandwiches, lemonade, and chocolate cake to my father. Sitting on the ground in the shade of the combine, we'd munch on the sandwiches, our backs resting against the tires. Sometimes my father would take a short nap, and I'd climb the metal steps to the top of the combine and leap into the grain hopper, nibbling on wheat kernels that tasted of nuts and earth.

Finally, I reach Sunny Slope Farm, home of our nearest neighbor and the final landmark before I turn north to drive the last mile to our place. At that junction, the fog rolls in, enveloping the car and blocking my vision. I park the car, get out, and stand in the middle of the road. I know that behind the fog, my father waits near our small, white farmhouse where pink hollyhocks stretch to my bedroom window and Creeping Jenny spreads over the sidewalk. There, the weathered granary, an old and faithful sentry, sags with the burden of keeping watch for vagabond masters who never come home. But the haze is impenetrable. I can't find my way. Time and again through the years, I awoke from this dream desolate and abandoned, my face wet with tears, the now familiar pain of loss and grief as intense as the day we buried my father.

Today, my dream no longer haunts me, for I have come to understand that my father is always with me in the stories I tell my grandchildren, stories of playing rodeo with him, he on all fours, and me riding his back and kicking his sides with my cowboy boots as he bucked and twisted and tossed me into my bed. Stories of my father kneeling by my bed whisking away my nightmares with soft words about angels that protect me and horses with wings that carry me away from danger. I will tell them stories of his adventures, riding the rails to the world's fair and hiking Black Elk's Peak, a mountain so high that when he reached the top he felt as if he had come to the end of the world. But he always came back to the patch of grassland where his story began. In the same way, my story circles me back to that piece of land and to the man who farmed it. Of all the lessons my father taught me the most valuable may be that stories are the bread crumbs that guide us home.

DOGGED STRENGTH

When I first saw that girl. . .
I didn't need a psychiatrist to tell me.
I knew what kind of mind I was dealing with.
But I have never dealt with one like that before.
Yes perhaps it even repelled me at the time.
But I have had medical literature I could study.
Samuel Masten's closing argument

It's a peculiar sensation, this double-consciousness
two souls, two thoughts, two unreconciled strivings;
two warring ideals in one dark body
whose dogged strength alone
keeps it from being torn asunder.
Leslie Feinberg
Stone Butch Blues

In early June of 2014, I drove through the
entrance to the Human Services Center in Yankton
where Bev lived for over twenty years. I was stunned
to see middle-school-aged athletes playing soccer in
an open field. Mothers cheered from the sidelines
while younger siblings tumbled in the grass laughing
and picking dandelions. Above me, the sky, wide and
blue as the seas, sparked memories of days on the
farm when I felt it might be possible to get pleasantly
absorbed into that dome of vibrant blue. I could
almost smell alfalfa blooming in a nearby field and

hear the cackling of pheasants sitting on nests. Instead of feeling confined or fearful as I had expected to feel, I sensed something welcoming about this place. When did this facility open to the public? And why?

The Yankton hospital was founded in 1879 and originally called The Dakota Hospital for the Insane. After complaints that the name denigrated other patients confined to the hospital—particularly alcoholics and epileptics—the facility was renamed The Yankton State Hospital. In 1974 the legislature changed the name once again to The Human Services Center to reflect more accurately the many services provided here.

I thought of the cruel language my friends and I used like the nut house, the booby hatch, the funny farm, and the loony bin. Adults used words like the lunatic asylum. Although the word asylum originates from Latin and French for sanctuary or haven, the definition meant something different to me. Asylums protected those outside the walls from people inside like Bev.

A memory came. March 1963, my friends and I drove by the campus on our way to a high-school basketball tournament. My stomach clenched at the sight of the imposing buildings and the lurid images they sparked of the patients behind those walls. Insanity loomed large in my imagination in those years most likely because of movies like *Psycho* with its soundtrack of violin strings plucked in shrieking staccato. It was a terrifying movie with a terrifying ending. Tony Perkins watches a fly crawl over his hand, then looks up with a demented grin. His mother's ghostly voice echoes in his brain. Nightmares about crazy people wanting to kill me murdered my sleep for weeks after that.

We stayed in an old hotel in downtown Yankton, a few miles from the hospital. Sitting cross-legged on the bed, we held flashlights under our chins. The lighting distorted our faces and made our eyes deep and hollow as skulls. We spooked ourselves with a story we all knew but told at every slumber party, a cautionary tale of teenagers parking in an isolated pasture not far from an asylum. An announcer interrupts the music on the radio to report that a male patient with a hook for a hand has escaped from the asylum. The young lovers hear a scratching near the passenger window and speed away. When they get home, they discover a hook hanging from the door handle. We shrieked and clutched one another at the story's end then crawled into bed whispering reassurances that we were safe. "It's ok," one girl said. "It's only a story." Still, I got up twice that night to rattle the lock on the door. I had no idea that the next year, Bev would be committed to the Yankton facility not far from where I had spent a fitful night.

~~~

After her sentencing, Bev entered the Nebraska Correctional Center for Women in York, Nebraska, a modest-sized community on the flat lands not far from the Kansas border. If Bev was our town's most notorious criminal, Caril Anne Fugate was the prison's most infamous inmate. In the winter of 1957-58, the fourteen-year-old Fugate joined or perhaps was forced by Charles Starkweather to go on a killing spree across Nebraska leaving ten people dead in eight days.

In a picture taken of Caril Ann and Charles, Caril might have been Gina or any teenage girl in the 1950's. She wears a checkered blouse, jeans cuffed at the bottom, and white socks with black flats. Her dark hair coils around her cheeks and sets off her wide eyes. She looks at the camera with a toothy grin.

What connects Caril and Bev, however, is not just that they spent time in the same prison, but that their similar backgrounds and experiences with the legal system reflect the consequences of being poor or disenfranchised in America. Both girls came from poverty. Neither had been in trouble with the law until the murders. Although she was so young, Caril was tried as an adult, as was Bev despite being described by the psychiatrists as having the emotional maturity of an eight-year-old. Like Caril, Bev was unable to understand the terminology and legal procedures. Neither woman had legal representation during their interrogations. Eager to solve the murder and reassure terrified Nebraskans, the police may have tampered with evidence in Caril's investigation. In Bev's case, the prosecution and judge erred in several ways before and during the trial making Bev's defense more difficult.

Although Caril was seventeen years old when Bev came to the prison and Bev twenty-four, it's easy to imagine that the women met at some time, perhaps in the lunchroom or the kitchen or in the exercise yard. Caril studied for her high school equivalency exam in prison. A few years later, Bev trained as a barber. Both expected to spend the rest of their lives in prison. But they didn't. Instead over time, they were released from the York facility. Caril eventually married and raised a family. Bev transferred to the state hospital in Yankton, South Dakota.

~~~

In his closing statement, Masten had made the case that he did not aspire to see Bev reenter society, but rather to find a place where both she and society would be safe. "I have come a long way to solve a problem. I didn't come out here as some hired lawyer to get somebody out so they could walk down the street."

For two years after the trial, Masten worked on an appeal of Bev's verdict. I like to imagine him in his smoke-filled office in Canton, SD. I envision the room cluttered with stacks of books piled on chairs and shelves and legal pads with scribbled notes scattered over the tops of file cabinets. But perhaps he was neat freak and his office was tidy and organized. He likely studied codified law, other precedent-setting cases, and the trial transcripts until he had the information that he needed to request a second trial. Among the assignments of errors that he cited in the first trial was this charge. "Where insanity through the evidence has now become an issue, it is the burden of the state to prove she was sane beyond a reasonable doubt."

In April of 1964, the South Dakota Supreme Court met to consider the appeal. Among those who participated in the appeal were South Dakota Attorney General Frank Farrar, who later was elected the twenty-fourth governor of the state. After considering Masten's argument that the judge erred in its instructions to the jury, the court reached a decision that read in part:

We are unable to conclude that these errors in the challenged instructions did not prejudice the defendant. They had the effect of placing on her the burden of establishing she was irresponsible for her act while under our rule, it is the burden of the state to establish her ... guilt beyond a responsible doubt.

The court overturned the original verdict of manslaughter. In the second trial, the jury found Bev not guilty by reason of insanity. After two years in the York Prison, Bev was transferred to the Human Services Center in Yankton.

Together Masten and Bev changed legal precedent. Her case would require judges in the future to make clear to the jury that the burden of proving the defendant's sanity at the time of the murder lay with the state. It was not up to the defendant to prove insanity. Bev and Masten protected others from being sent to prisons instead of hospitals where like Bev they could be rehabilitated. Masten was certainly astute enough to understand the impact of what he'd done for future trials. I doubt Bev ever realized that she who possessed so little power throughout her life might one day be cited in law classes and legal texts. But Bev never forgot Masten's kindness. For many years, even after Masten's death, Bev sent his family Christmas cards, illegible and incoherent messages of gratitude and friendship.

~~~

When Bev lived in Yankton, rolling hills separated the hospital from the community.

Although the campus felt isolated then, its solitary presence distinguished the campus as something of social and medical importance. Highway 81 runs past the facility. Today, driving into Yankton on this road is like driving into any mid-sized town across the country, a road lined with fast-food restaurants, chain motels, and big-box stores. Nothing sets this neighborhood apart from any other. On the other hand, this sprawl of buildings prompted by commerce serves to integrate the campus into the community. Perhaps patients can walk to the Mongolian Barbeque or the coffee kiosk a few blocks away. Perhaps they chat with the locals or the wait staff. Maybe they share pictures of family or stories of hometowns.

In my memory, a fence enclosed the campus. But if so, it has since been removed. I thought of how fences and walls, both visible and invisible, keep those we fear or misunderstand locked away. In our community, people with cognitive or physical disabilities were often institutionalized or isolated in their families' homes. Some, however, defied our narrow expectations for what was "normal" or "abnormal." Bobby the Sweeper spent his day sweeping the sidewalk in front of his parents' house whistling to the rhythm of straw sweeping against concrete. Alice the hearing-impaired woman sat on the front stoop making guttural, unintelligible sounds, her fingers flying to shape words. Like Bev and her public and confounding gender bending, they refused to closet themselves even at the cost of disapproval or ridicule. Although they made me anxious when I saw them, they also sparked my curiosity. Why didn't they hide? How could they seem so unaware of their strangeness? Over time, I have come to understand their courage.

Intangible fences of racism or social and doctrinal mores are subtle yet often more effective than barbed wire and bricks. For years, unseen fences of disinformation imprisoned gays and transgender men and women and made them invisible. Churches and societies locked women in often not so subtle misogyny. Manifest Destiny gave white people not only permission but a sacred duty to steal land from native people and build invisible borders that caged them. Reservation borders are particularly insidious because they have allowed South Dakotans to look away from the injustices tribal people face. A visible fence, however, would force us to examine the reason for the border's existence and in the process to face our ignorance or indifference to our history of subjugation and genocide.

I came to the Human Services campus to walk on the same ground, the same green, tree-covered, rolling hills that Bev once walked, to hear what Bev might have heard—trucks motoring down the highway to the south and cows calling to calves in pastures. I wanted to inhale the aroma of pork chops or hamburger wafting from the kitchen, and maybe tour the old barber shop with its aura of maleness in the hair-oil-stained chairs and tattered magazines. I wanted to close my eyes and see Bev with clippers in her hand tilting a man's head so she could shave the fine hairs on the back of his neck. I hoped to tour the locked ward where "violent" patients including Bev had once been housed, to hear the click of a lock behind me, to experience the walls closing in around me. Then it might be possible to feel, not just speculate, what Bev's life had been like here. But today most of those buildings have been condemned and the others remodeled for a different function.

The regal Mead Building now wrapped in scaffolding as part of a major restoration project still reigns over the campus. Built in 1909 to house women patients, the building reflects hospital administrator Dr. Leonard Mead's thinking that visual beauty offered a sense of serenity, a vital therapy for mental illness. A marble, split staircase much like the one in *The Sound of Music* dominated the lobby. The terrazzo floors featured a geometric pattern. Hand-painted stencils lined the ceilings, and art work purchased over the years by Dr. Mead covered the walls. It was here that patients participated in dances, receptions, and concerts. Did this building soothe Bev? Or unnerve her? No matter the doctor's good intentions, the building represented a classicist view of beauty that may have seemed unwelcoming to Bev. Girls who grew up on the river often find comfort in natural beauty: the sun glistening on the river's waves, the green cedars dotting the grassy bluffs, and the trilling of red-wing blackbirds perched on cat tails. This ornate structure with its artificial light and quiet hallways may have made Bev feel even more like an outsider.

I walked further thinking that somewhere beneath my feet was once a dimly-lit tunnel that connected the buildings. One of those little girls shooed away from the murder scene that night was on a nursing rotation at the state hospital during Bev's confinement. She was walking through the tunnel when she saw Bev coming toward her. She took a stutter step backwards terrified that Bev would remember she had witnessed the crime. She realized, she later said, how silly it was of her to fear Bev who didn't seem to notice her presence. Perhaps Bev was used to startled looks on people's faces when they saw her. Likely she had seen others step nervously aside as she approached. Even in a place inhabited by those who lived on the far edges of society, Bev was alone.

What was Bev's treatment here? Hoping to get an answer to that question, I stopped at an office and spoke to a case worker who was reluctant to share information. Privacy matters he said. I didn't press him. In my research I discovered thorough information on the "curative" treatments given to gay and lesbians over the years. Reparative therapy included encouraging patients to be intimate with someone of the opposite sex, even fellow patients, then praising them when they did so. Aversion therapy involved attaching an electric wire to the patient's body and plugging the other end into a slide projector. Whenever an image of homosexual behavior appeared on the screen, the machine shocked the patient on the arm, the leg, fingers, and sometimes the male genitals. Nothing documents patients at the Yankton facility being subjected to any of these therapies. But shock treatments were used at the hospital when Bev lived there, so it's easy to imagine Bev lying on a table, a rubber heel in her mouth to keep her from choking as she convulsed to electrical currents running through her body, easy to envision Bev who once crackled with nervous energy slumped in a chair groggy and confused.

I was a senior in high school when Bev entered the violent criminal unit at the Yankton hospital. While she sat in her cell, I stuffed Kleenex into chicken wire for the prom and spent late hours editing the school newspaper. While I was fuzzy-minded from too much beer at college parties, Bev was probably lethargic from strong doses of Thorazine, a drug commonly used to keep patients calm and less likely to be disruptive. During the years of Bev's confinement, doctors learned how to adjust the strength of the drugs to levels that improved the lives of patients. Perhaps the medication helped Bev to become a trustworthy patient given the freedom to roam the grounds and to work as a barber. While teaching at a university fulfilled my life's ambition, Bev at long last entered a man's world of shaving cream and the fragrance of aftershave, of cigarette smoke and talk of fish and pheasants.

After twenty-some years, Bev was released from the hospital leaving with the handful of her possessions: two centavos, a cigarette lighter, a shot gun shell, a jackknife, and for some reason her school records. They say she moved back to Chamberlain where she prompted rumors that she walked the bluffs in the moonlight, a rifle over the shoulder. That was a just another untrue story in the life of a woman defined by rumors. At loose ends and homeless, Bev checked herself in and out the hospital for many years continuing to work as a barber when she lived in the facility. It must have felt like home and the staff and other patients like family.

Eventually, she moved into a small house in Yankton and spent her days fishing beneath the river bluffs. A neighbor wrote in the guest book on the funeral home website: "Bev was our neighbor when we lived in Yankton. We could not have asked for a better neighbor and friend. She was always so very kind and loved sharing her catch of catfish." Bev's life in Yankton appears to have been quiet and satisfying until ill health forced her to enter a nursing-care facility in Sioux Falls where she died.

~~~

I left the campus disappointed to have found no answers to my questions. Nor did I know for certain that I had walked where Bev walked. I drove by a barn of concrete blocks, freshly painted white, nestled in blue stem, thistle, and milkweed. The windows and sliding doors were still intact and the shingles on the roof looked almost new. I had been to the campus before and had a memory of a wooden barn, paint gray from age and boards sagging into the open field. The smell of manure and traces of sour milk seemed to linger that day. Why had this image of decay stayed with me and not a memory of this carefully tended barn? Perhaps my fondness for old barns wedged itself into my subconscious. Weathered barns on abandoned farmsteads are failure written on the landscape and belie the promise or myth of the West that drew people to settle here. But old barns also remind us that someone had once striven to survive in a hostile place the way Bev endured living on the fringes all her life.

My last stop was a cemetery along the side of the road. Several rows of concrete blocks the size of bricks spread over the grass. Numbers, not names, were engraved in the stone. Of course, the facility needed to protect the patients' identities. Their names did not survive them. Why were these people buried here so far from family? In many cases, the family couldn't afford transportation costs to bring the body home. In others, they were ashamed and left relatives at the hospital rather than acknowledge their existence. Those rows of nameless graves reminded me of words Leslie Feinberg wrote, "There's other ways to be than either or. It's not so simple otherwise there wouldn't be so many people who don't fit in."

To the south of the cemetery, the Missouri River rushed toward the Gulf seeking its home. Bev had fished where tree roots clung to the sides of the bluffs, the ground beneath them eroded by currents. Some argue that those who have different cognitive or physical abilities, different gender or sexual identities, emotional or mental problems weaken the solid ground of society. They underestimate these people, as I had once underestimated Bev's inner strength to survive and Bobby's and Alice's courage to live in the open. In the same way, the majority culture has misjudged the native people's determination to not just survive cultural destruction and genocide, but to thrive; in the way men have miscalculated a woman's strength to endure and overcome the challenges of patriarchal cultures. For like the massive roots of trees clinging stubbornly to bluffs, the oppressed seek out ground that allows them to flourish. And when the roots of the older trees finally let go and tumble into the water, more saplings take root in their place.

KNOWING AND NOT KNOWING

It wasn't the way we looked.
It was just a feeling we got
that would let us know who was and who wasn't.
It was scary, but wonderful--
operating in a straight world, being totally undetectable
by them,
but knowing and trusting each other.
F.L., a UCLA graduate student in the early 1960's
Odd Girls and Twilight Lovers: A History of Lesbian Life in
Twentieth-Century America

If I have done nothing else
but bring one light of understanding out to your area,
it's been worth my time. If there is just a flicker of
understanding so
we can understand the reality of that word we call
justice,
my task has been well performed.
Samuel Masten in closing argument

Summer 2015. I arranged a white ceramic coffee cup and spoon to my left and three sharpened pencils to the right, my compulsive ritual before taking notes, writing, and revising a manuscript. I sat in a booth by the front window of the Anchor Grille, called the Rainbow Café in my youth. Much has changed in the years between when the Rainbow Café became the Anchor Grille. A teenage boy is serving tables, not a middle-aged woman with a ruffled apron and sturdy shoes. The neon rainbow sign hanging above the entrance is gone, replaced by a simple display with black lettering and an illustration of steaks. The café's walls and upholstery are earth-toned, the chairs and booths, wood. White beams crisscross the ceiling. A tall ship sits on the countertop suggesting a nautical theme. The room where teenagers once danced at café-sponsored sock hops is dark. Venetian blinds cover the windows, the slats open to let in the light and scenes from Main Street.

Main Street, however, is much the same as it was when I was sixteen. Mothers haul groceries down the sidewalk, children tagging along behind them, some screaming, some sucking their thumbs. Gaggles of girls stroll past the store fronts, cracking gum and giggling. Across the street the State Theater's posters of upcoming movies fade in the bright sun. I recall rushing out of Catechism class and dashing down the street to pay fifteen cents for the movie and ten cents for popcorn. Western movies dominated my Saturday afternoons the way super heroes fuel the imagination of today's young people.

An old model Chevy drives slowly down Main. A young man slouched behind the steering wheel manages to look both bored and alert as if looking for trouble. A memory, unbidden and unwanted, comes to me. The Duke has picked me up as I walked home from a late choir practice one night. Maybe he said something like "Do you want to cruise town for a bit with me?" Or maybe he said nothing but just assumed that when he pulled over, I would hop in his car like the other girls always did. He made the right assumption.

We loop Main several times when he spots Bev's car ahead of us and says, "Hey, look. There's the It who walks the West. Let's give The Dyke some flack."

I never heard her called "dyke" before and wasn't certain what he meant. I didn't ask.

He guns the engine and pulls up next to her. "Hey, Bev, how ya doing?"

When she turns to us, her dark eyes are shining like a child surprised and pleased by something unexpected—ice cream before supper perhaps, or the gift of a baseball mitt for no reason except that summer had begun. Before she can answer, The Duke flips her off, yells "Fuck you, Butch," and spins away, tires squealing. I laugh hard because I am a chubby freshman girl in the presence of a cool senior boy. The woman I am today wants to shake that girl. To tell her how she should have yelled at The Duke for his cruelty and demand he pull over and let her walk home, should have named his words as malicious, should never have ridden with him again. Instead, I sighed with relief that his nastiness had not been aimed at me, and I jumped in his car the next time he beckoned to me.

~~~

The Anchor Grille became my temporary office during my many trips to Chamberlain for my research. I spread the trial transcripts over the table top and read and reread them. My reading list included several books that provided valuable information and a solid basis for the memoir. Particularly helpful was *Odd Girls and Twilight Lovers* by Lillian Faderman a well-researched, comprehensive history that traces the arc of lesbianism in the twentieth century America, beginning with "romantic friendships" common at women's universities in the early 1900's. A landscape unto its own where men seldom appeared, the campus offered an insularity that promoted intimacy between women. In fact, some considered this attraction a normal part of the maturation process for young girls, a rehearsal in a sense for marriage. A senior sorority sister picked out a freshman woman who would be her "partner" that year. They were inseparable or "smashed." The older woman courted the younger with bouquets of flowers, boxes of candy, and locks of her hair tucked in sweet notes she'd written and slipped under her door. At the end of the year, the older woman donned a tuxedo, slicked back her hair with butch wax, bought a corsage for her date, and filled in her dance card at the annual prom. These "romantic friendships" were rarely considered sexual, although evidence suggests that many couples were physically intimate. Still the affairs were tolerated or more likely ignored by the campus, family, and even boyfriends.

Gina's affair with Bev began at a time when Myron was often gone and Gina was bored and lonely. It grew stronger after a car accident had traumatized Gina, and she seemed to turn to Bev for emotional support. Parental disapproval likely made Bev more attractive to Gina the way my father's concerns about Nick made him more desirable.

At the time, I couldn't understand how Gina could be intimate with both Bev and Myron. I measured my life as a straight woman in a monogamous relationship against hers and expected her to follow my path if she wanted to be "normal." As a college teacher, I met a few young women who were involved in lesbian relationships during college. Some then committed to heterosexual relationships when they graduated. Lesbian until graduation, (LUG) is considered a cultural phenomenon which according to researchers has many possible explanations: experimentation, personal expression of social-political views, rebellion against parents and society, an awakening of their own feelings, and a natural progression from the intense intimacy of young women's friendships to intimacy with a man. These possibilities may offer one way to understand the brief and intense relationship between Bev and Gina.

In the 1930's, Sigmund Freud addressed lesbianism from the viewpoint of a traditional male. Women were becoming too ambitious and independent. Athletic prowess for females was abnormal and suggested homosexual tendencies. Perhaps fear of turning girls into lesbians through physicality may explain my high school physical education class, segregated by gender and requiring little strenuous exercise. We wore one-piece, pumpkin-orange bloomers and exercised daily to a record called "Go you chicken fat go." Touching our toes, doing jumping jacks, and high stepping to the lyrics *Give that chicken fat back to the chicken* most of us still kept our chicken fat. In fact, I managed to gain a few pounds by eating baskets of broasted chicken during my shift at the A & W.

During World War II, women donned work shirts and overalls and went to factories to build planes and munitions for the war. It wasn't uncommon to see women holding hands or walking down the street with arms wrapped around one another's waists. Physical displays of affection among women generally were ignored by employers as they were by military officials who were ordered not to bother women involved in "close" relationships. After all, women were critical cogs in the war machine working as military clerical staff, truck drivers, airplane mechanics, and even test and transport pilots. Firing them for being lesbian would create a shortage of labor and likely delay the end of the war.

When the war ended, President Dwight D Eisenhower ordered commanders to weed lesbians out of the troops calling them "security risks." Female personnel infiltrated lesbian bars to act as decoys who could then identify lesbians in the military. Women suspected of being lesbian were threatened with court martial and warned that the military would expose them to their parents.

Did my mother and her friends understand how the freedom lesbians enjoyed during the war spilled over into more independence for heterosexual women? Likely the few mothers I knew who worked outside the home had discovered the value of being relevant in the larger community and the pride in making money and choosing how to spend it. I, however, the daughter of a stay-at-home mom pitied the children whose mothers worked. I had heard the critical tone in my mother's voice when she said to a friend, "I never thought she would give up on her children," by which, I think she meant abandon them for a "career." It may be no coincidence that by the 1960's women were prescribed valium, "mother's little helper," twice as often as were prescribed to men. I have memories of walking into a dark, hushed house and seeing my friend's mother lying on the bed in the middle of the afternoon, the shades pulled. My friend hustled me outside. The look of shame or horror on her face told me not to ask what was wrong with her mother.

In the 1950's, one psychiatrist wrote, "The new freedom that women are enjoying serves as fertile soil for the seeds of sexual inversion." In other words, strong, independent women should be controlled so they don't become lesbians. Words like inverts, perverts, and queers made their way into the language. Magazines published articles with titles like "New Moral Menace to Our Youth" which presented lesbianism as leading to drug addiction, burglary, sadism, and murder. Any printed material that depicted gays in a positive light was considered pornography and subject to prosecution. Secrecy once again closeted the LGBTQ+ community whether through not acting on one's feelings toward a same-sex person or not seeking a change in gender identification. Transmen and transwomen and homosexuals suffered violence in the streets and bars. and discrimination at the work place reared its head once again. All were potholes in the bumpy road toward equality for LGBTQ+ members.

Since the 1962 murder of Myron Menzie, Congress has passed laws to protect the civil rights of all Americans regardless of race, gender, sex, or religion. Positive changes also emerged for the LGBTQ+ communities, most notably the 2015 Supreme Court decision regarding same-sex marriages. However, today politicians and prominent clergy use words like bestiality and sodomy to argue for bills discriminating against LGBTQ+. Restricted bathroom bills continue to be introduced and debated in state legislatures. Former US Attorney General Jeff Sessions ruled that the Civil Rights Act of 1964 did not apply to LGBTQ+ people, which threatens their right to employment without fear of discrimination as well as their right to marry, adopt children, or purchase goods and services. At a time when the rights of LGBTQ+ people are in danger and when members of their communities live with the threat of violence, understanding and making connections seems more crucial than ever.

~~~

The waiter stopped by my table and topped off

my cup of coffee. He glanced at the pictures on the books' covers, one of two women sitting at a table holding hands, their images overlaid with shades of green and pink. The other cover featured a black-and-white photo of Leslie Feinberg resting his check in his hand, his face in shadows, and his deep-set eyes hollow. "Whatcha readin?"

"I'm doing research for a book about a murder that took place just a block away from here. A love affair between two women prompted this murder."

He thought for a second then nodded his head. "Cool."

Had I been in the classroom with this young man, I could have told him that current research explains that genitals and our gender identity may be misaligned due to biological processes. We all begin essentially genderless until about six weeks after conception when hormones begin to shape sexual differentiation of genitalia. During gestation, hormones and up to fifty genes influence our development, but it's the last pair of chromosomes that ultimately determine the sexual or gender identity. This happens at about six weeks. Sexual differentiation of the brain, including gender identity, occurs later in the development of the fetus again largely due to hormones. Environmental circumstances might alter the development as well. These processes take place at different times and through different pathways. Generally, they match, but a variety of biological events can alter the outcome. The result is multiple variations of brain and anatomy structure and alignment. For transgender men and women sexuality and gender identity do not fully align.

I should have explained this to him, but I didn't. By now I understood that sexuality and gender identity do not lend themselves to a brief explanation. As I immersed myself into research, I discovered a plethora of terms that describe different ways of being: gender dysphoric, lesbian, homosexual, nonbinary, sexually fluid, asexual, cisgender, pansexual, and intersex. I learned about pronoun preference and how using the right pronoun matters. I understood that naming oneself is an act of courage and pride. I also understood that I risked offering faulty information despite the reading I've done and that I had much more to learn. More importantly, I wanted to avoid appearing to speak for LBGTQ+ people and to avoid appropriating their stories.

I smiled at the young man and he moved on to the next table. I poured cream into the cup and watched the white liquid swirl through the dark until it merged into a lovely, caramel-colored drink, a blend of sweet into bitter and light into darkness.

STORIES ARE THE BREAD CRUMBS

Authors do not choose a story to write,
the story chooses us.
Richard P. Denny
"Writing Forever," blog

Now all those I love and did not understand are dead,
but I reach out to them.
Norman Maclean
A River Runs Through It

The daughter of a natural storyteller, I lived in a world rich with stories, true and imagined. I crave stories well told. Stories with illusive meanings. Stories with memorable characters. Stories set in evocative places. Like a detective poring over bits of cloth and muddy footprints to solve a mystery, I study words on billboards, magazine ads, literature, and song lyrics with the writer's need to decipher the intention behind the words. Perhaps that's why I am drawn to small, country cemeteries and to ancient tombstones settled into the earth like vertebrae on the crooked backs of old farmers. Tombstones tell stories if we take the time to interpret them. I kneel and like readers of braille spider my fingers over the letters and numbers etched in stone eroded by years and harsh weather. Who is the person buried here? What is the narrative of his life or her sorrows?

My obsession with epitaphs on tombstones likely began after the death of my cousin Fran who lies in the Reliance Cemetery near her Woster parents and grandparents. Fran, a red-headed sprite with freckles sprinkled over her nose, died at fifteen from measles complications. She spent her last days trapped in an iron lung, the line between life and death a thin layer of air that mechanical bellows breathed for her. Many years later, I stopped at Fran's graveside. Engraved on my cousin's stone were the simple words "Our Fran." I puzzled over those words for some time. Then I recalled the wintery day we buried Fran. My Aunt Margaret and Uncle Frank leaned against one another clutching rosaries. Engulfed in the stretch of grasslands that surrounded them, they seemed tiny somehow as if diminished by grief. The heartbreaking, possessive pronoun "our" speaks volumes about the need my aunt and uncle felt to claim their daughter even in death.

On newer stones are photos or images that also contain clues to the lives of those buried beneath them. Myron's brother William's tomb lies in the clipped grass of the Pleasant Lawn Cemetery in

Geddes, South Dakota. Engraved on his stone are the words Saddle Bronc Rider and an image of a cowboy on a bronco's back, the horse's hind legs vertical to the ground, the rider thrown back against its flanks. William defined himself in those few words and that image. He was a cowboy. In the same way, a sheaf of wheat on my father's stone tells the story of my father as farmer, a man who every year brought life from the earth. The Celtic cross on my mother's stone speaks of her great pride in being Irish and of a homesickness she felt for a country she'd never known. But those are my interpretations. In years to come, others may pass by these stones and find a different story within them.

Not far away from William's grave, Myron Menzie's gray tombstone lies flat against the ground. His name and years of his birth and death—1941 to 1962— are engraved in the granite. Beneath is the inscription "May He Rest in Peace." The iron cross enclosed in vines and chrysanthemums on Myron Menzie's grave suggests a crown on the head of a king, perhaps the golden future his parents once dreamed for their son. How often did Bill and Gladys kneel at Myron's grave weeping? How deeply did they feel the injustice of Bev being released one day from the institution just two hours away from their son's grave?

Like many parents of teenagers, the Menzies

must have feared and expected that phone call on July 30, 1961, telling them that Myron and Gina had been in a car accident. Myron having once outrun the pale horse his parents may have believed he was destined for a long life. They couldn't have imagined Myron killed by a jealous lover or the circumstances that triggered the murder. Myron's little sister had teased him about Bev applying for a license to marry Gina, but his parents probably didn't comprehend what prompted her teasing until they sat in the courtroom and Masten asked, "So, Gina, Myron was fully advised as to the relationship between you and Beverly Waugh. . . and he had known for some time, hadn't he?"

"Yes."

"He knew down to its intimate details, isn't that right?"

"Yes."

How painful it must have been to hear the defense attorney say, "She told the young man all about it and yet he continued to go with her. How degraded can we get?"

Even though Gina admitted to Myron that she and Bev spent nights on lovers' lane "kissing and petting and other things," he still planned to marry her. Popular culture suggests that men find something titillating at the thought of the two women tangled in the car's back seat or the soft grass of the ditch. Some people suggested that Myron might have been gay and Gina was his "beard." Or maybe, despite Bev's masculine appearance and exaggerated swagger, Myron thought of her as just a woman and no serious threat for a man. Such speculations or narratives are troubling. Myron couldn't speak for himself and no family member testified on his behalf. Of Myron we know only what was revealed in the courtroom—that he was handsome, athletic, hardworking, and a beloved son. His motives for keeping his commitment to Gina may never be known.

If Myron's parents had heard the story of Gina's indiscretions and their son's intentions to marry her anyway, what could they have done? Call her parents? Confront their son about the rumors? Myron was an adult. He made his own choices. If he bore any responsibility for the tragedy, it may have been that he believed in the western myth that as a man he could reshape Gina the way he changed the landscape by building a dam to contain the river's flow. Or perhaps he was being stubborn in insisting Gina marry him despite her affair with Bev. It's possible that he was simply a good man willing to move forward with the girl he loved.

The cemetery's website added this notation: *Myron Mellette "Chuck" Menzie. Murder—shot by Beverly J. Waugh.* Who posted this and why? To preserve history? To flesh out the story? To make certain this horrific crime was never forgotten?

The notation gave me pause as did the prosecutor's words when he expressed admiration for Masten's skill in presenting Bev as a sympathetic person manipulated by her lover. "We are asked to show sympathy (toward Bev), but that won't give life back to Myron Menzie." Had I made Bev more sympathetic than she deserved, this woman whose instinct toward violence and gut-level response to race were revealed or intensified by the stress of losing Gina? *Stay away from that half breed. And that half breed better stay out of my way to hon. You're mine and only mine. If he doesn't stay away from you. He's going to get hurt.*

Had I forgotten Myron in telling this story?

~~~

I left Myron's grave and drove to Pukwana where spiffed-up ranch houses with flower beds and cottonwood trees offer a sense that this small town may yet recover. The survival of small towns in South Dakota is the story of perseverance. As I drove through Pukwana's quiet streets, I thought about Gina's strength during the trial and in the years that followed. Although we didn't know each other, more connected us than divided us. Gina and I both married a few years after the murder. Gina left the state while I left my hometown. Neither of us moved back. We raised our children and moved on to be adoring grandparents. Like me, she returns to her little town to see friends and visit the graves of family including her parents Sadie and Joe. We both have painful and joyful memories of growing up in a little prairie town where innocence often collided with reality.

One way to understand and empathize with Gina is through her letters which reveal a young girl like many girls in the 1960's. I hear myself in her naughty, adolescent voice, *my sister . . . had only 3 hours sleep last night . . . Keith gave her a hickey. Oh, Oh. Does that sound like anyone you know?*

I see the willful, teenage daughter, challenging her mother the way I had my father. *Mom is mad at me again. When she came into my room I didn't look up or talk to her.*

The rebellious worker. *Yep, the old hen gave me heck—AGAIN. Grr.*

Her last letters reveal a panicked girl responding to Bev's anger. *I tried to call you already but there is just a funny like sound over the line. . . don't get shook baby. I'm thinking of you and wishing you were here.*

And a girl who writes of heartbreak whether because of a disastrous love affair or fear of Bev acting out on her threats. *When we are together nothing else in the world matters but when we aren't which is most of the time, what then?*

Neither of our mothers was forthcoming about sex. Sadie said she answered questions when Gina asked them, but Gina later said she didn't ask her mother about sex. In the same way, my mother's tight-lipped silence made clear to me that talk of sex was off limits. We knew little about our bodies and sexuality and had no concrete information about gender dysphoria or homosexuality. We were puzzled by what we didn't know. Gina was likely confused about Bev's gender bending because she never saw Bev undressed. Gina didn't have the language to understand her feelings about Bev and had nobody to help her make sense of them.

Once I was inclined to think that the relationship between the two women was the emotional closeness that many girls experience, a "romantic friendship" between two women that was not always physical. I blamed the gossip about their relationship on a cultural shift that interprets all tenderness between two women as sexual. Then I reread their letters.

Gina wrote, "I wish honey we were at the drive-in like last summer, don't you, a cool breeze blowing in your partly rolled down window but it was never too cold we sat too close. Well close but not too close."

Bev responded, "I know you really love me. When I hold you in my arms I know you really care.

And when I kiss you honey. Our love is strong for each other and let's keep it that way."

In the trial, Bev and Gina were forced to talk about necking and "other things" and cigars wrapped in tape. Those details strongly suggest that their relationship was physically intimate at some level. But does that really matter? How does it make their suffering less overwhelming? How does it change the outcome of this tragic story?

If Gina and I had been the same age, if we had attended the same school, we might have sat next to each other in study hall and chatted about our first dates. I might have whispered to her about Michael Sean O'Donnell who never snapped the back of my bra, never called me Olive Oyl because my feet were so large, never made cracks about my troubled skin. Gina could have told me stories about Myron Menzie, the football star with brown eyes and broad shoulders who jogged across the football field, waist narrow, thighs bulging beneath pads; she might have blushed at remembering how she waved her pompons as he ran through the tunnel of fans. Maybe she would have trusted me enough to speak of her conflict over loving both Bev and Myron or experiencing the terror of those days before the murder. I might have been the "one person" to whom she could tell her story. Maybe, but not likely. My teenage self would have slowly disentangled myself from her. I would have been too fearful of what other girls might think of her being my friend. I wouldn't have risked being seen as "one of them."

~~~

I often drive by Bev's home when I am in Chamberlain. I study her house grappling with her story and my compulsion to tell it. Although in 2002 I campaigned against a constitutional amendment banning same sex marriage, my support was on a philosophical and intellectual level of equal rights. I didn't truly empathize with those who dealt with this issue on a personal level because I had never experienced the longing for another woman, nor had I felt out of place or misaligned with the gender assigned to me at birth. So much separated Bev and me, and yet I had a sense that our lives were intertwined in ways I hadn't understood. I felt driven to know more.

I had always assumed that Bev was a lesbian who dressed and acted like a man. I have since come to a new way to consider Bev as revealed in the trial transcripts. Bev's psychiatrist first triggered this insight. "Beverly is a sexual deviate with reactive depression due to the stress of her male identification. Her dress was that of male attire with the possible exception of a curl on her forehead. Her gait and mannerisms were male. Her orientations were strictly male in terms of thinking. And this had

344

been her way of thinking for the majority of her life."

What a struggle her gender misalignment must have been for Bev. Renee Baker a transgender woman I've known for years described her experience with gender dysphoria this way. "The problem is a mental closet. You're living a life inside your head, and eventually you have to align your inside world with your outside world. I think people have a hard time adjusting to the idea that trans is a real thing. People believe that male to female designation means that a male has transitioned to female, not a female who was assigned male by mistake."

What defines gender? Is it traditional and social behavioral markers—men are assertive, decisive, and strong, and women are pliable, weak, and nurturing? Do we define gender mostly by genitalia? What does that mean for intersex people? Do certain hormonal levels divide us into male and female and if so, what are those levels? Does the line between those levels ever bend or swerve?

In Lakota tradition, a transgender person was called a *winkte*, a two-spirit person blessed with the power of being both male and female. The Lakota respected the Winktes for their gifts as healers, interpreters of dreams, and teachers of children. Would Bev's life have been different if our community had known the story of *winktes?* Would she have been honored among us, not misunderstood as an oddity and an outsider? Probably not. Most of us knew little about native cultures and cared even less. We viewed their dancing and chanting, their burning of sage and vision quests, and their reverence for nature as superstitious. Learning that native people admired a transgender person would have cemented our sense that they were pagans practicing dangerous rituals. Our ignorance about native people reassured us that being white, Christian, and heterosexual (we assumed) made us superior.

~~~

On a spring day in 2016, I stood at Bev's grave on the bluffs of the Missouri River. Thistle, clover, and dandelion shoots pushed up through the dried grass around her grave. The branch of a cedar tree hung over the pink-and-black speckled tombstone the word "Daughter" engraved in no-frills letters above her name. Bev's parents had already died. Who then chose the word daughter? Perhaps her siblings selected the word as a relationship clue for genealogists. It may have been chosen to show that Bev, an outsider most of her life, belonged here in this place with these people. Maybe there's no story behind the word at all.

All of Bev's immediate family have died in the years since the murder. Her brother James passed in

1992. Helara and her brother Darrell in 2001, brother Jerry in 2018, and her sister Norma in 2016. Frank died in 1971 while Bev lived in confinement in Yankton. I have knelt in the viewing room of the funeral home where his body lay, have prayed the rosary in the smell of carnations and candle wax and heard the murmuring of the funeral director as he guided mourners to the guest book. Bev didn't attend the service. Because she had committed a crime that resulted in death, she was denied by law the release time needed to be at her father's funeral. Maybe keeping her behind institution walls at this sorrowful time punished her fairly for the pain she caused. Perhaps the Menzie family found some comfort in that. Or maybe, and I think this is more likely, denying her the right to grieve with her family was one more cruelty in her generally merciless life.

Bev's funeral service was November 11, 2014. November days in central South Dakota can be glorious with air as crisp as parchment paper, and the earth smells of snow that will soon bleach the landscape white as an altar cloth. When I thought of Bev's burial on that November day, I could only imagine a small group gathered around the grave and the odor of rotting leaves in piles under trees entangling with diesel fuel from semis driving down the hill. Her life seemed so bleak I couldn't envision the sun shining as she was lowered into the ground.

I regretted that I had not attended her funeral although I am not sure I had the right to be there. I especially regretted that I hadn't spent more time looking for Bev instead of focusing on transcripts, books, newspapers, and interviews. I told myself I wanted to understand the story before I contacted her. Maybe I was reluctant to remind her of those painful days, falling back on my instinct to be silent about suffering. More likely, I was a coward. I didn't want to confront her. Perhaps I still feared her the way I did years ago when she dragged Main. So it was that the grief I felt for a woman known mostly through legal documents and letters caught me off guard.

Who was left to mourn Bev? I pulled out my cell phone, googled the funeral home website, and clicked on a few entries. A fellow patient or perhaps a staff member at the Human Services Center wrote: "I met Bev in early 80s as I also worked at HSC then, we often ate lunch together. She was a kind person with a very big heart."

Loving, thoughtful words from one who knew her in a different time and place, who knew her better than I did, words that said Bev was not lonely in her last years.

I knelt at her grave thinking of something Carson McCullers wrote about the burden of loneliness for those who are born and live as outcasts: "The hearts of children are delicate organs. The heart of a hurt child can shrink so that forever afterward it is hard and pitted as the seed of a peach .. . or fester and swell until it's a misery to carry within the body."

Her words strike at the heart of understanding Bev who was surely altered by her earliest experiences of being disenfranchised from society and even her own body, who suffered from the humiliation of being either the object of ridicule or pity. Her sad past does not excuse Bev. Her jealousy and desperate need to control Gina ended in the death of an innocent man. At the same time, she was a slow-witted, lonely, and vulnerable girl who shared all of my yearnings but none of my possibilities. In the end, she may have believed she had only one chance to save her life: put down Myron Menzie or die from the loss of love. She pulled the trigger.

I picked up a stone. Three irregular sides were connected at three points the way that three lives shaped the narrative of a perilous love triangle. I dug two more rocks out of the dirt and stacked them at the base of Bev's tombstone. By night, curious critters would most likely scatter the rocks over the grass or bury them in the sod. But it comforted me to know that for a few hours I had left a prairie cairn to tell the story of three people triangulated by love.

EPILOGUE

I drive up the Highway 16 hill past Sanborn Street and beyond to the Dairy Queen where I had gathered with friends the night of the murder. How many times in high school had I driven up and down that hill, a carload of teenage girls gossiping and sharing woeful tales of broken romances and difficult parents? Cars were our refuge. At a time when the only telephone in the house was often in the living room, cars were our only means of finding privacy from nosey siblings and parents who might eavesdrop on our conversation and subvert our plans for the night. But if cars offered seclusion, they also offered connections. Cars were our cell phone, our Facebook, Twitter, and Snapchat. Most of my memories of high school involve cars.

In one memory, I am dragging Main with my friends not long after my transition into a girly-girl. We scream at boys who pull up beside my car, the engine stuttering. One boy flips us off and we pretend to be offended. "Oh, my God, you're such a pig," one girl yells. He laughs and gives us the bird again as the car spins away, tires squealing.

We spot Bev's Oldsmobile a block ahead of us. I had often peeked out the corner of my eye when Bev dragged Main with us, fascinated by how the points of her collar touched her ears and how the butch wax in her duck ass glistened in the dashboard's lights. There was always a cigarette dangling between her lips and a pack of smokes tucked in her shirt pocket. She didn't drink yet for some reason I still imagine a six-pack of Blue Ribbon on the seat beside her or maybe nestled between her thighs. Likely she had propped a rifle in the back seat.

"Come on, pass her," says one girl. I step on the gas pedal and pull up beside her. Mostly Bev stares straight ahead when she drives the loop. But that night she looks at my bleached and lacquered hair, turquoise eye shadow, and pink lips. She squints as if trying to remember where she had seen me before. I press harder on the gas pedal, speed away from her, and pull into an alley to wait until her taillights fade. The alley is dark, but street lights on Main cast distorted shadows over the walls. I can't remember if I was trembling or simply numb with fear of those dark eyes.

The girls look out the back window. "Did you see how she stared at us? Mary Alice, don't leave yet. She might be coming back, so we have to hide."

We are in no danger from Bev. We invent the threat of her to provide a bit of drama in our small-town lives the way horror movies took us into a world where blue-blooded men became vampires and scientists altered human forms into massive flies. Still, I watch in the rearview mirror. Would I recognize her headlights turning into the alley? Did she carry her gun in the car? Fear locks me in that shadowy place for at least twenty minutes. During that time, I don't hear the other girls babbling. I am wrestling with the truth. I am not hiding from Bev and the threat of violence, but from the girl Bev recognized beneath the layers of makeup and platinum hair. In transitioning to a male, Bev risked ridicule and rejection in order to align her inner and outer self. Prompted by the jeers of boys, I transformed from a tomboy who tromped the prairie and climbed the granary roof into a girl constrained by girdles and garters, a girl whose long strides were hampered by heels and her hair so stiff with spray that not a strand moved in the wind.

The memory of that brief encounter with Bev in our cars stays with me now as I pass the turnoff to Old Highway 16. I think of the many times I traveled that highway with my family, our Pontiac station wagon bulging with children and dogs. As a child, I knew exactly how many miles separated one small town from another. I knew the grassy hills and river bluffs, the twists and curves of the road, and the pasture where a single tree rises from the buffalo grasses, the only vertical object for miles. This place contains my stories and knows me as no other place can.

But I don't take that road. Instead, I guide my Malibu onto I-90 which stretches for miles ahead of me, a straight and predictable road with few bends or hills. Nestled against my thigh is the newspaper with Bev's picture. I touch her image thinking how this photo drew me into pursuing a story I never intended to tell. But why me? Fate? Timing? Magic? I didn't ask such questions. I simply said yes.

I look in the rearview mirror. A scrim of color falls over the bluffs, but even that brilliant coral can't capture this brief moment when day surrenders to night. This sunset, this natural progression from endings to beginnings, mimics the path that I am now compelled to follow. The next morning at sunrise, working backwards from Bev's death to her birth, I will begin to write in a room cluttered with books on shelves and totems scattered over the desktop—sage from the Badlands, statues of Guan Yen and Buddha, and a ceramic scarab—symbols of the timelessness, wisdom, and renewal I hope will inspire and permeate my writing. I hit the cruise control, roll down the window to let the wind sweep the fragrance of spring through the car, and drive east toward home where Ken waits for me.

AUTHOR'S NOTE

When I found the old photo of Bev Waugh, I knew there was a story that needed to be told. I had planned on writing a nonfiction, true-crime book. Then I discovered a number of true-crime memoirs in which murders prompt the authors to tell a story beyond the facts of the case and into the author's life. I realized this book was a memoir.

The story is true. All the events and information about family and the murder is based on my research. None of the dialogue between Bev and Gina was invented. Every word they, the families, witnesses, and legal teams speak comes from letters and trial transcripts. I did not make grammatical changes on other's dialogues because I wanted their voices to be authentic. I do at times weave lines from letters into scenes involving actions that connect to their words. The dialogue in my own narrative is reconstructed from my sometimes-faulty memory, but always with faithfulness to the way the people in that time and place used language.

Understanding the importance of language for the LBTGQ+ community, I struggled particularly in choosing the appropriate pronoun for Bev, but finally settled on the female pronoun. I made this choice for several reasons. This story occurred in the 1960's when gender identity was not clearly diagnosed and there was no awareness of pronoun preferences. All the documents, the testimonies, the newspaper accounts, and members of the community referred to Bev as she. Also, Bev was never diagnosed as transgender because that term did not exist in 1962. Finally, gender identity is complicated and I can't assume that Bev totally rejected a feminine identity.

Leslie Feinberg, wrote, "I care which pronoun is used, but people have been respectful to me with the wrong pronoun and disrespectful with the right one. It matters whether one is using the pronoun as a bigot, or if they are trying to demonstrate respect."

Renee Baker echoed Feinberg's words. "Your sensitivity to the people in this story overshadows any concerns about language."

I obsessed over privacy issues and so I changed the names of several people in this book. Sixty years after the murder, I assume I have also if unwittingly compressed two people into one character and two events into one.

BIBLIOGRAPHY

Odd Girls and Twilight Lovers: A History of Lesbian Life in Twentieth Century America, Lillian Faderman; *Stone Butch Blues,* Leslie Feinberg; *Becoming Nicole: The Transformation of an American Family,* Amy Ellis Nutt; *What Becomes You,* Aaron Raz Link and Hilda Raz, and *Murder Over a Girl: Justice, Gender, Junior High,* Ken Corbett.

The Fact of a Body: A Murder and a Memoir, Alexandra Marzana Lesnevich; *Green Fields: Crime, Punishment, and a Boyhood Between,* Bob Cowser, Jr.; *Love in the Sunshine State: The Story of a Crime,* Cutter Wood; *Visiting Hours: A Memoir of Friendship and Murder,* Amy Butcher; *Love and Terror on the Howling Plains of Nowhere,* Poe Ballantine; *Son of a Gun: A Memoir,* Justin St. Germain; *We Are All Shipwrecks: A Memoir,* Kelly Gray Carlise; *Down City: A Daughter's Story of Love, Memory, and Murder,* Leah Carroll; *She Left Me the Gun: My Mother's Life Before Me,* Emma Brocks; *The Twelfth Victim: The Innocence of Caril Fugate in the Starkweather Murder Rampage,* Linda Battista and John Stevens Berry, and *In Cold Blood,* Truman Capote.

STUDY GUIDE

Discussion Questions for *Out of Loneliness*

1. Is the author trying to elicit a particular response from the reader? If so, what? If so, how does she accomplish that?

2. Was the story compelling? Discuss the effectiveness of the author's language and style. Is her voice authentic? Is the imagery evocative? Are the characters presented well? Which passage seemed particularly effective?

3. How does memory function in a memoir? What decisions did the author make in choosing the events that would best frame her narrative? Was there any time at which you thought the author was not being truthful?

4. What is the relationship between the past and the present in the author's life? How does the structure of the novel make that relationship clearer or foggier? Were there any gaps in the story or pieces of information that were missing?

5. What is the role of setting in this book? Was it effective?

6. What is the author's purpose in writing this memoir?

7. Discuss the author's stance toward the people in the community, her family, and Bev, Gina, Myron and their families?

8. What strategies does the author employ to set the context for this story?

9. The author wrestles with her impulse to write the book. How does she resolve that conflict?

10. What are the ethics of writing a story about other's tragedies?

11. How did the author define masculinity as a child? As an adult?

12. What central themes emerged in your reading of this book?

ACKNOWLEDGEMENTS

Out of Loneliness began several years ago as an essay I submitted to *River Teeth: Journal of Nonfiction Narrative*. I am grateful to Dan Lehman who encouraged me to consider writing a book.

My appreciation to Dan Lehman and Joe Mackall for publishing my work in their fine journal and for including my essay in their anthology *River Teeth: Twenty Years of Creative Nonfiction*.

Robert Root, in gratitude for seeing value in this story and for ushering me through the process of making it better.

Steven Harvey, The Humble Essayist, for including an except from my essay on your website and for your encouragement and support throughout the process of writing and publishing this book.

Kent Meyers who has been a great source of encouragement and a willing reader for nearly twenty years. I am grateful for your wisdom, advice, and your friendship.

Linda Hasselstrom, thank you for sharing your ranch and your generous spirit. You were the first person to say, "You need to call yourself a writer."

I could not have completed the book without those many who read my often clumsy and wandering early drafts of this story: They include my Brookings group of fabulous writers Christine Stewart Nunez, Amber Jensen, and Darla Biel; Kate Hopper, for editing the early draft; The Fifty+ Writing Group at the Loft Literary Center which includes Deborah Hersey, Bonnie Wilkins Overcott, Jeri Voci, Ted Hovey, Carol Hazard, and Linda Holmes; and finally, Ruth Harper and Ginny Hatch my good friends and thoughtful readers.

Jeff Masten, the son of Samuel Masten, provided essential background information on his father's personal and professional life as well as details about Bev that were not recorded in the transcripts.

Meghan Woster Roche, Assistant US. Attorney in Sioux Falls for always answering my legal questions.

Renee Baker, transgender counselor and author, who read an early draft of my manuscript and spent many hours talking with me about this book and answering my many questions.

Lara Widman, an activist for the LGBTQ+ community who read the manuscript and helped me understand how that community might respond to my book.

Larry S., Bev's cousin, for providing personal and specific information about Bev's behaviors and struggles.

Leo Woster, whose memories of my father brought richness to his story.

Taylor Livingston for finding a way to illustrate what this story means.

Jonathon Burns for your technical support, creativity, and good heart.

And to my siblings, Jim Woster, Jeanne Woster Chaussee, Terry Woster, and Kevin Woster for never challenging my right to tell our family's stories.

And finally, Ken and Maura without you nothing is possible or meaningful.